Cast of Characters

Ronen Ladarna

Aiymie Ladarna

Master Ze

The only son of Aiymie. His mother tells him his father is a great man and has always promised that one day, they will be reunited with him.

Mother of Ronen. She has made it her life's work to get Ronen to his rightful family.

How this mighty warrior came to be in Irdne and why he is crippled is unknown.

Baroness Mazza Mesozora

Baron Ermont Mesozora

Proud siblings of the mighty Mesozora clan that rule Irdne.

Tenny Nanaru

Zeb Hahn

These two children were adopted as infants and raised by Master Ze. They help him run his desert ranch.

Drego

Aramas

Ferr

Ronen and Aiymie's loyal servants who have been with the family for many years. Each is endowed with considerable fighting skills as well as knowledge in planetary farming.

www.princeofheroes.com

Chapter 1

Irdne

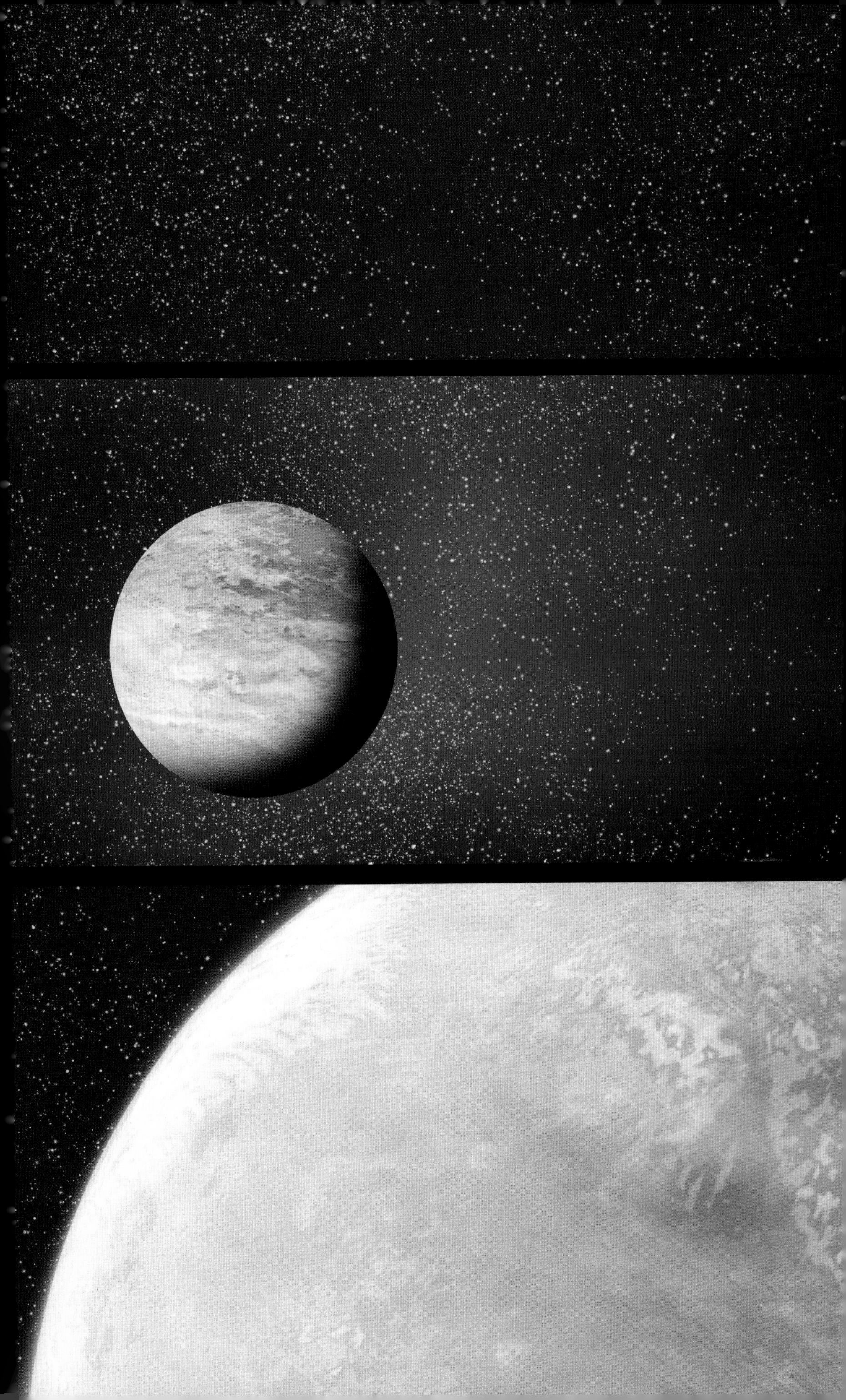

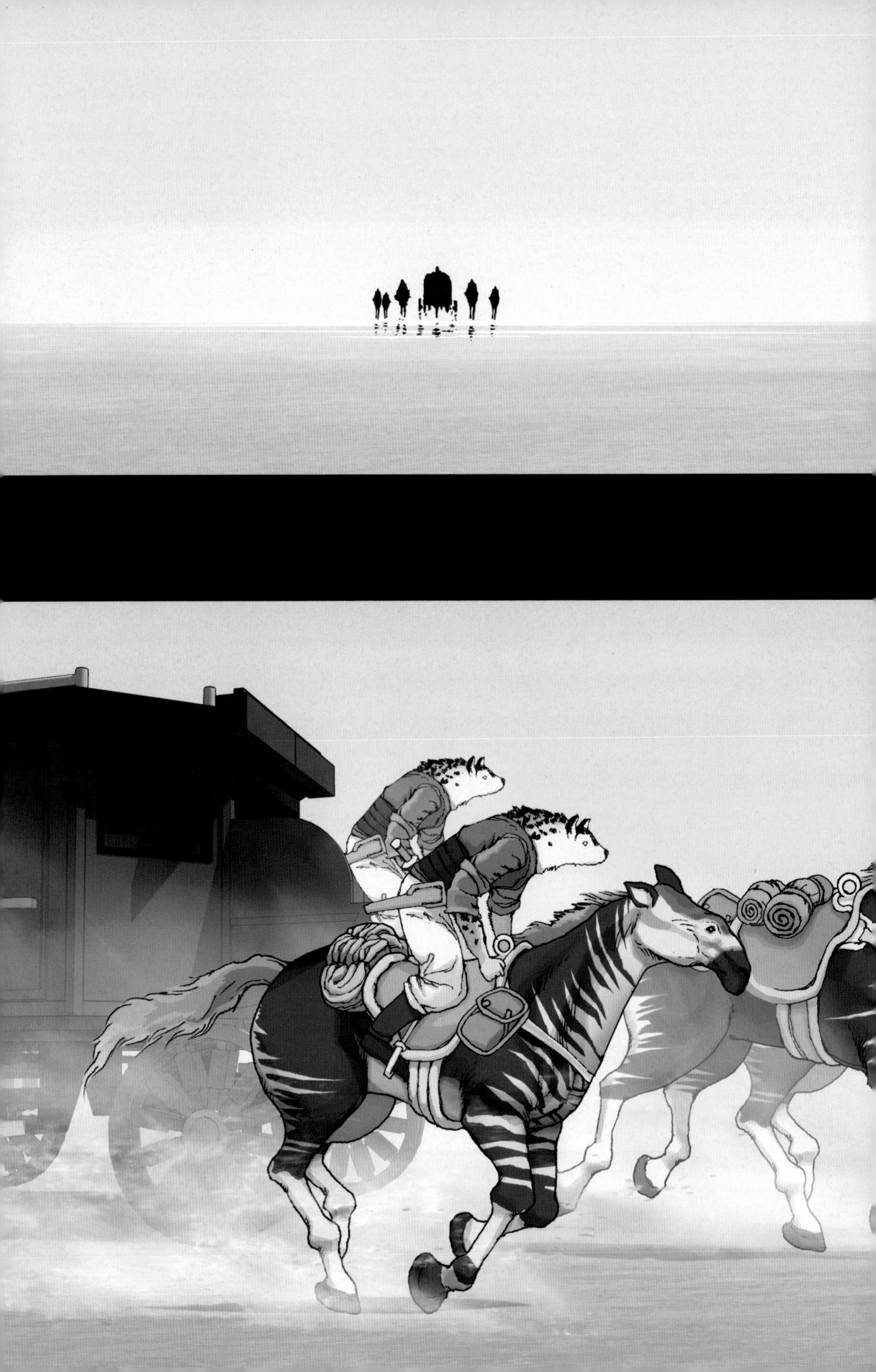

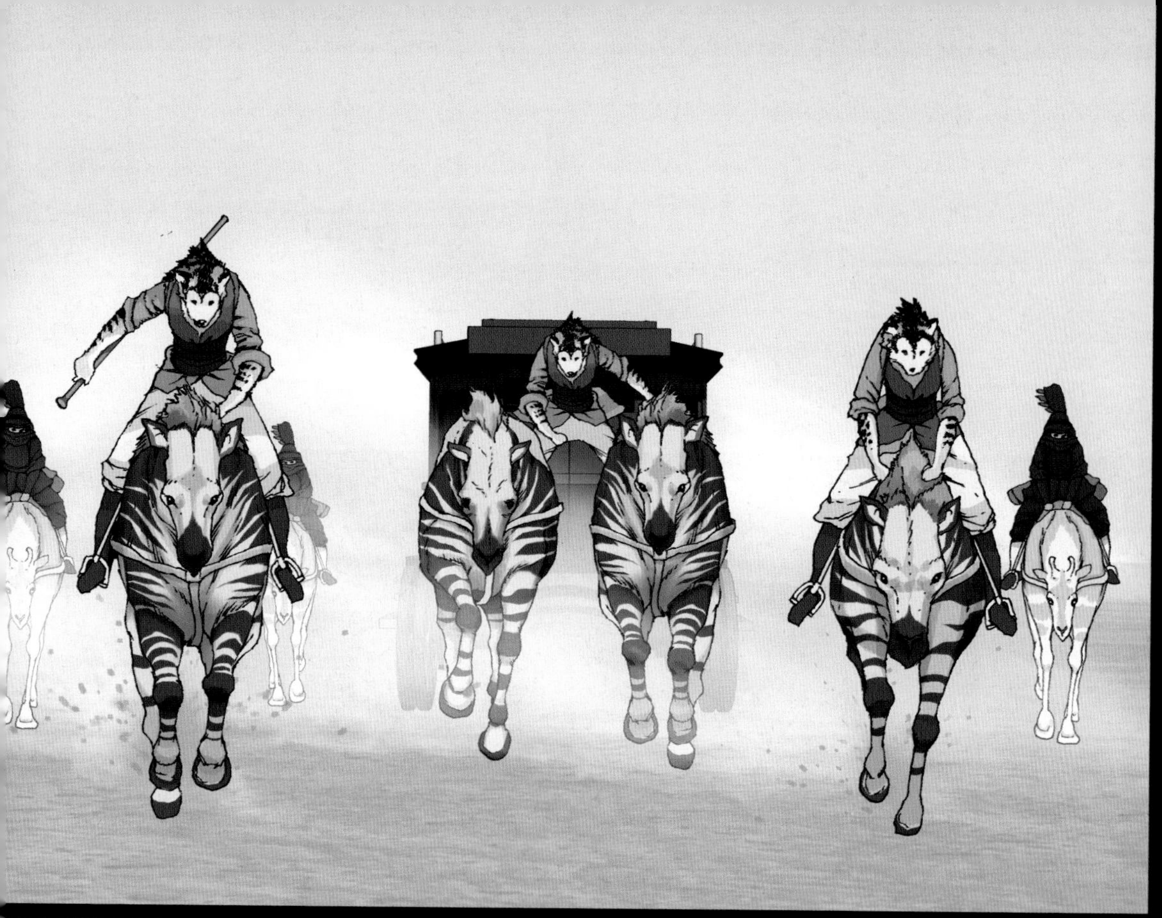

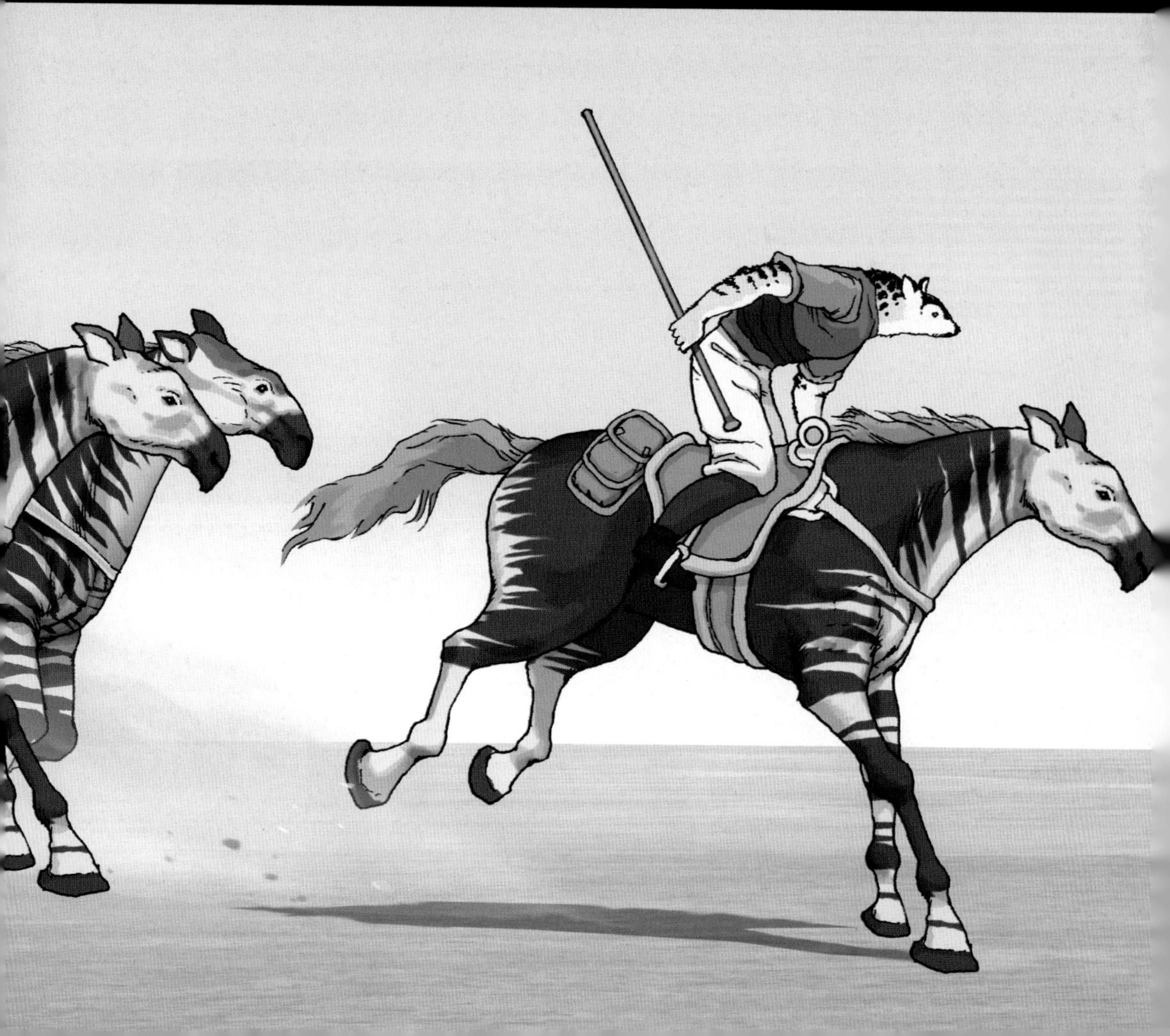

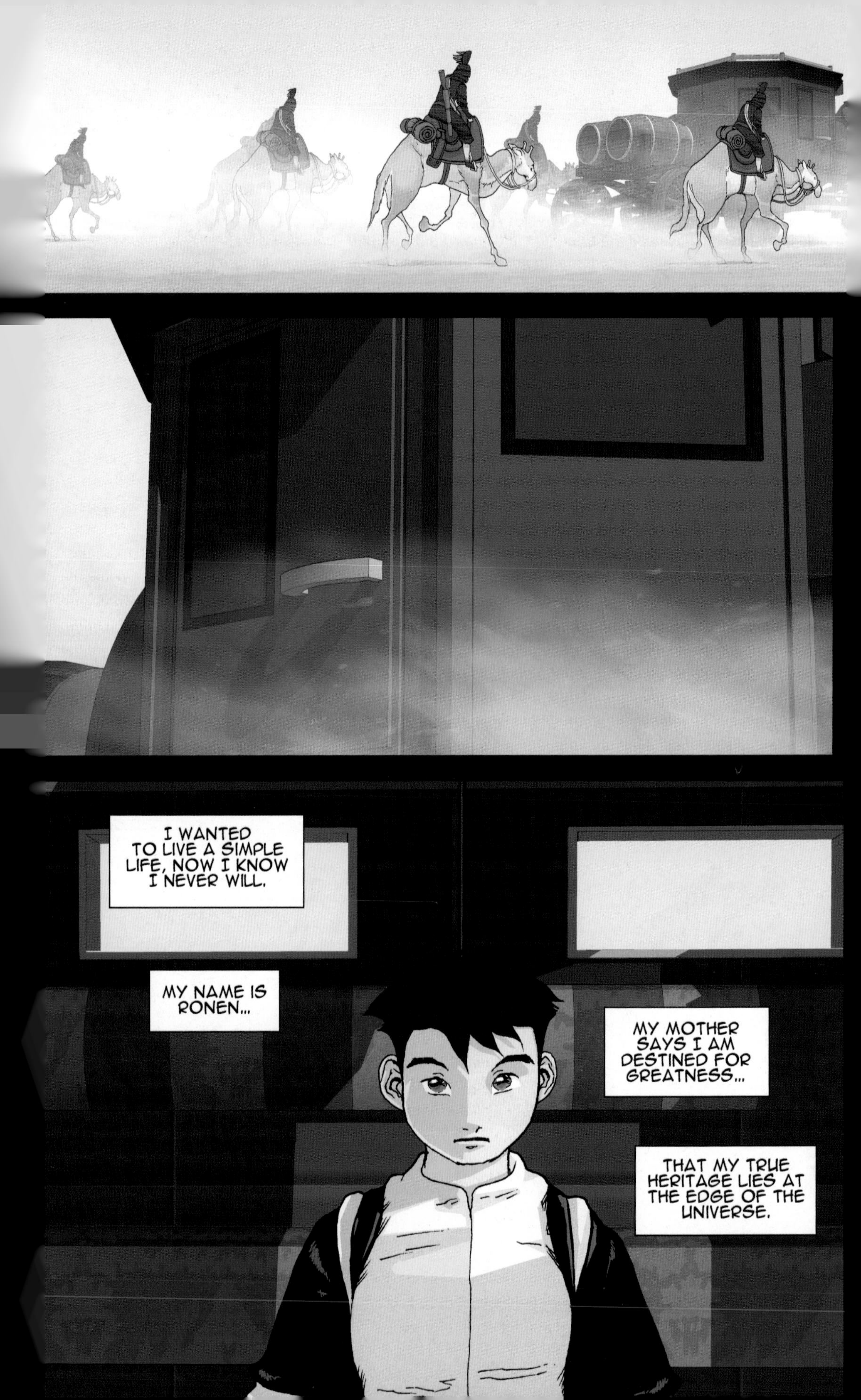
I WANTED TO LIVE A SIMPLE LIFE, NOW I KNOW I NEVER WILL.
MY NAME IS RONEN...
MY MOTHER SAYS I AM DESTINED FOR GREATNESS...
THAT MY TRUE HERITAGE LIES AT THE EDGE OF THE UNIVERSE.

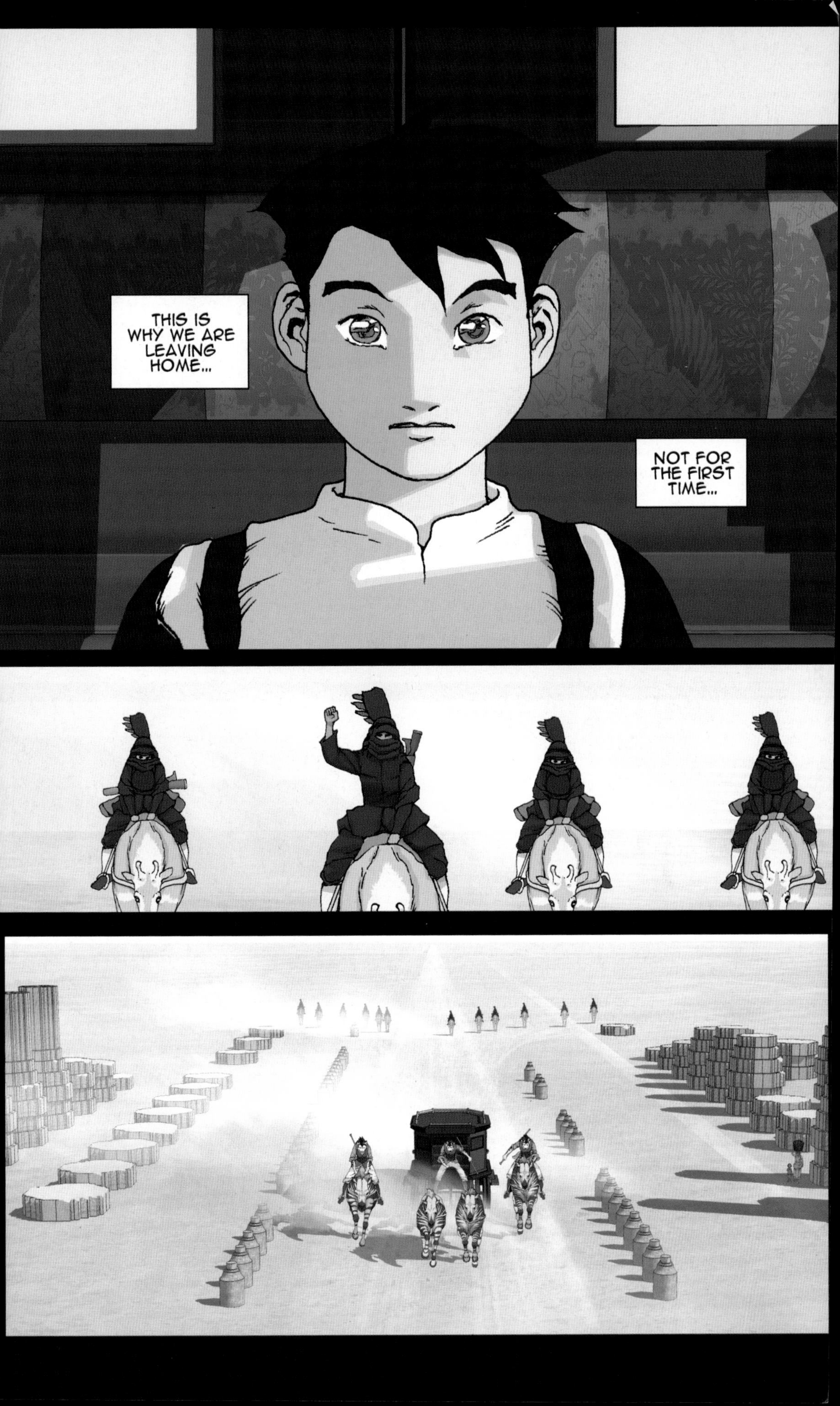
THIS IS WHY WE ARE LEAVING HOME...
NOT FOR THE FIRST TIME...

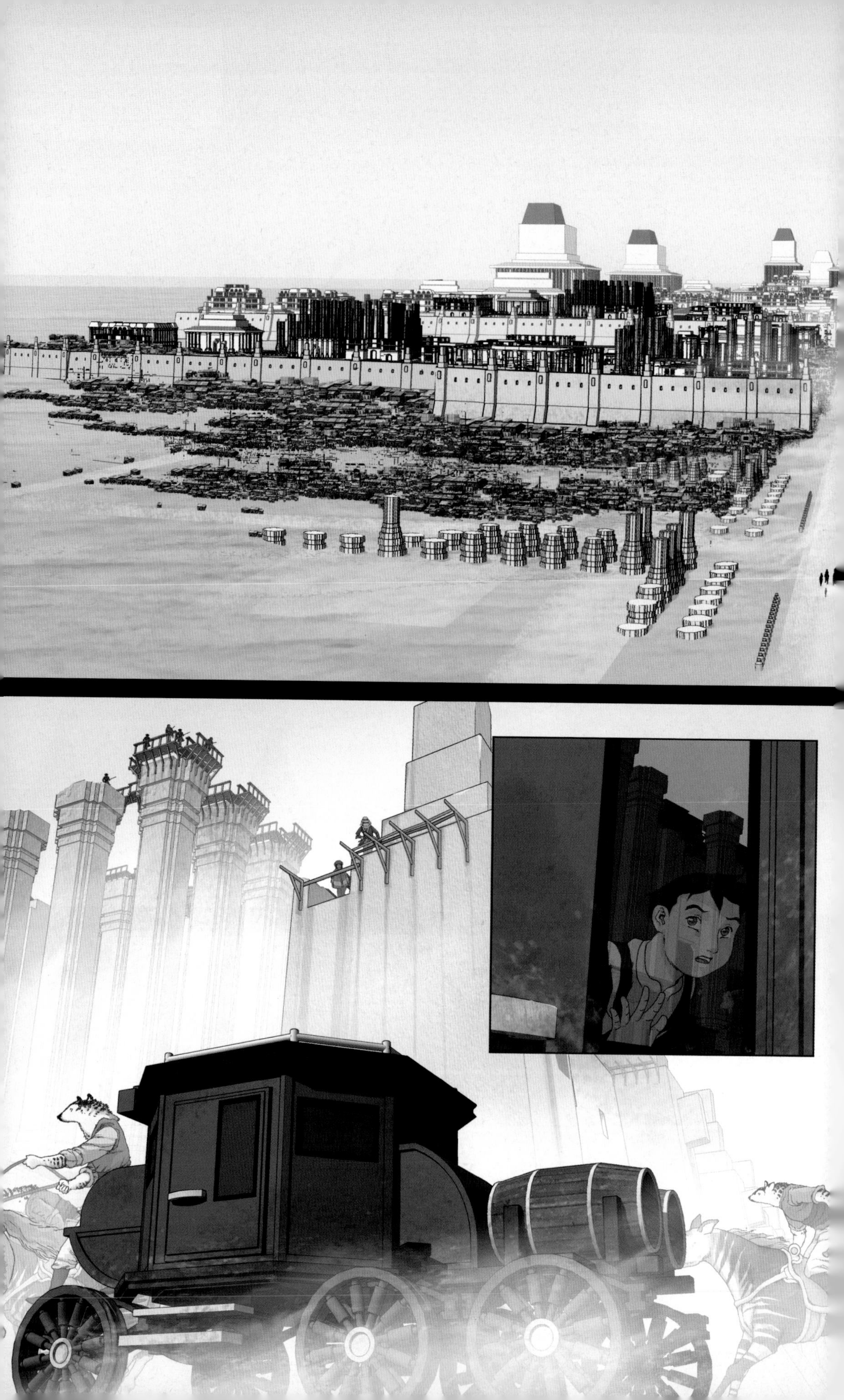

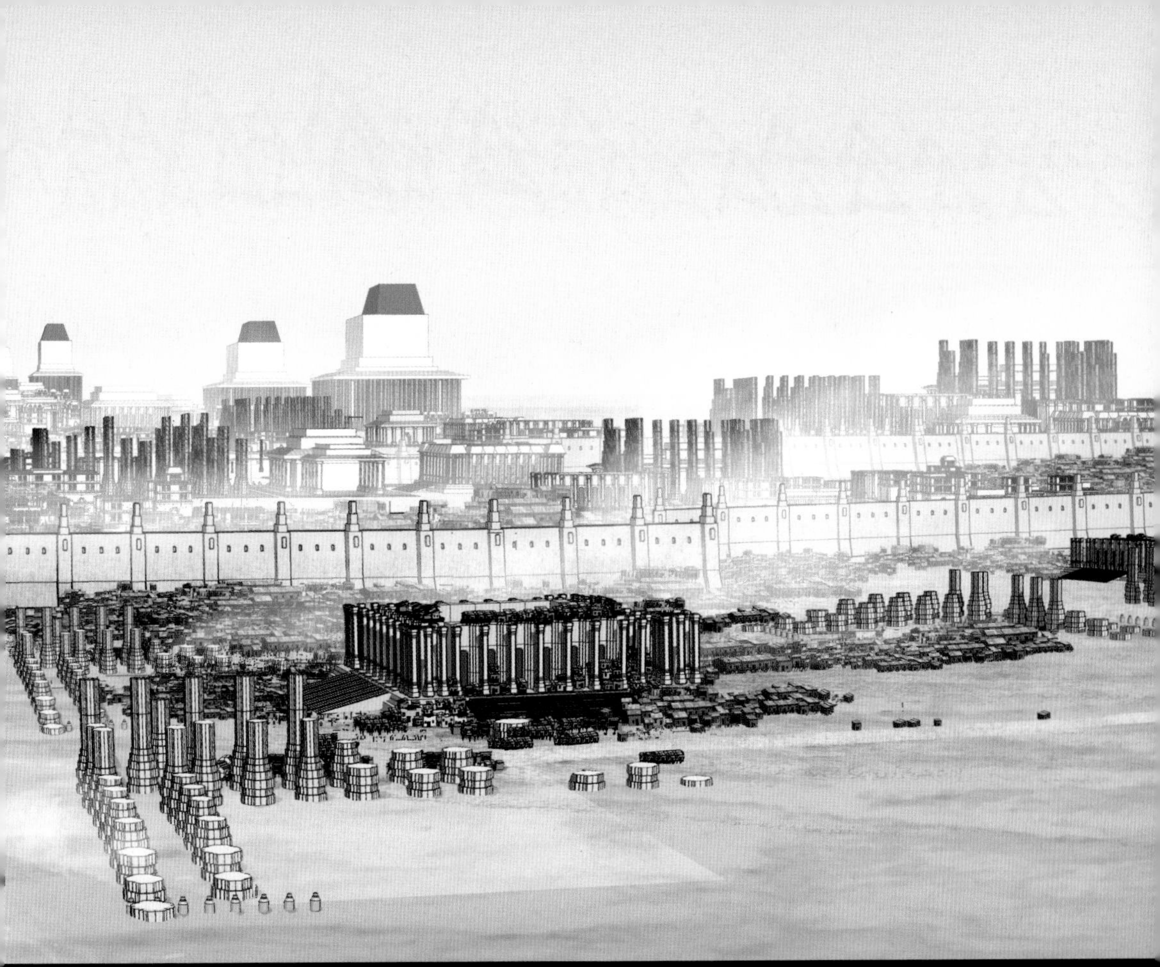

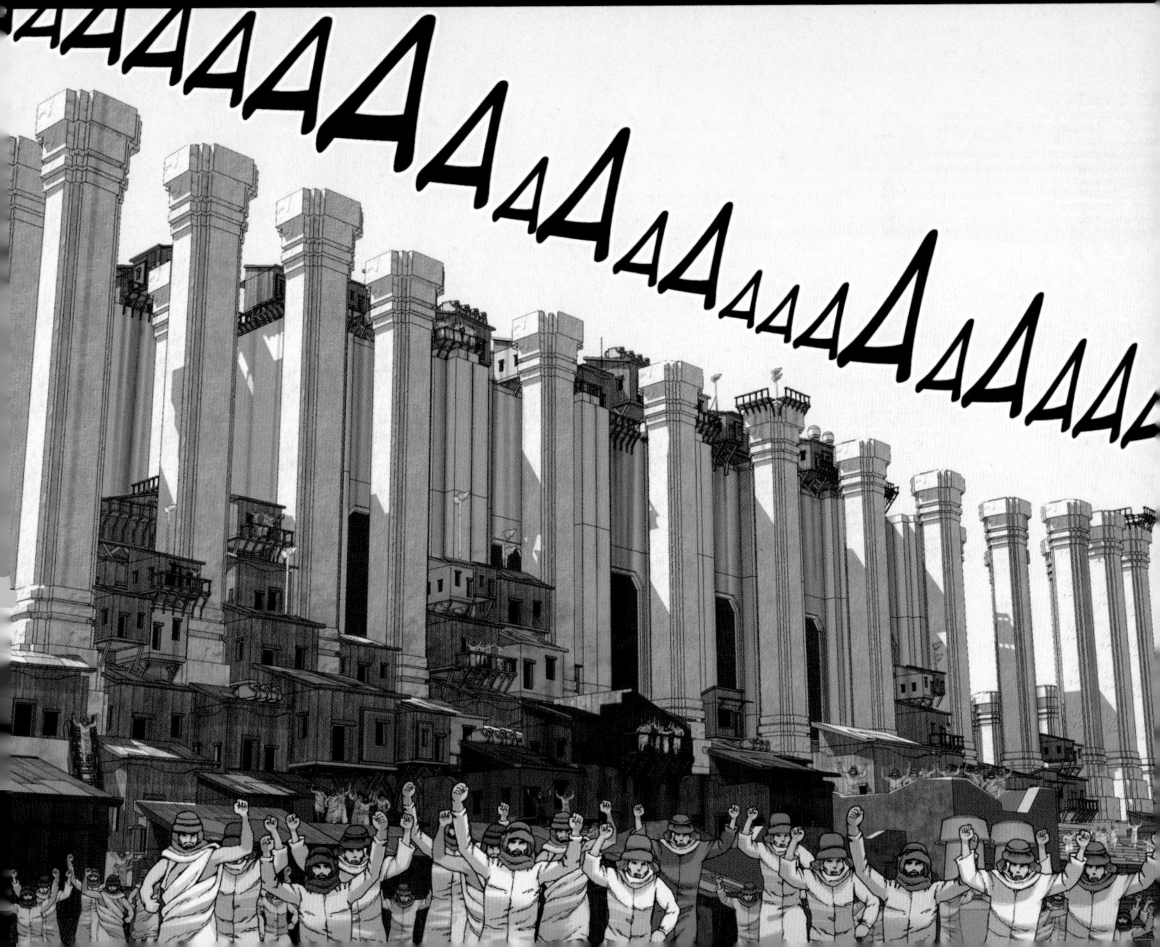
AAAAAAAAAAAAAAAAAAAAAAA

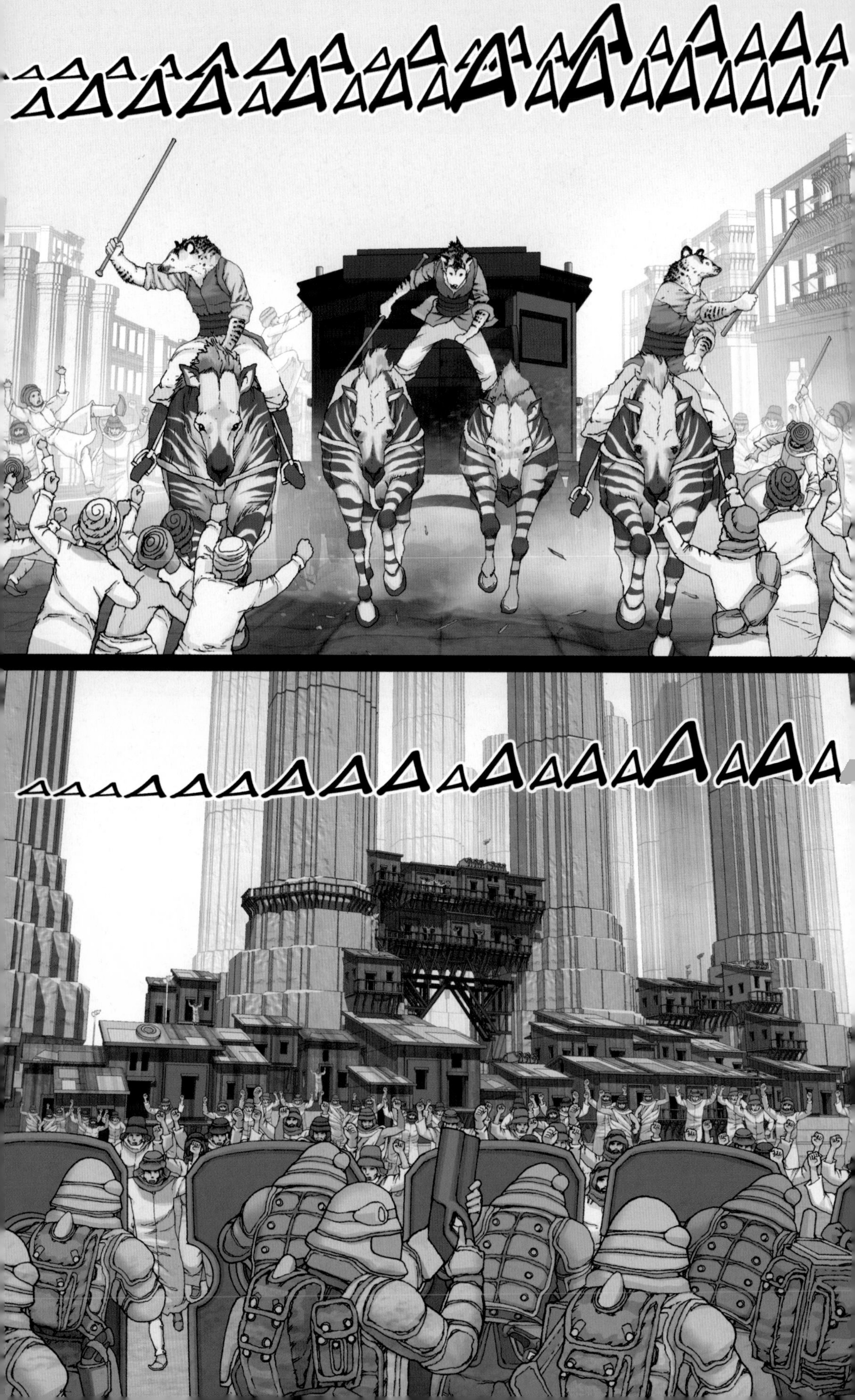
AAAAAAAAAAAAAAAAAAAAAAAAAAAAAAAAAAAAAAAAAAAAAAAA!
AAAAAAAAAAAAAAAAAAAA

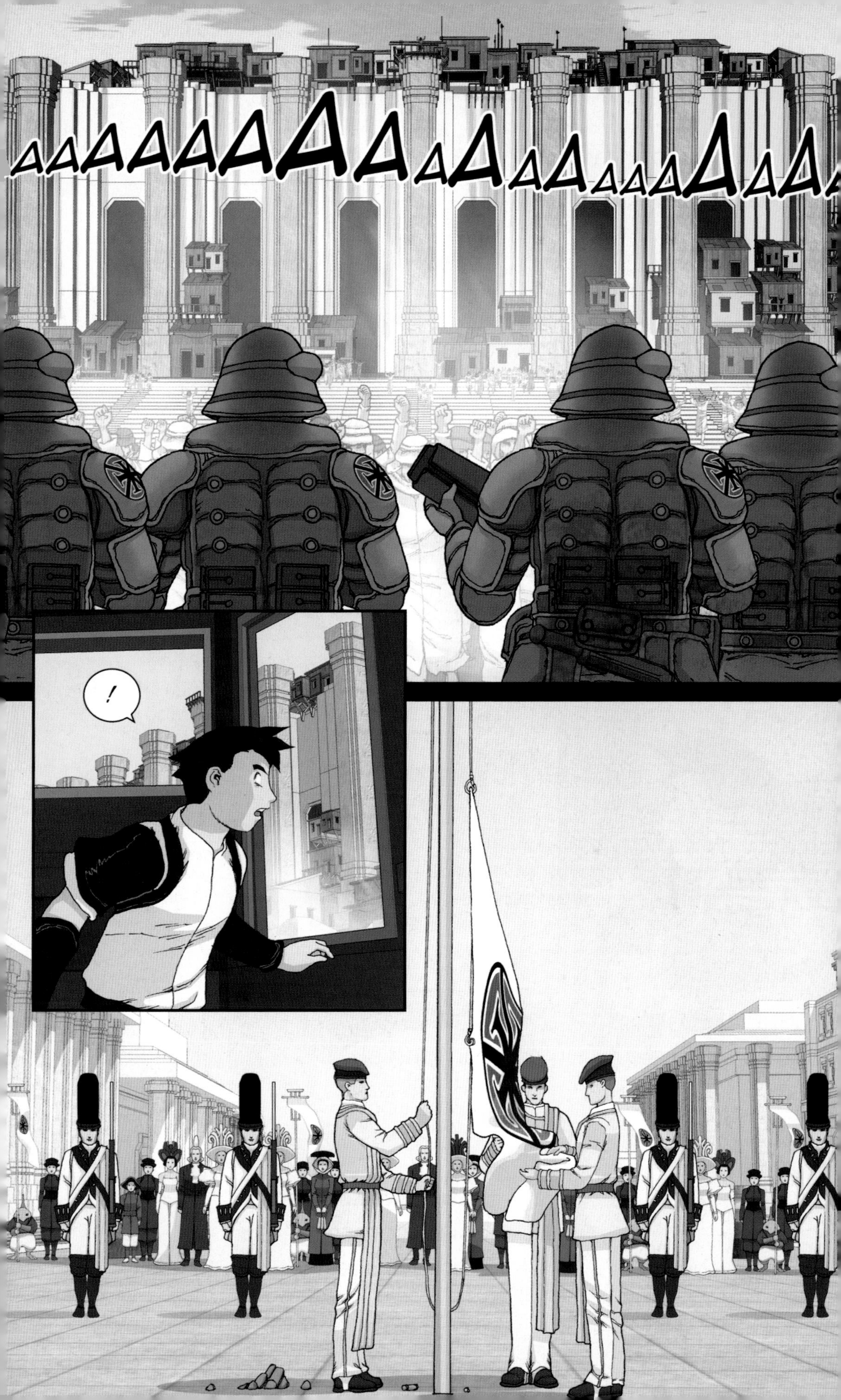

AAAAAAAAAAAAAAAAAAAAA
!

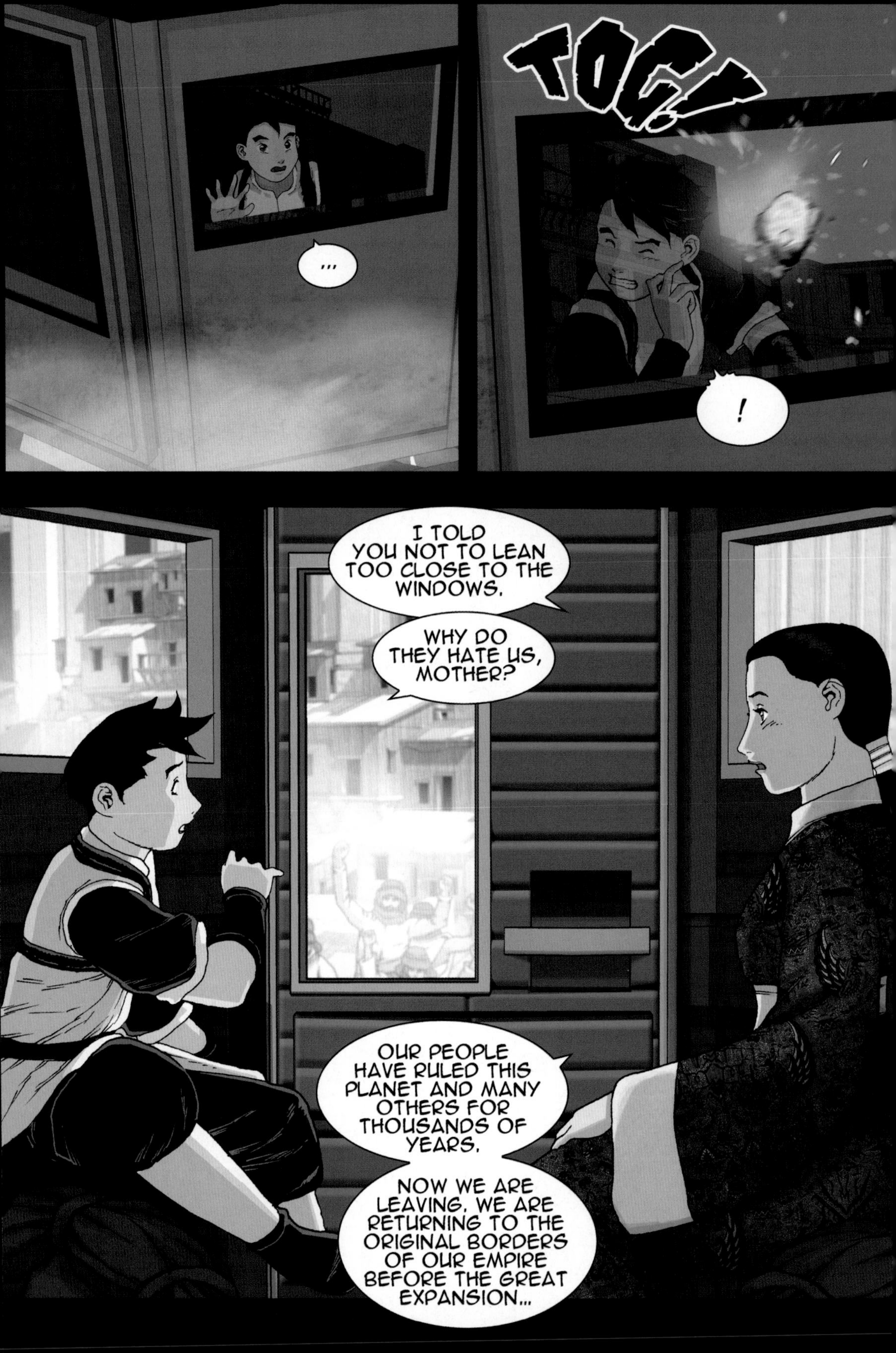
...
TOG!
!
I TOLD YOU NOT TO LEAN TOO CLOSE TO THE WINDOWS.
WHY DO THEY HATE US, MOTHER?
OUR PEOPLE HAVE RULED THIS PLANET AND MANY OTHERS FOR THOUSANDS OF YEARS.
NOW WE ARE LEAVING. WE ARE RETURNING TO THE ORIGINAL BORDERS OF OUR EMPIRE BEFORE THE GREAT EXPANSION...

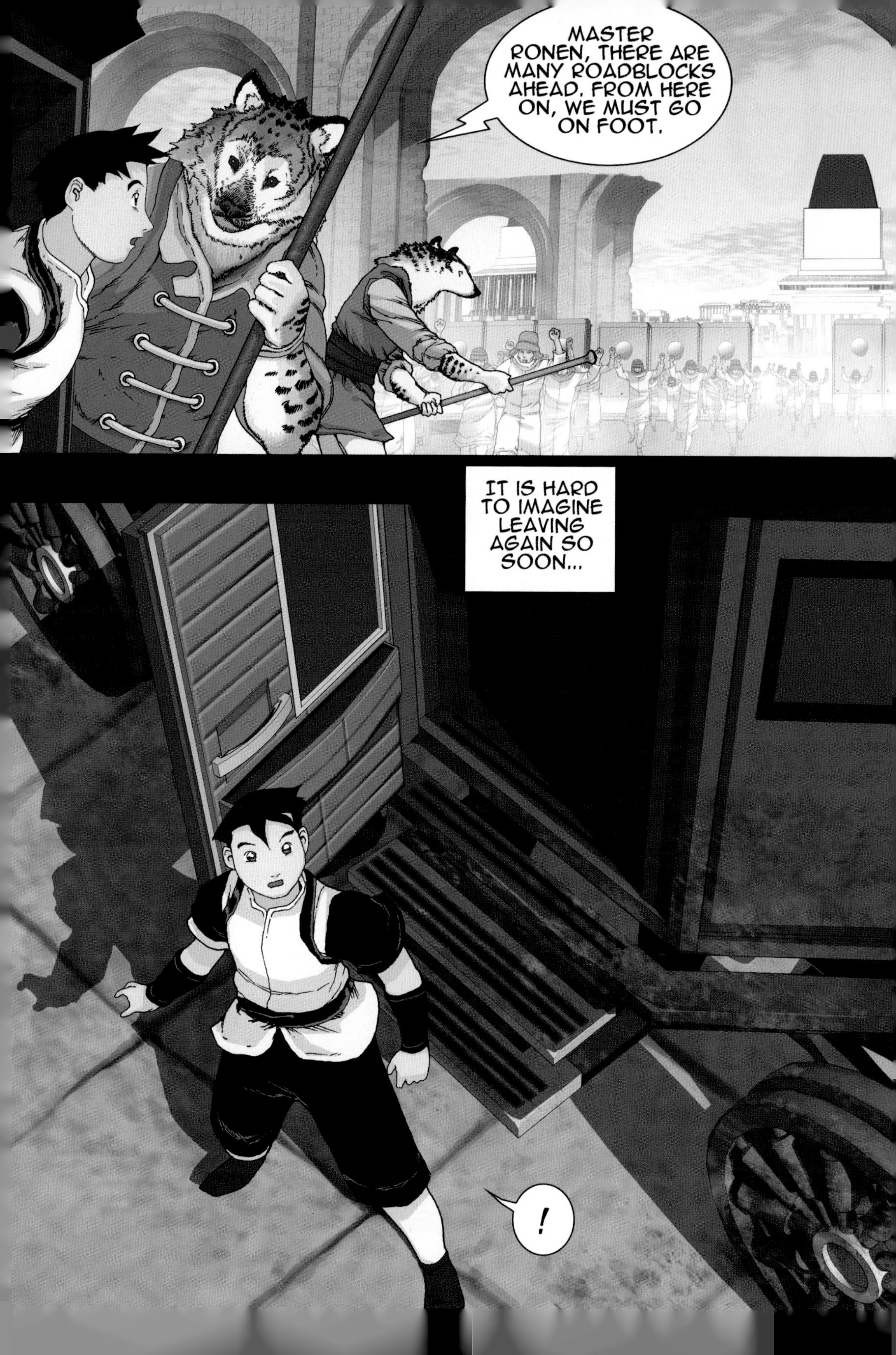
MASTER RONEN, THERE ARE MANY ROADBLOCKS AHEAD. FROM HERE ON, WE MUST GO ON FOOT.
IT IS HARD TO IMAGINE LEAVING AGAIN SO SOON...
!

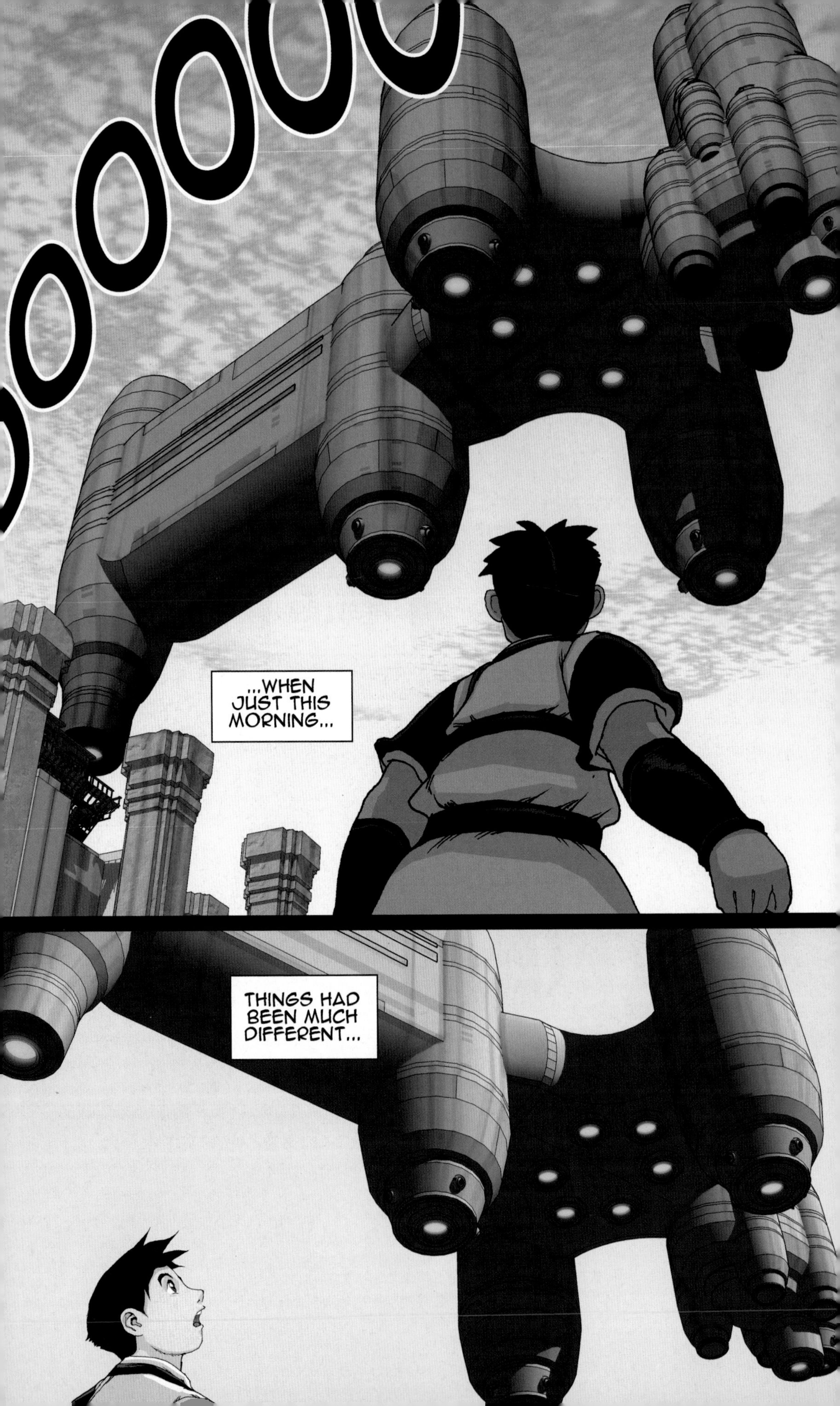
...WHEN JUST THIS MORNING...
THINGS HAD BEEN MUCH DIFFERENT...

Rod Espinosa
Presents

The
Prince of Heroes

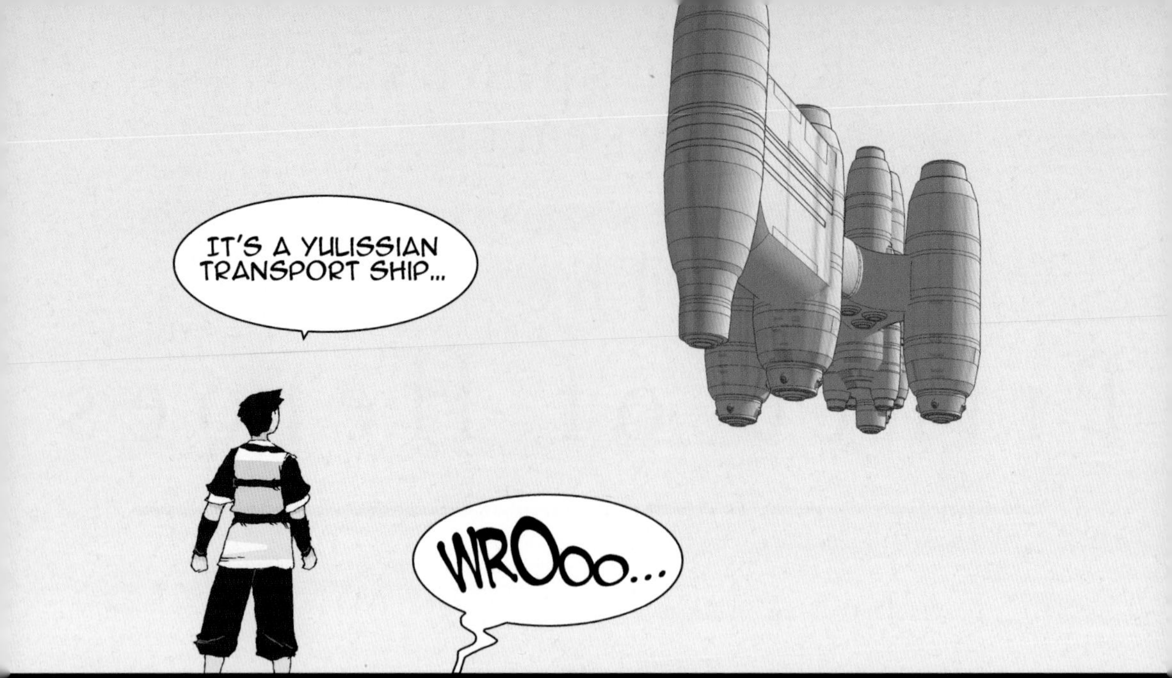
IT'S A YULISSIAN TRANSPORT SHIP...
WROooo...

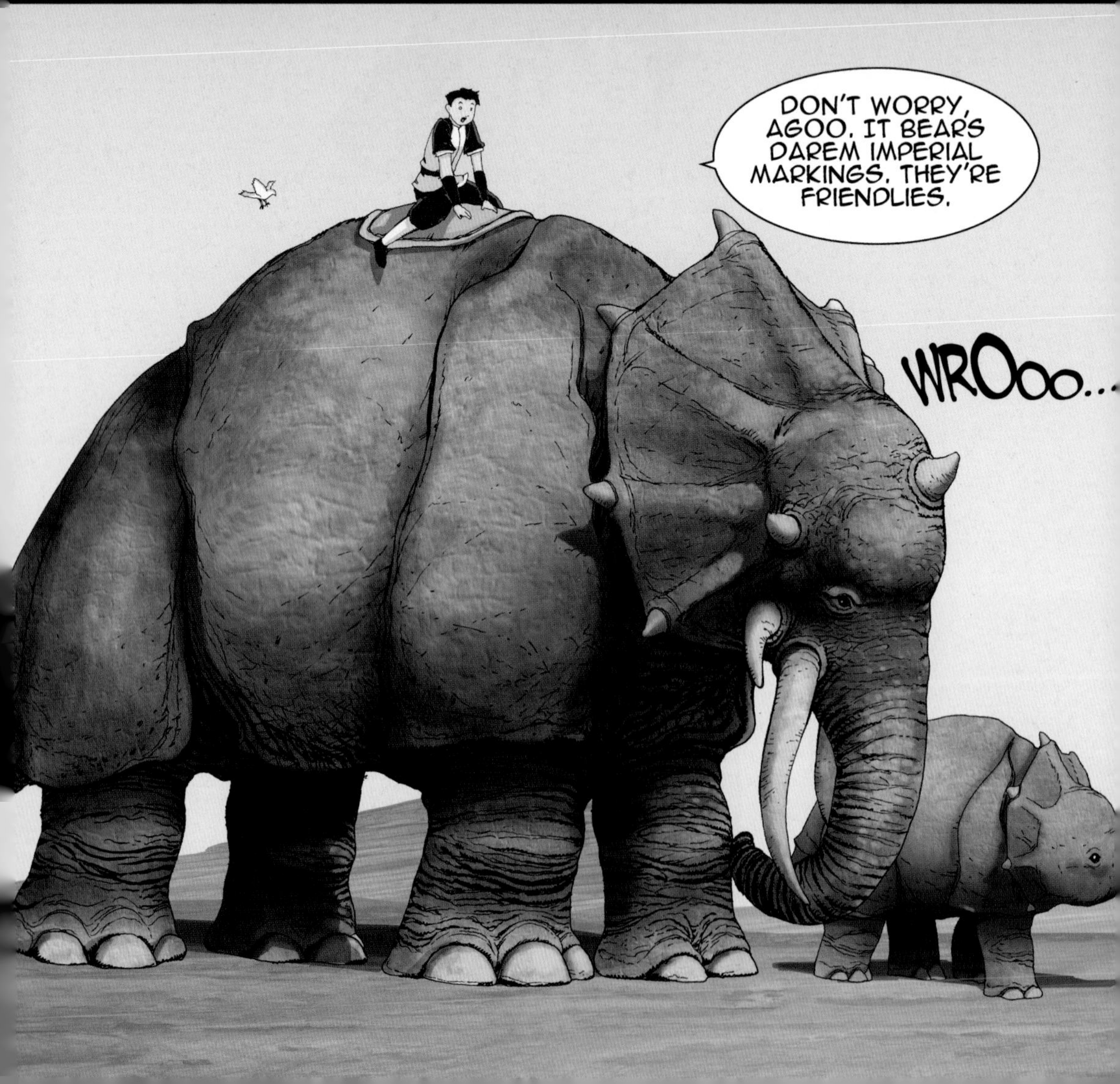
DON'T WORRY, AGOO. IT BEARS DAREM IMPERIAL MARKINGS. THEY'RE FRIENDLIES.
WROooo...

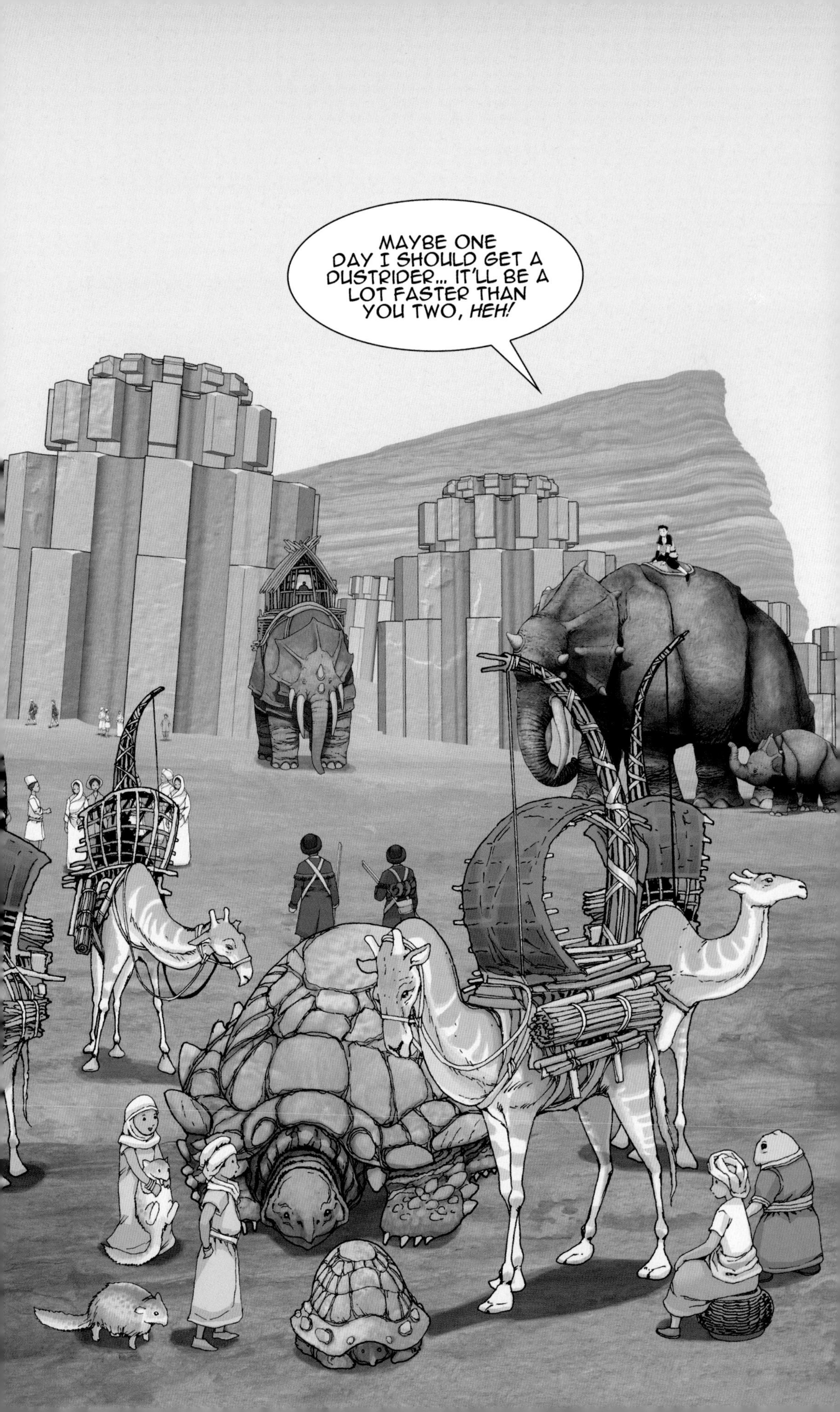
MAYBE ONE DAY I SHOULD GET A DUSTRIDER... IT'LL BE A LOT FASTER THAN YOU TWO, *HEH!*

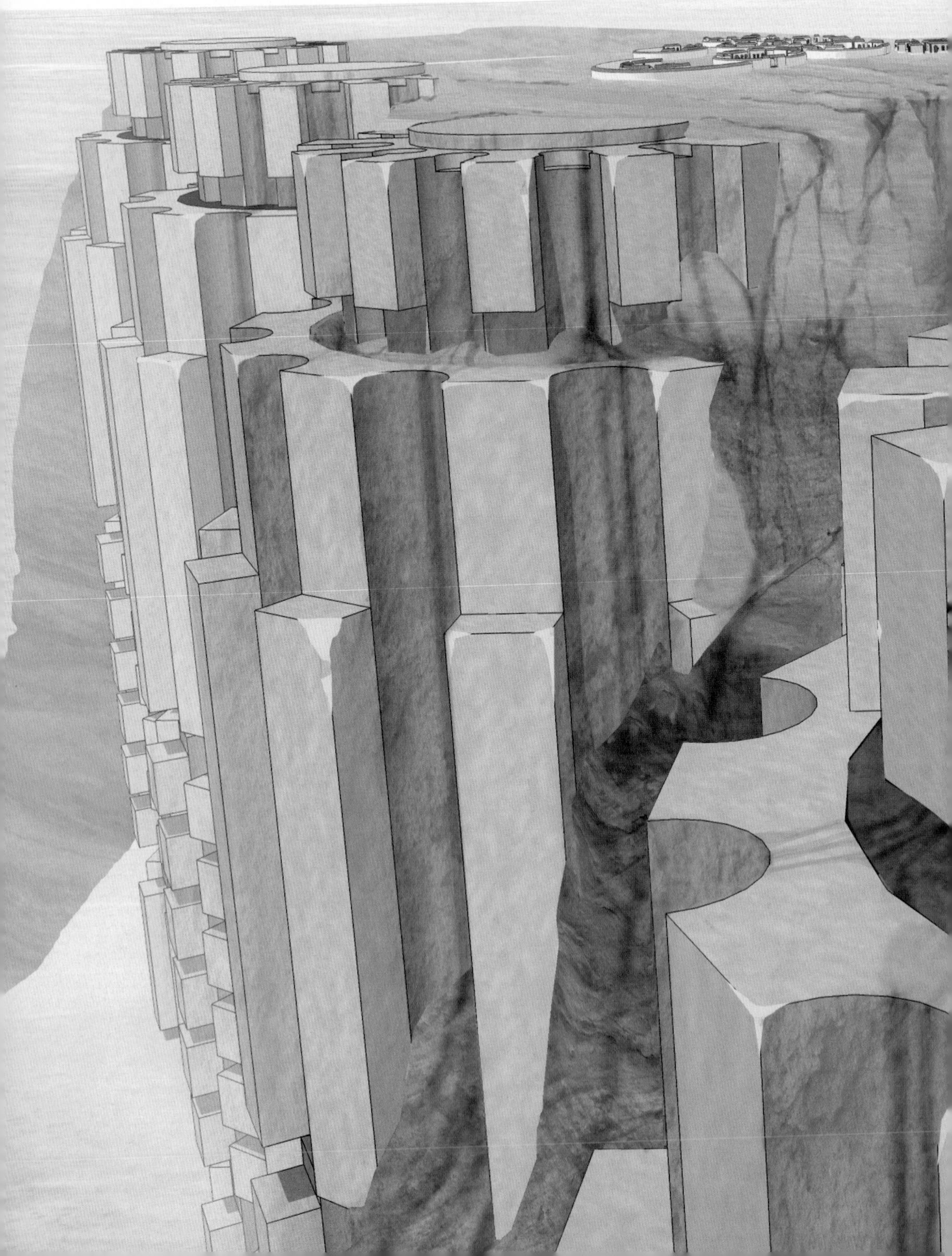

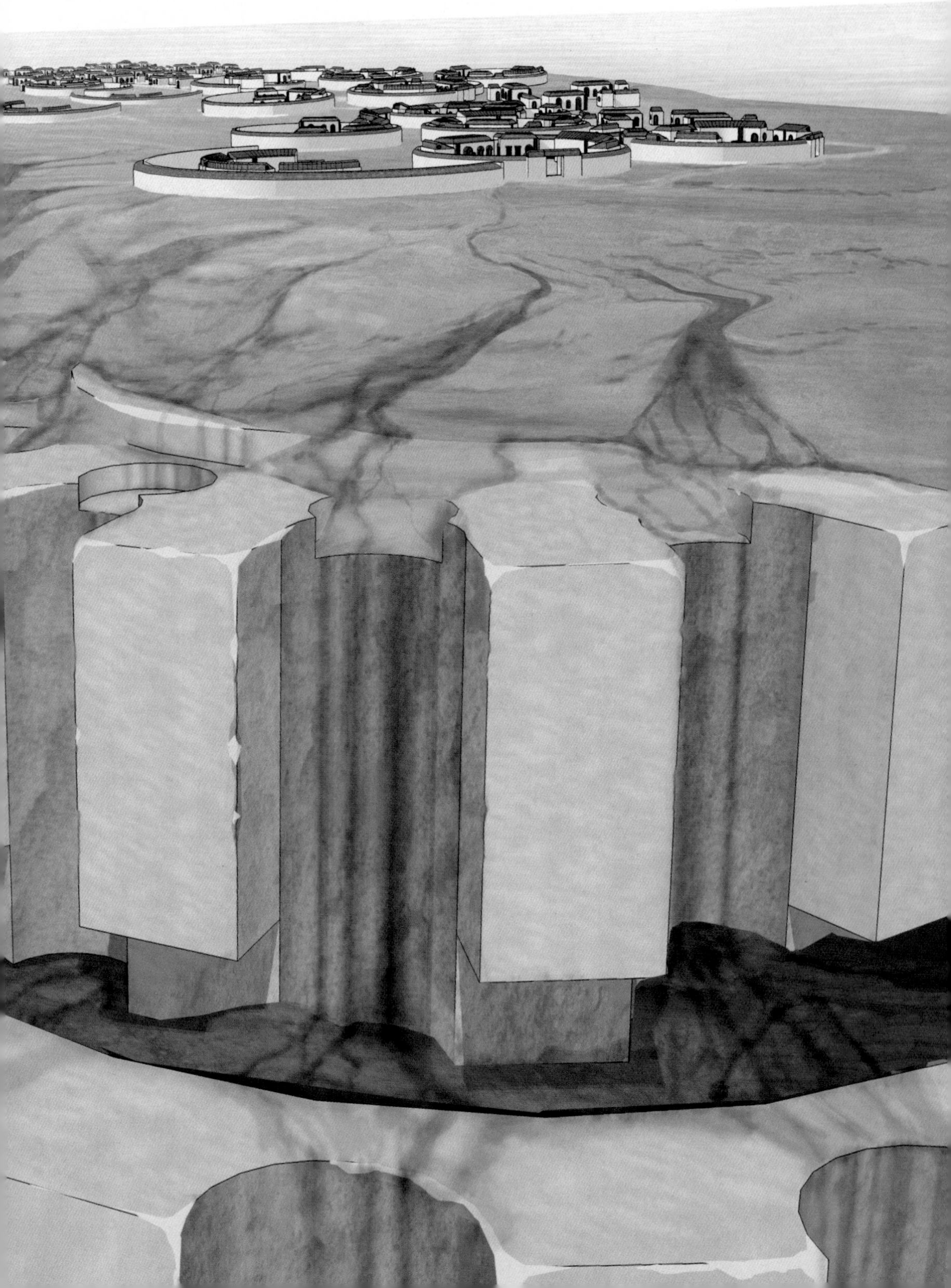

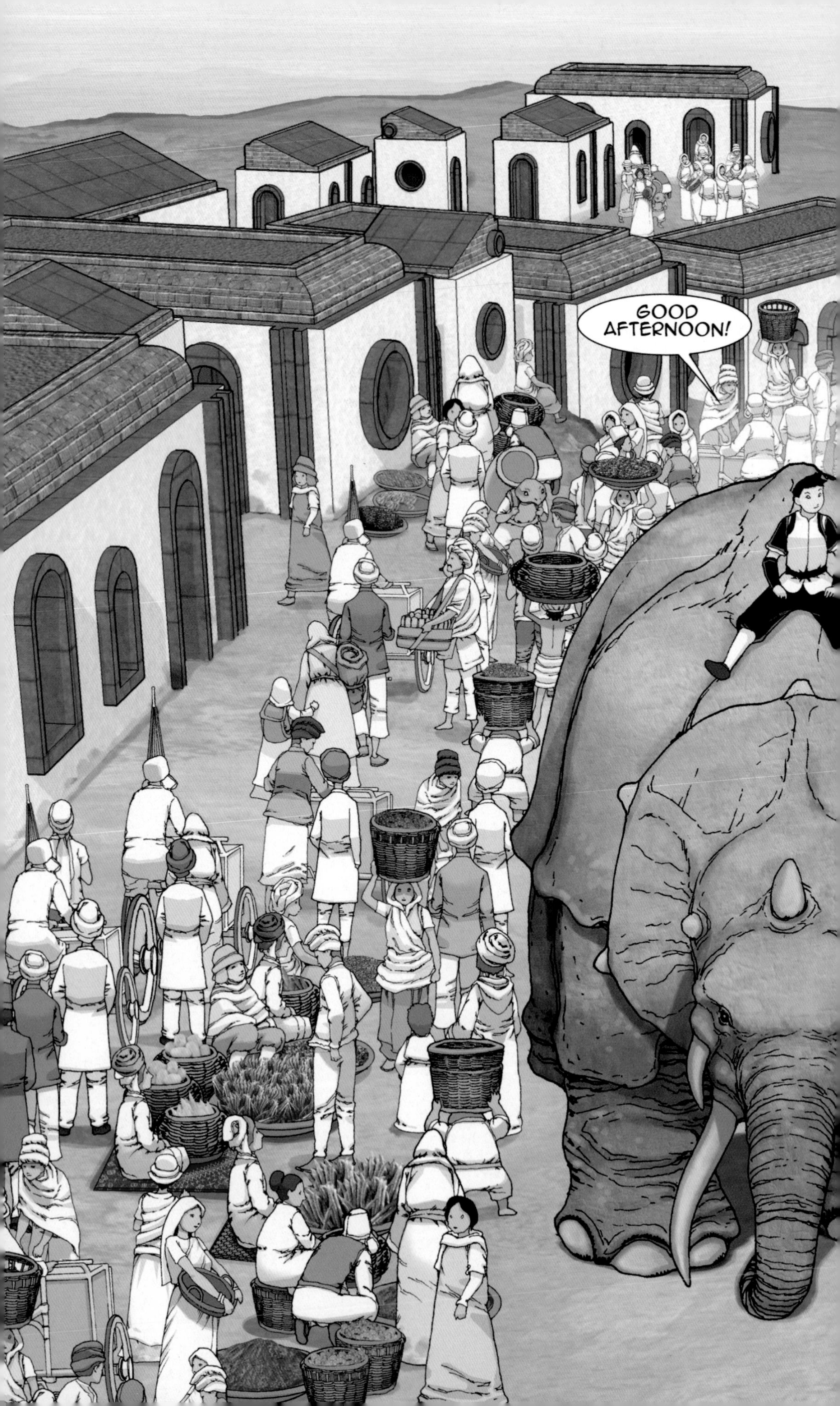
GOOD AFTERNOON!

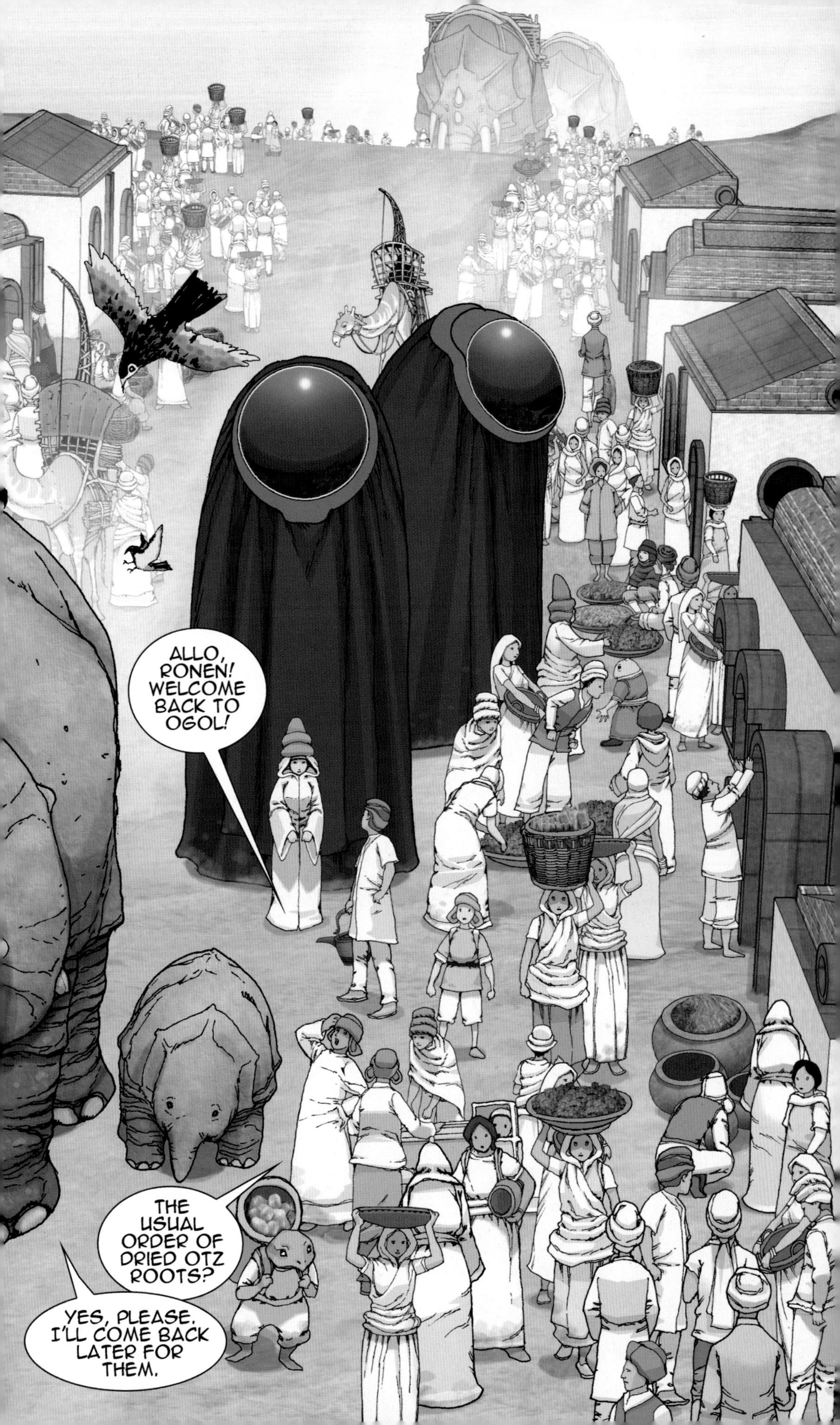
ALLO, RONEN! WELCOME BACK TO OGOL!
THE USUAL ORDER OF DRIED OTZ ROOTS?
YES, PLEASE. I'LL COME BACK LATER FOR THEM.

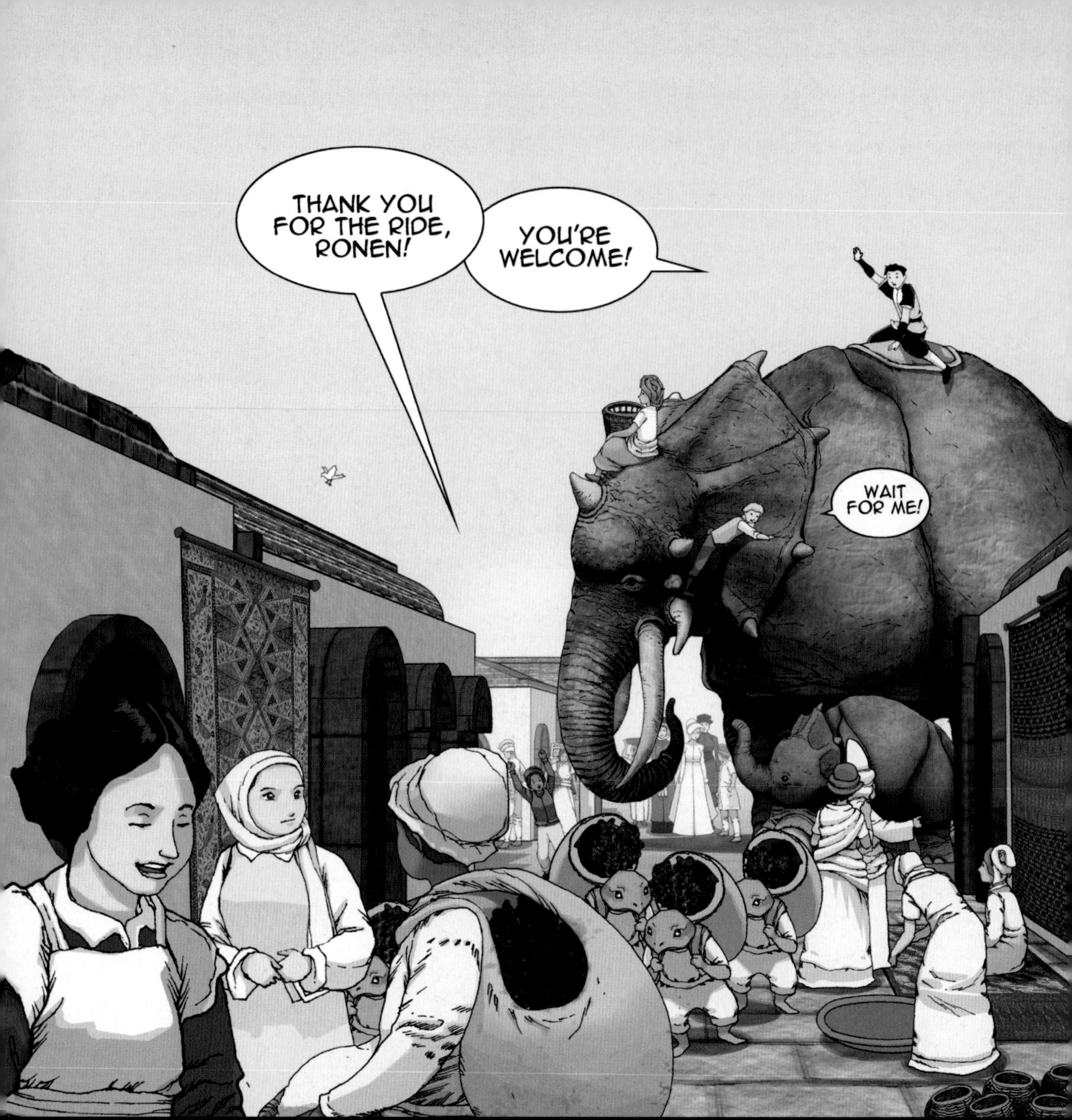
THANK YOU FOR THE RIDE, RONEN!
YOU'RE WELCOME!
WAIT FOR ME!

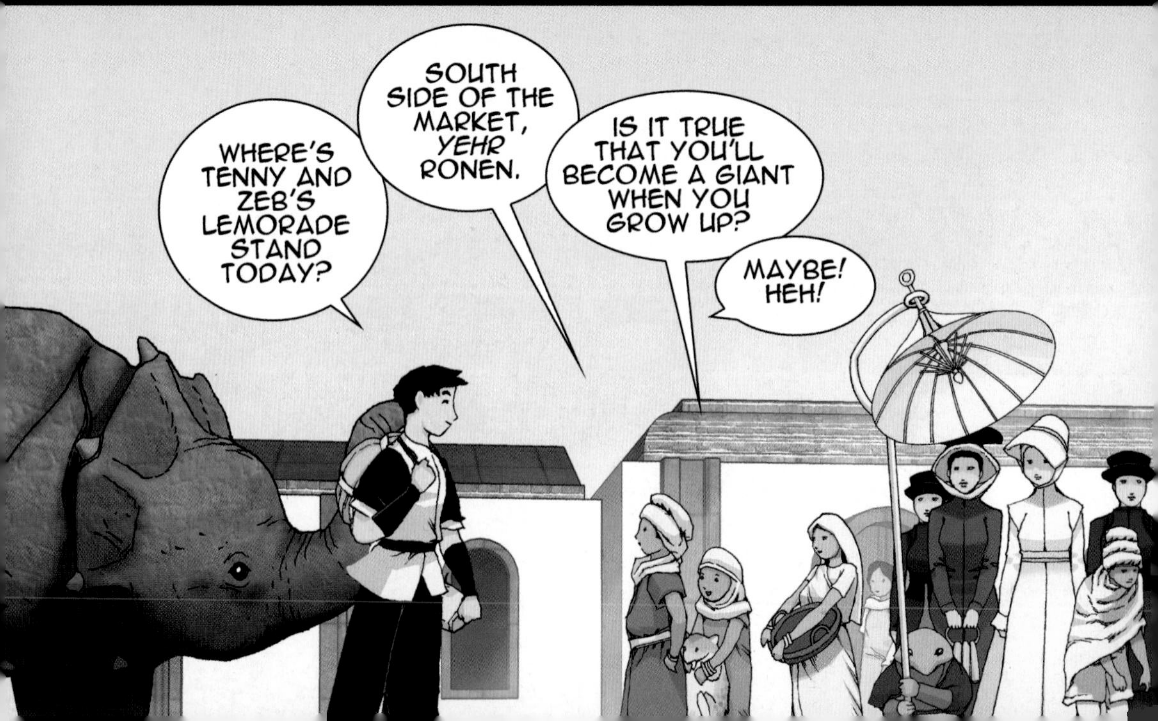
WHERE'S TENNY AND ZEB'S LEMORADE STAND TODAY?
SOUTH SIDE OF THE MARKET, *YEHR* RONEN.
IS IT TRUE THAT YOU'LL BECOME A GIANT WHEN YOU GROW UP?
MAYBE! HEH!

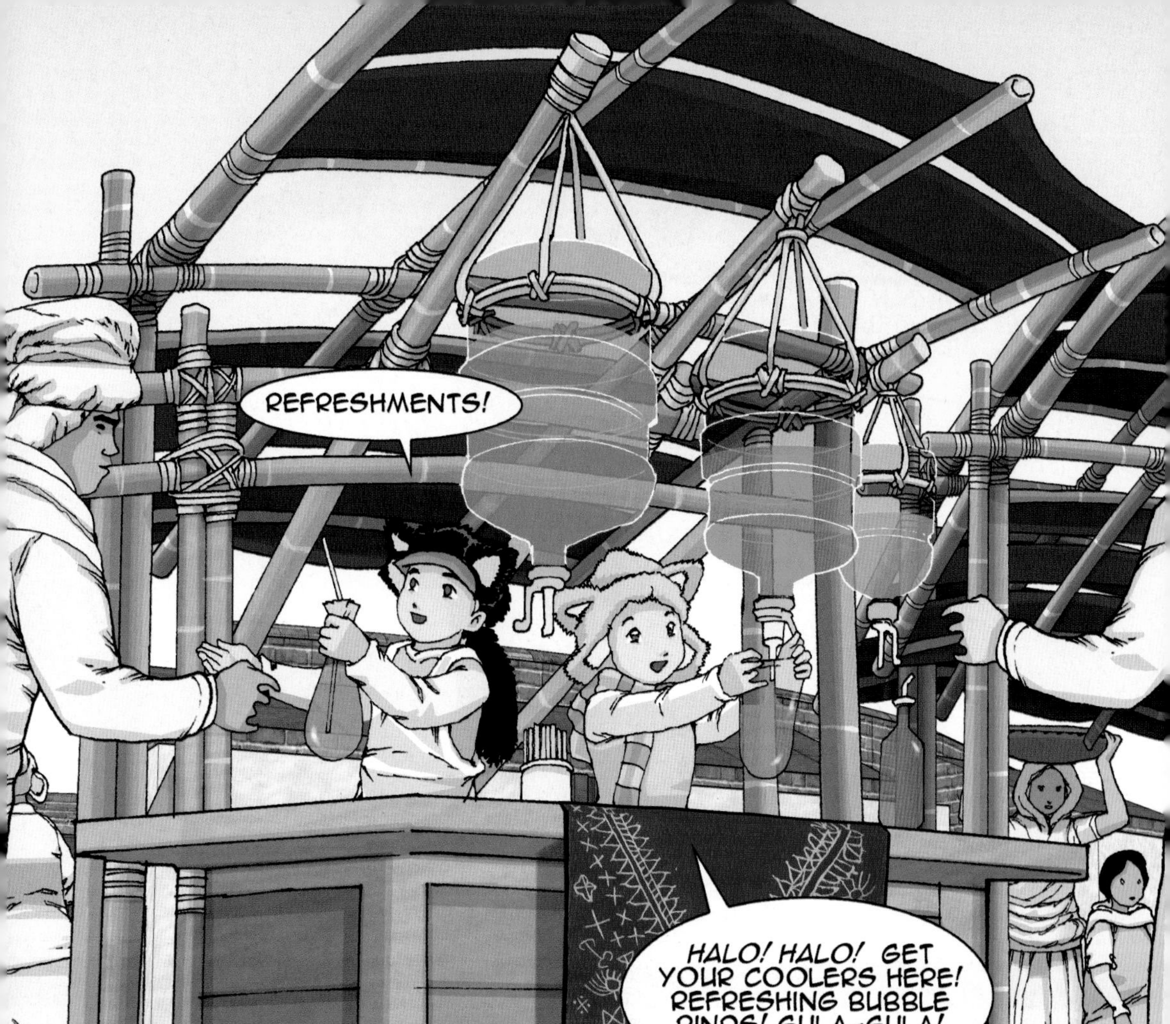
REFRESHMENTS!
HALO! HALO! GET YOUR COOLERS HERE! REFRESHING BUBBLE RINDS! GULA-GULA! LEMORADE!

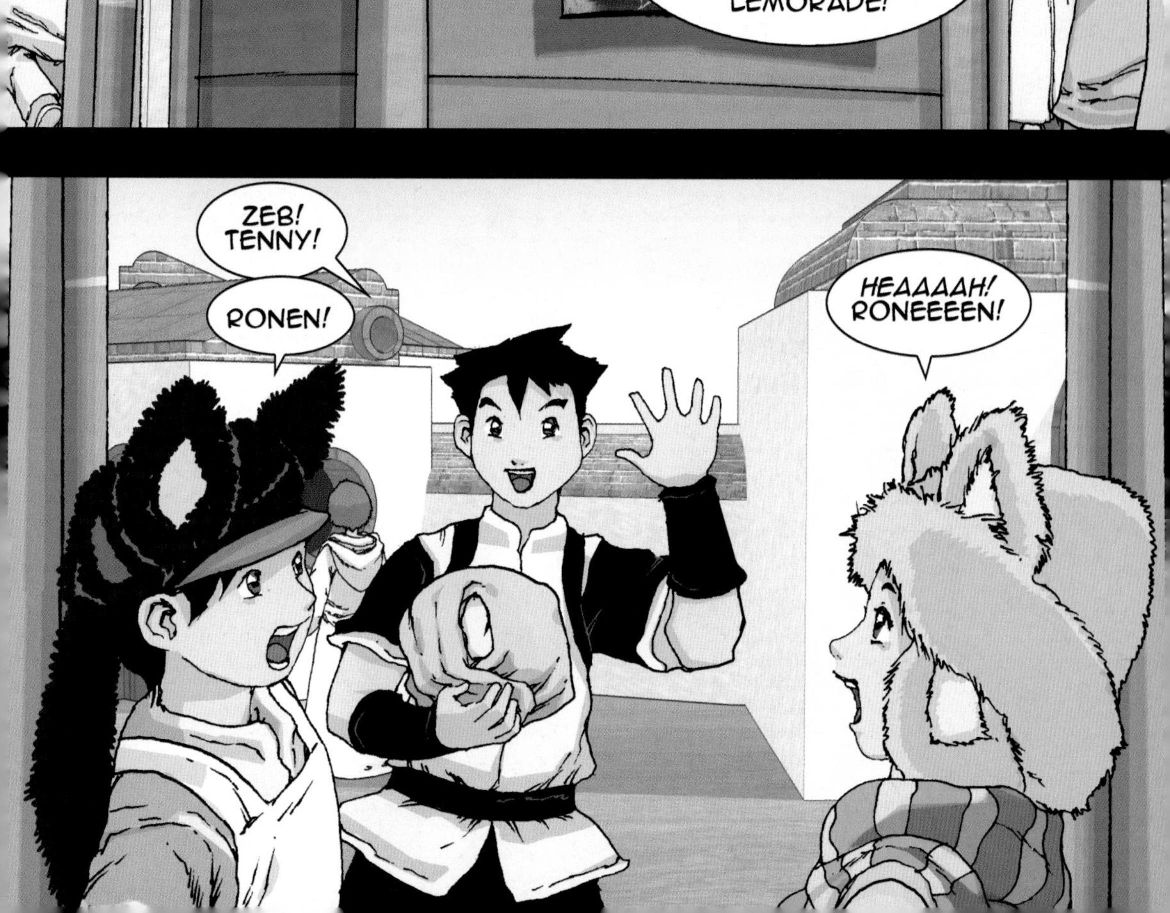
ZEB! TENNY!
RONEN!
HEAAAAH! RONEEEEN!

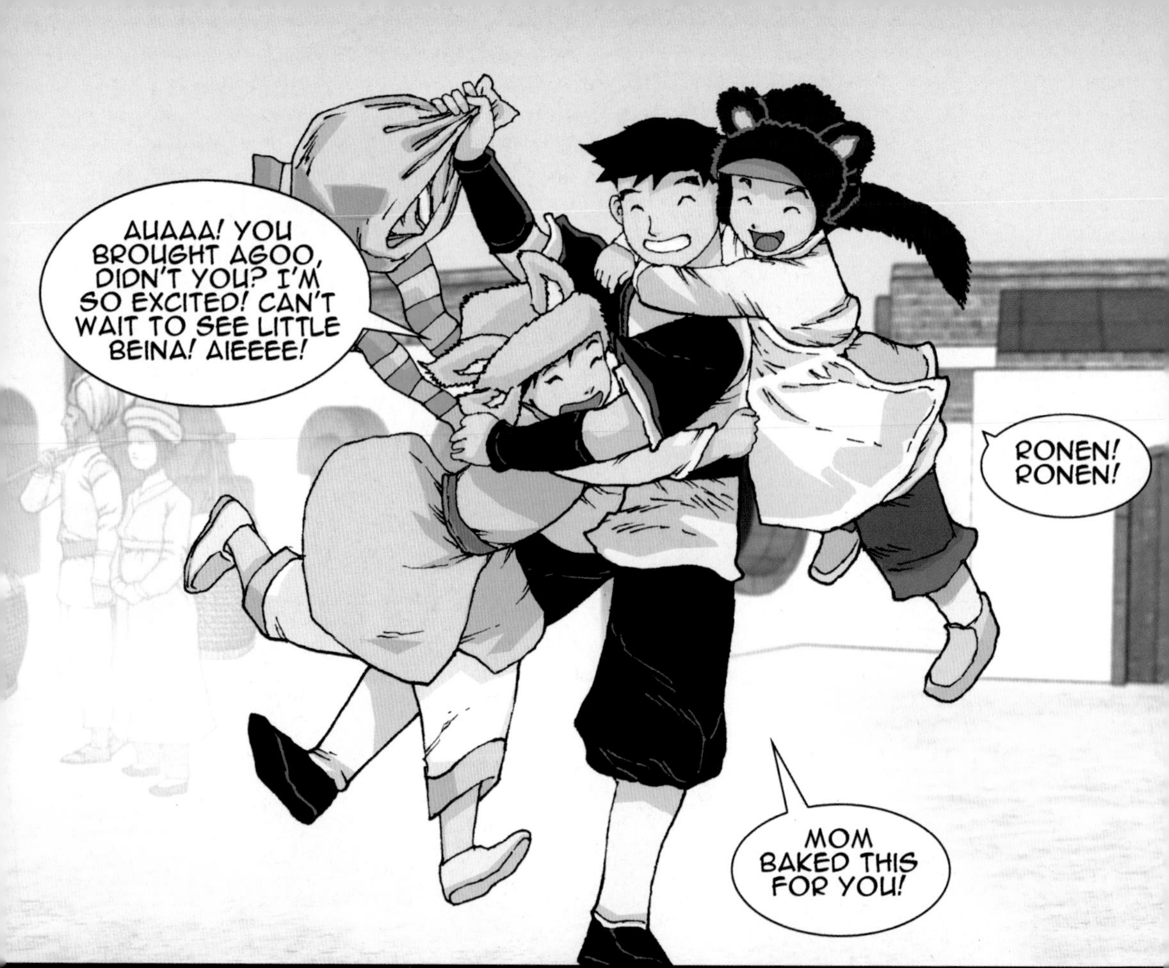
AUAAA! YOU BROUGHT AGOO, DIDN'T YOU? I'M SO EXCITED! CAN'T WAIT TO SEE LITTLE BEINA! AIEEEE!
RONEN! RONEN!
MOM BAKED THIS FOR YOU!

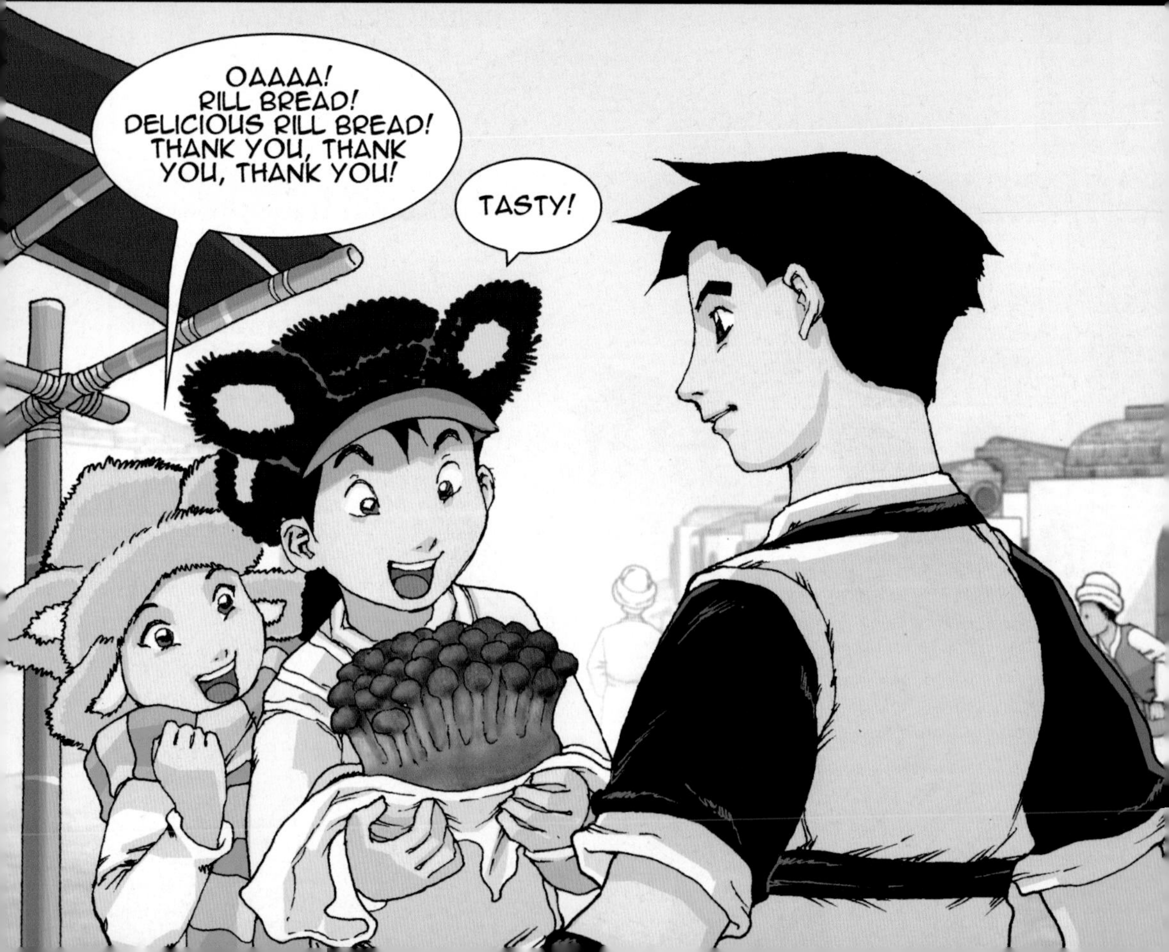
OAAAA! RILL BREAD! DELICIOUS RILL BREAD! THANK YOU, THANK YOU, THANK YOU!
TASTY!

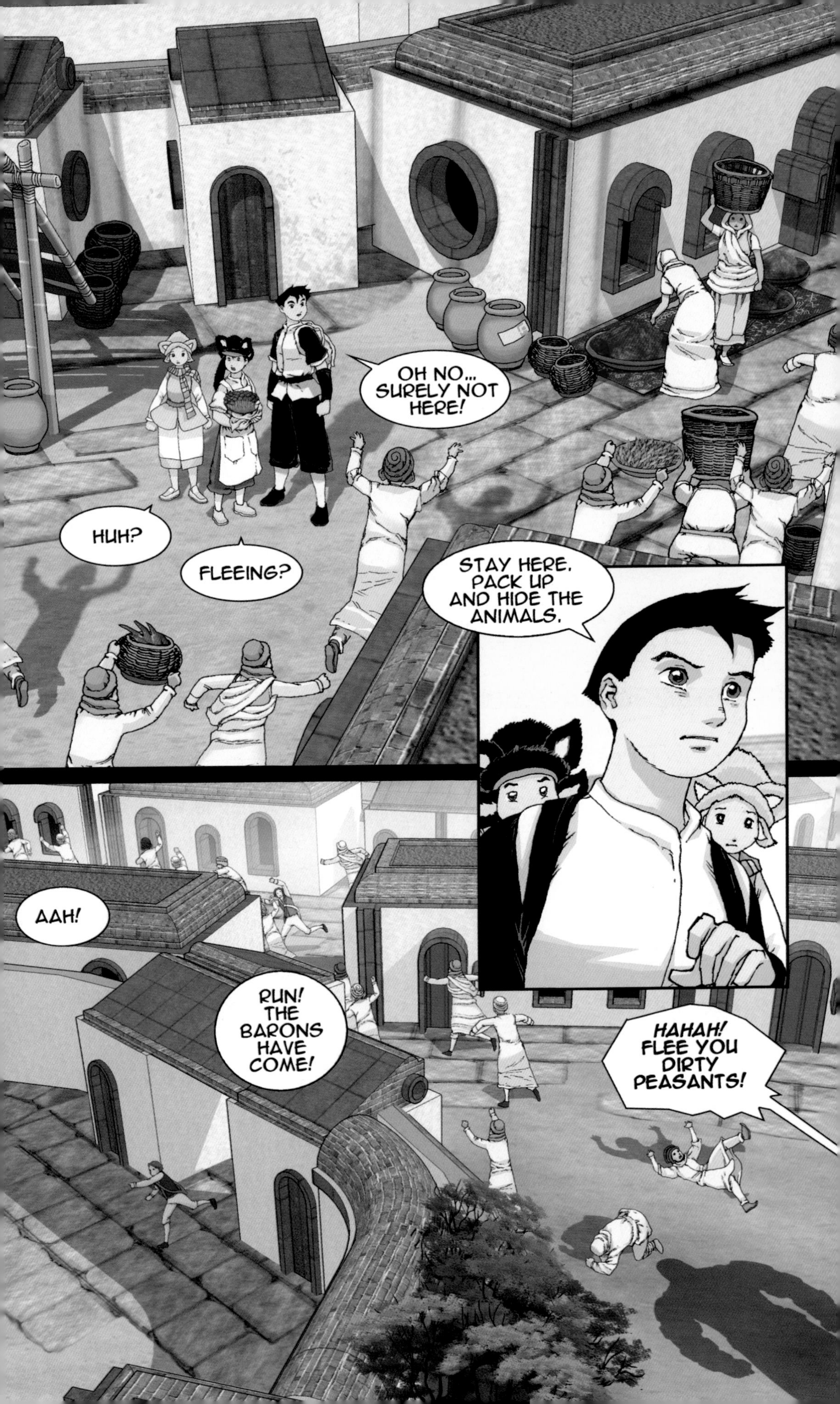

OH NO... SURELY NOT HERE!
HUH?
FLEEING?
STAY HERE. PACK UP AND HIDE THE ANIMALS.
AAH!
RUN! THE BARONS HAVE COME!
HAHAH! FLEE YOU DIRTY PEASANTS!

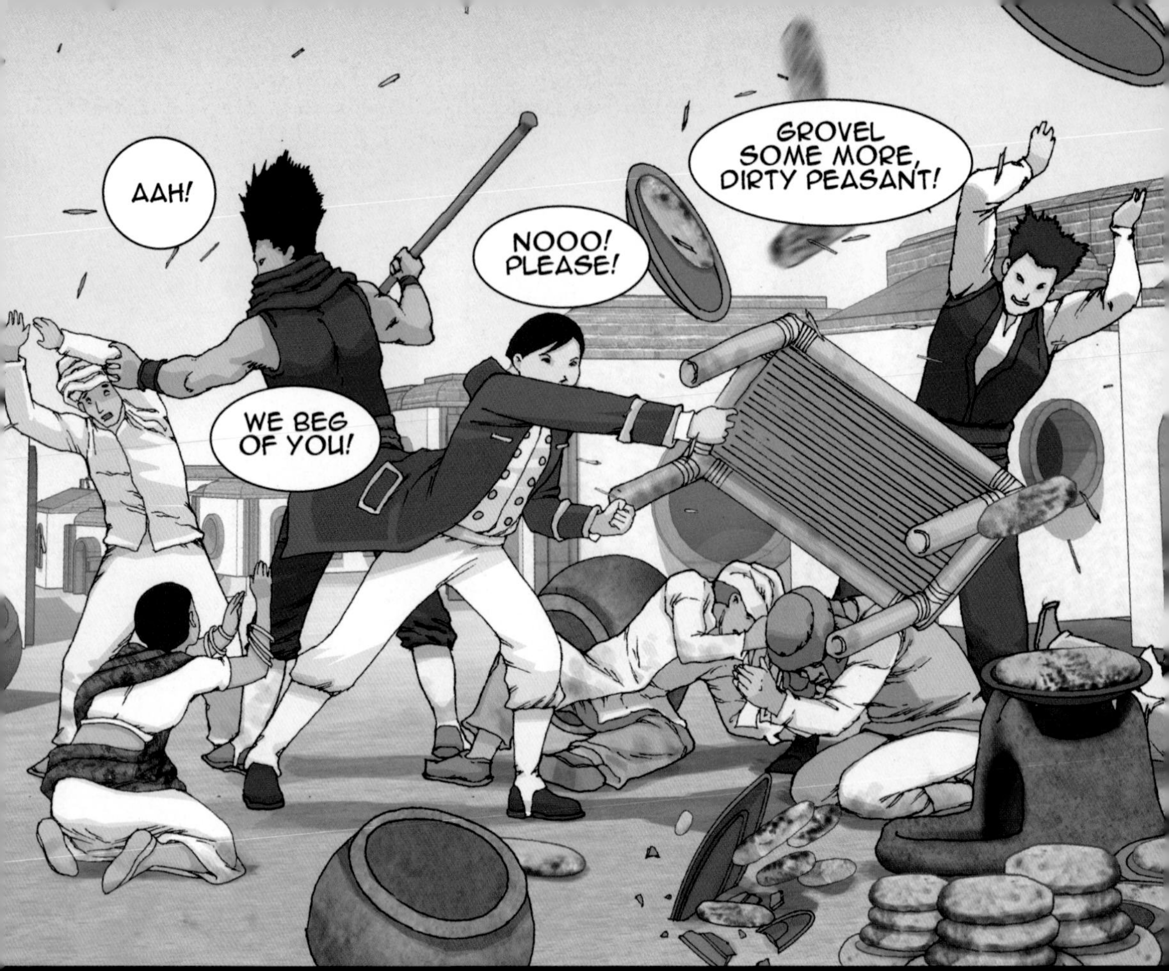
AAH!
WE BEG OF YOU!
NOOO! PLEASE!
GROVEL SOME MORE, DIRTY PEASANT!

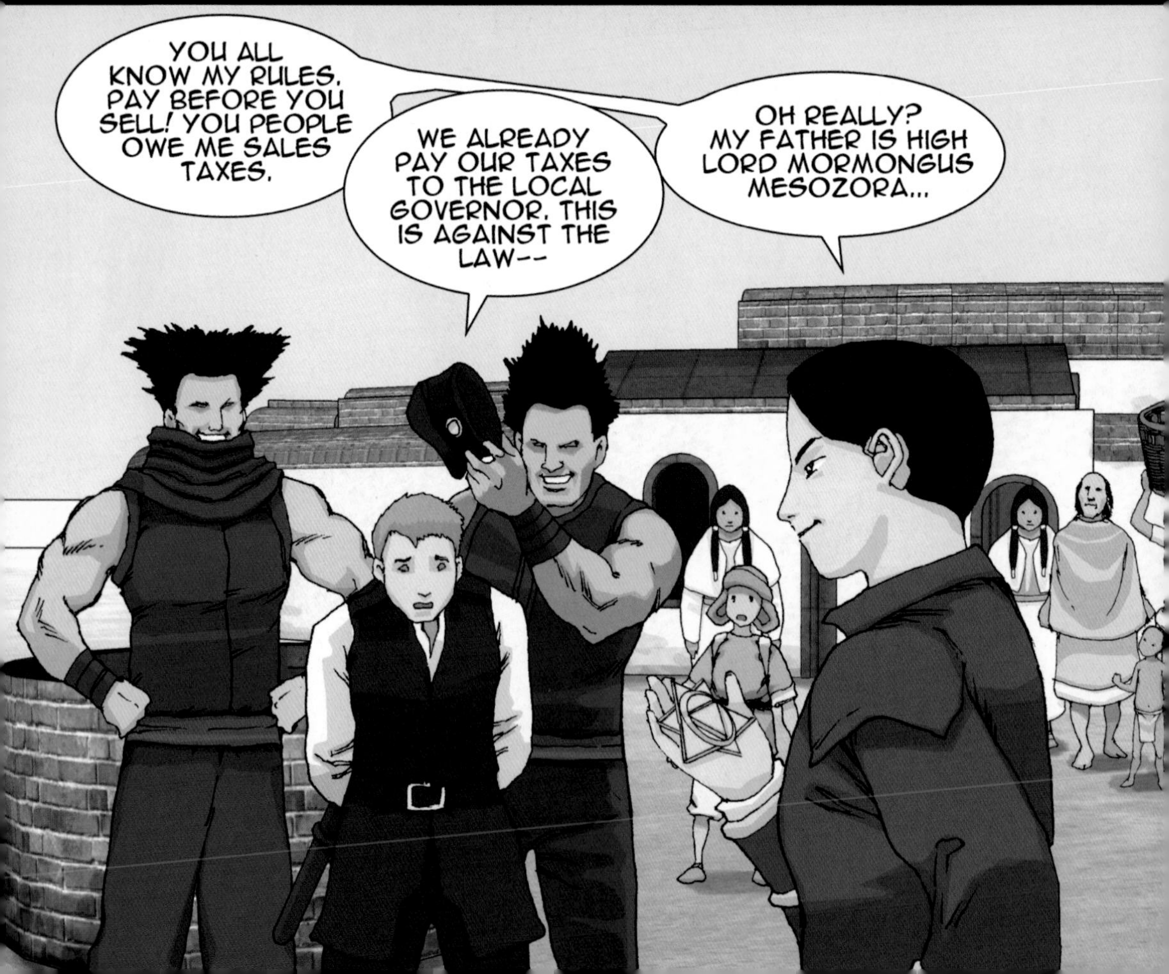
YOU ALL KNOW MY RULES. PAY BEFORE YOU SELL! YOU PEOPLE OWE ME SALES TAXES.
WE ALREADY PAY OUR TAXES TO THE LOCAL GOVERNOR. THIS IS AGAINST THE LAW--
OH REALLY? MY FATHER IS HIGH LORD MORMONGUS MESOZORA...

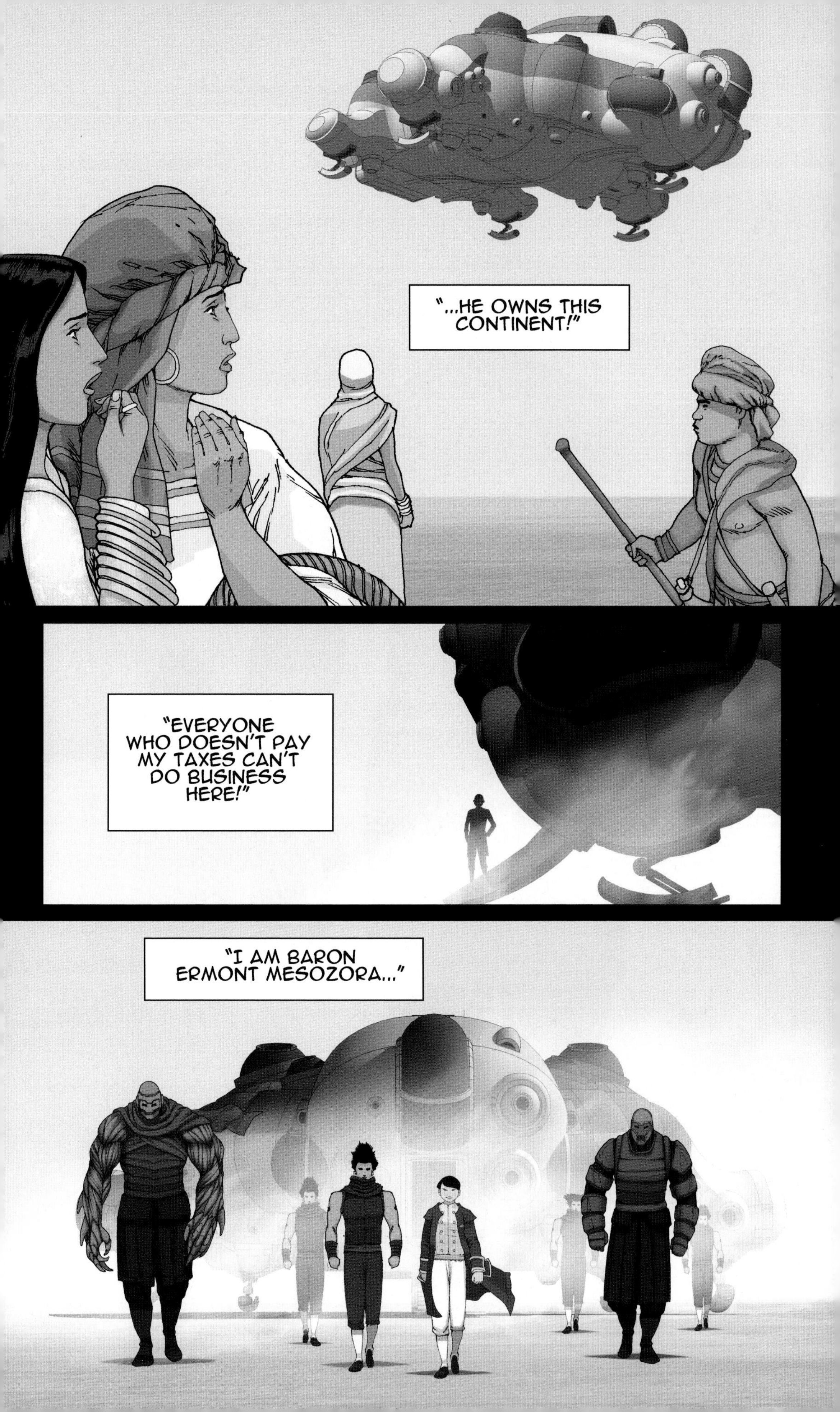
"...HE OWNS THIS CONTINENT!"
"EVERYONE WHO DOESN'T PAY MY TAXES CAN'T DO BUSINESS HERE!"
"I AM BARON ERMONT MESOZORA..."

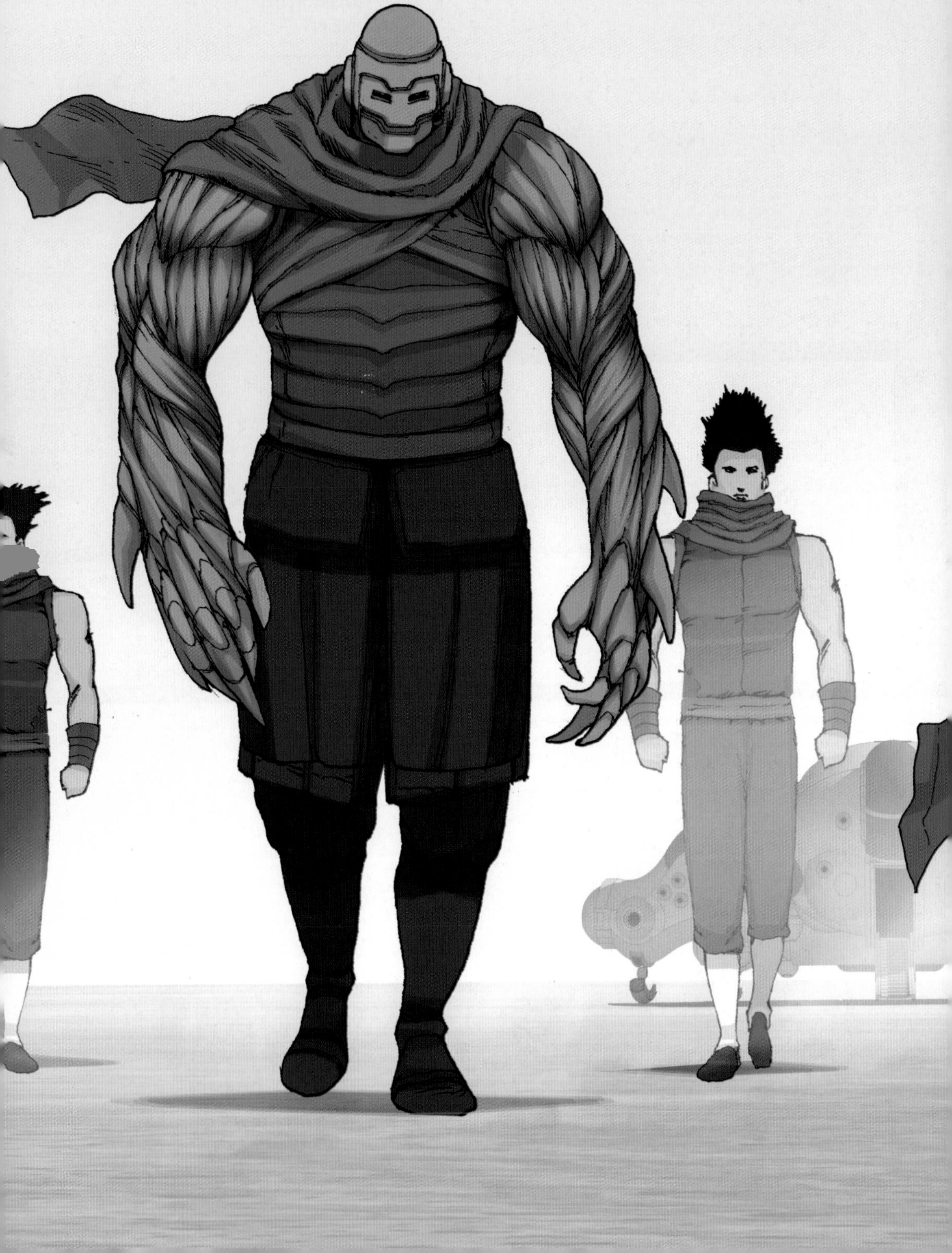

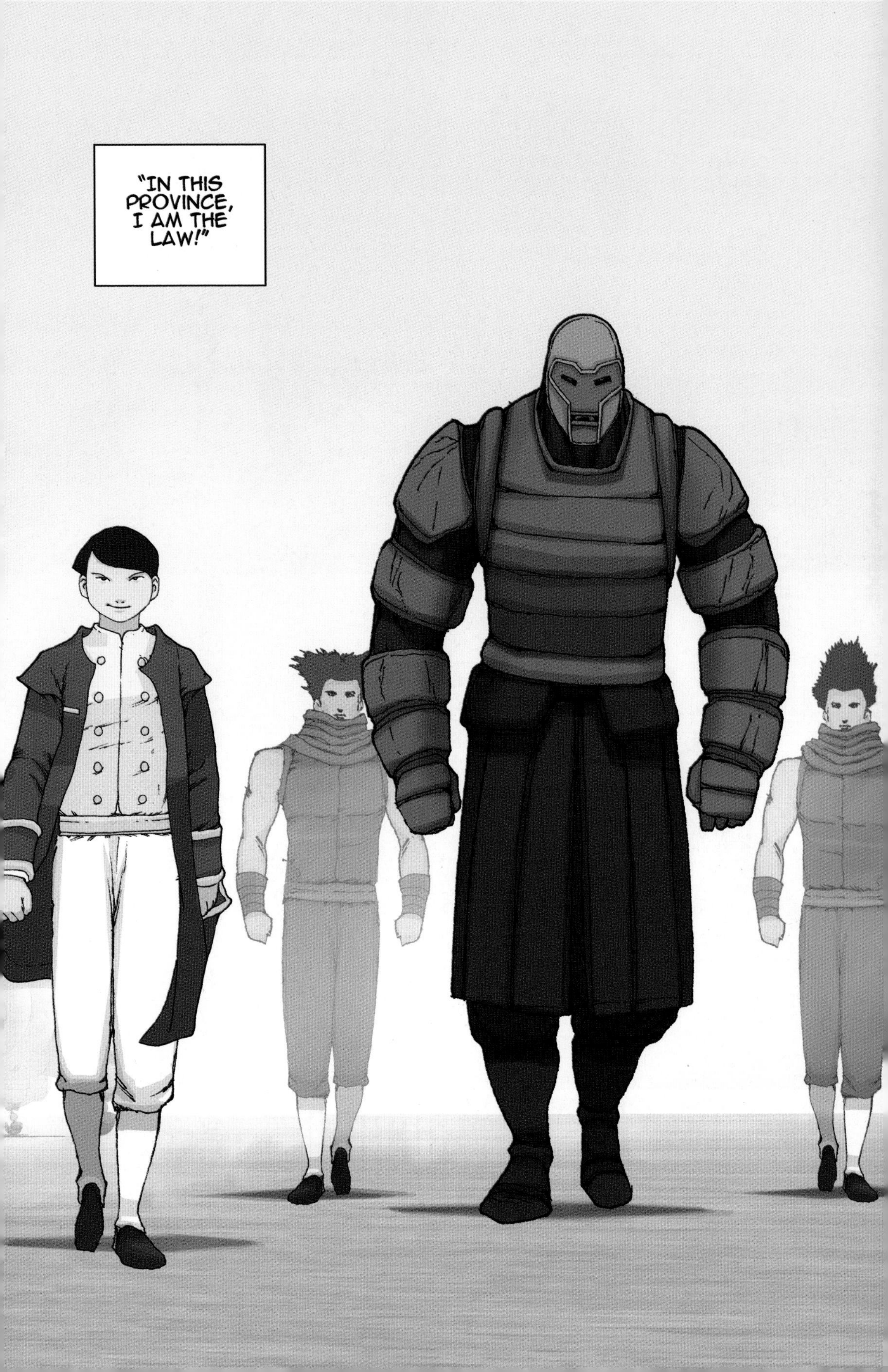
"IN THIS PROVINCE, I AM THE LAW!"

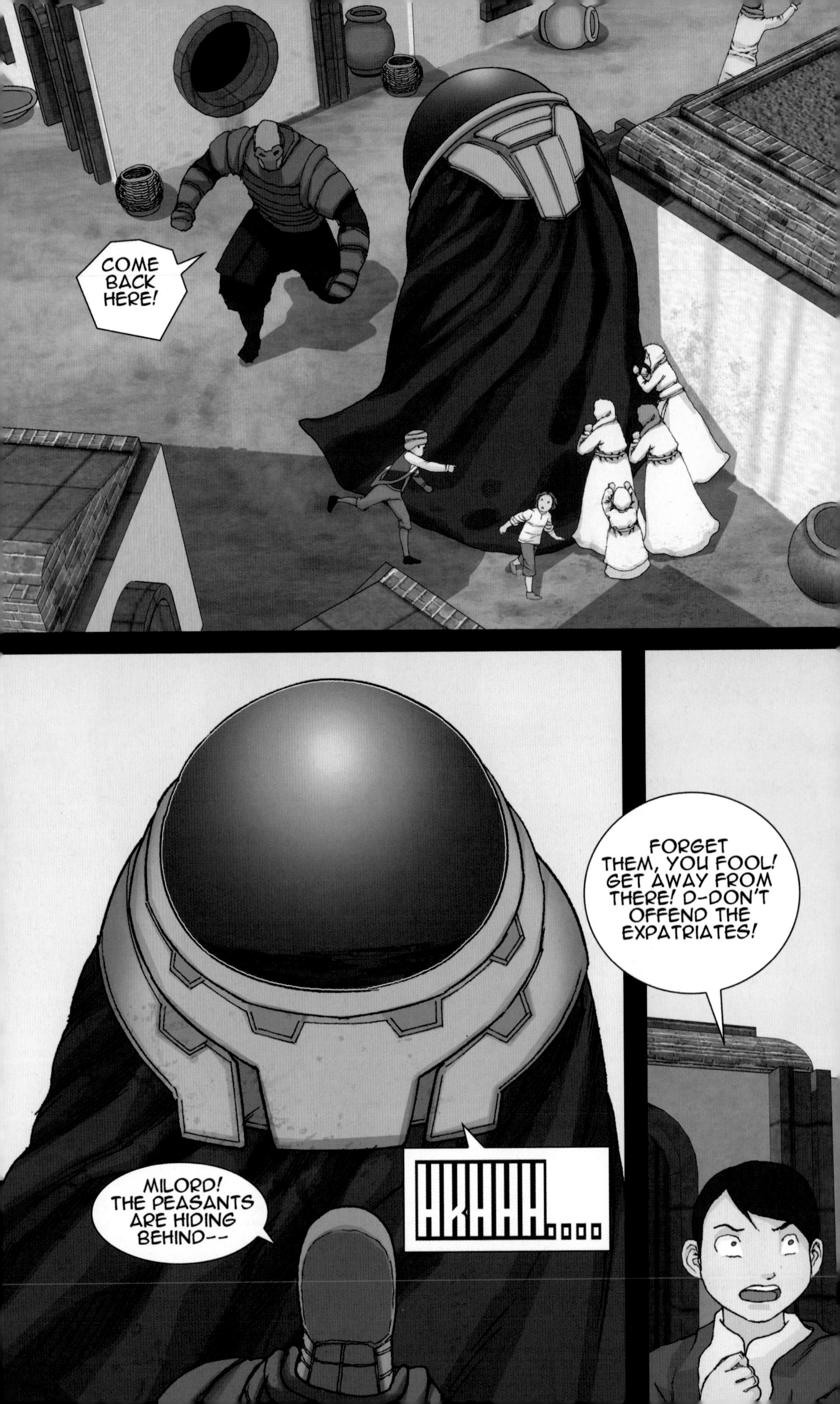
COME BACK HERE!
FORGET THEM, YOU FOOL! GET AWAY FROM THERE! D-DON'T OFFEND THE EXPATRIATES!
MILORD! THE PEASANTS ARE HIDING BEHIND--
HKHHH...

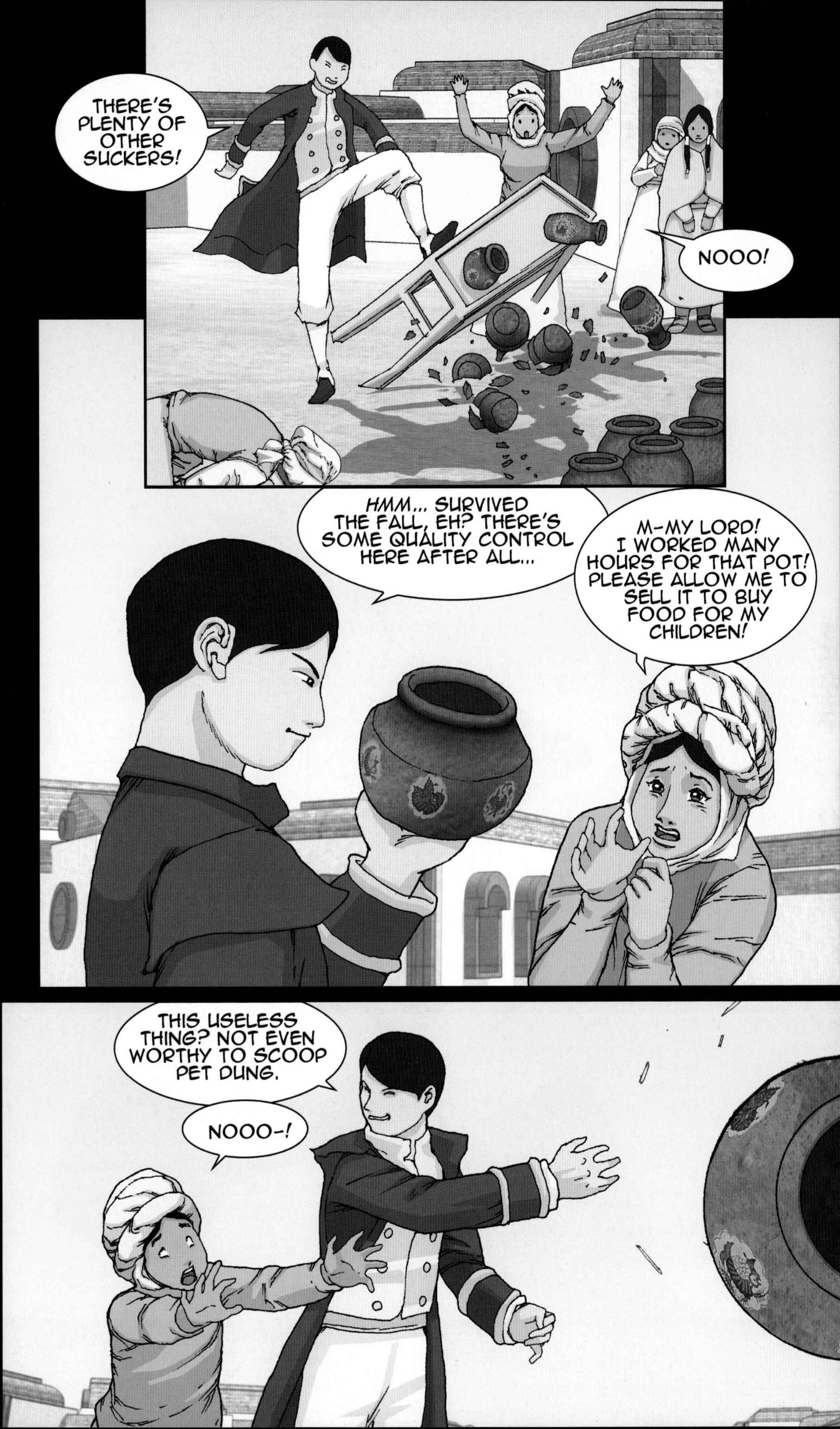
THERE'S PLENTY OF OTHER SUCKERS!
NOOO!
HMM... SURVIVED THE FALL, EH? THERE'S SOME QUALITY CONTROL HERE AFTER ALL...
M-MY LORD! I WORKED MANY HOURS FOR THAT POT! PLEASE ALLOW ME TO SELL IT TO BUY FOOD FOR MY CHILDREN!
THIS USELESS THING? NOT EVEN WORTHY TO SCOOP PET DUNG.
NOOO-!

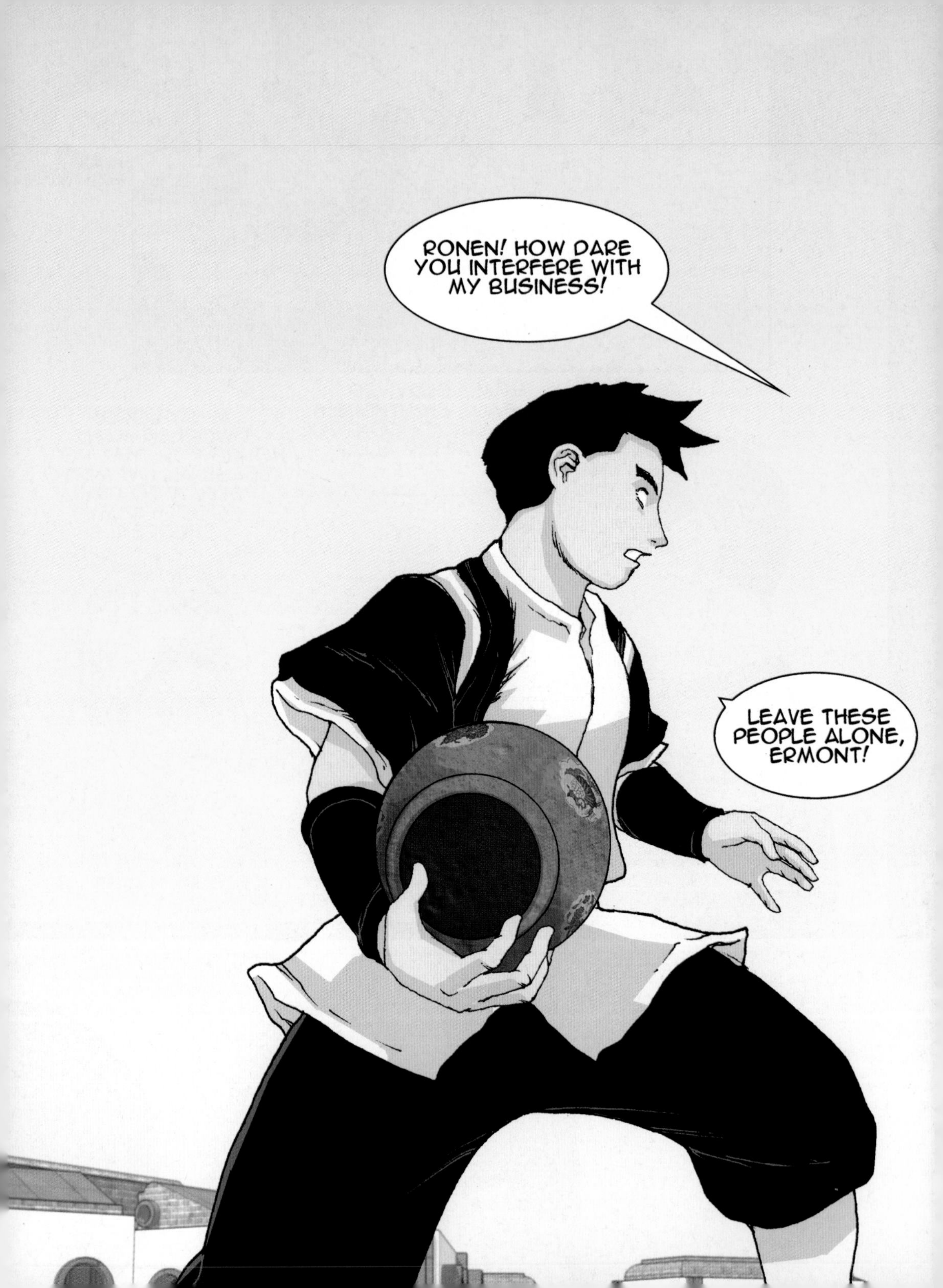
RONEN! HOW DARE YOU INTERFERE WITH MY BUSINESS!
LEAVE THESE PEOPLE ALONE, ERMONT!

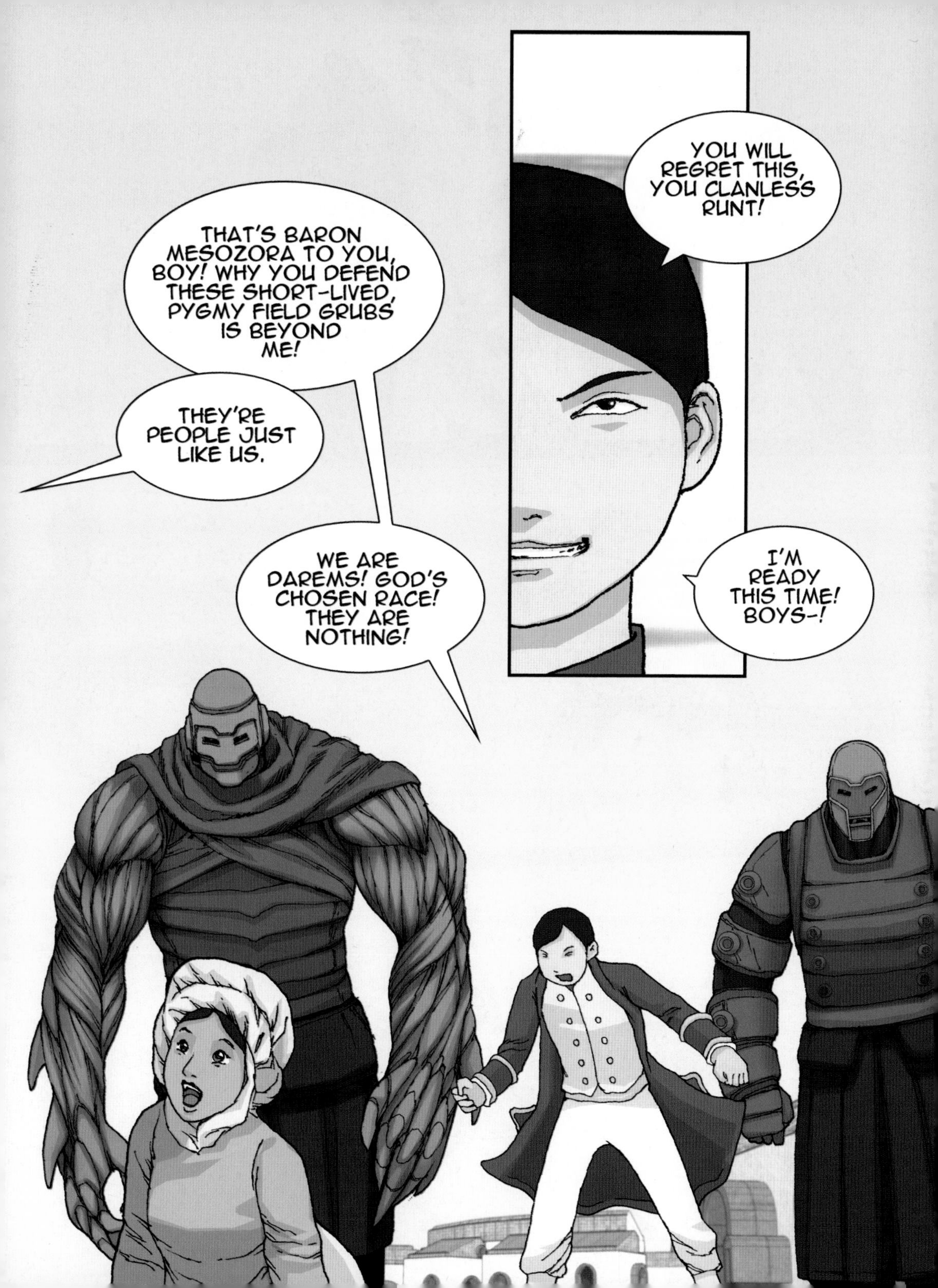
THAT'S BARON MESOZORA TO YOU, BOY! WHY YOU DEFEND THESE SHORT-LIVED, PYGMY FIELD GRUBS IS BEYOND ME!
YOU WILL REGRET THIS, YOU CLANLESS RUNT!
THEY'RE PEOPLE JUST LIKE US.
WE ARE DAREMS! GOD'S CHOSEN RACE! THEY ARE NOTHING!
I'M READY THIS TIME! BOYS-!

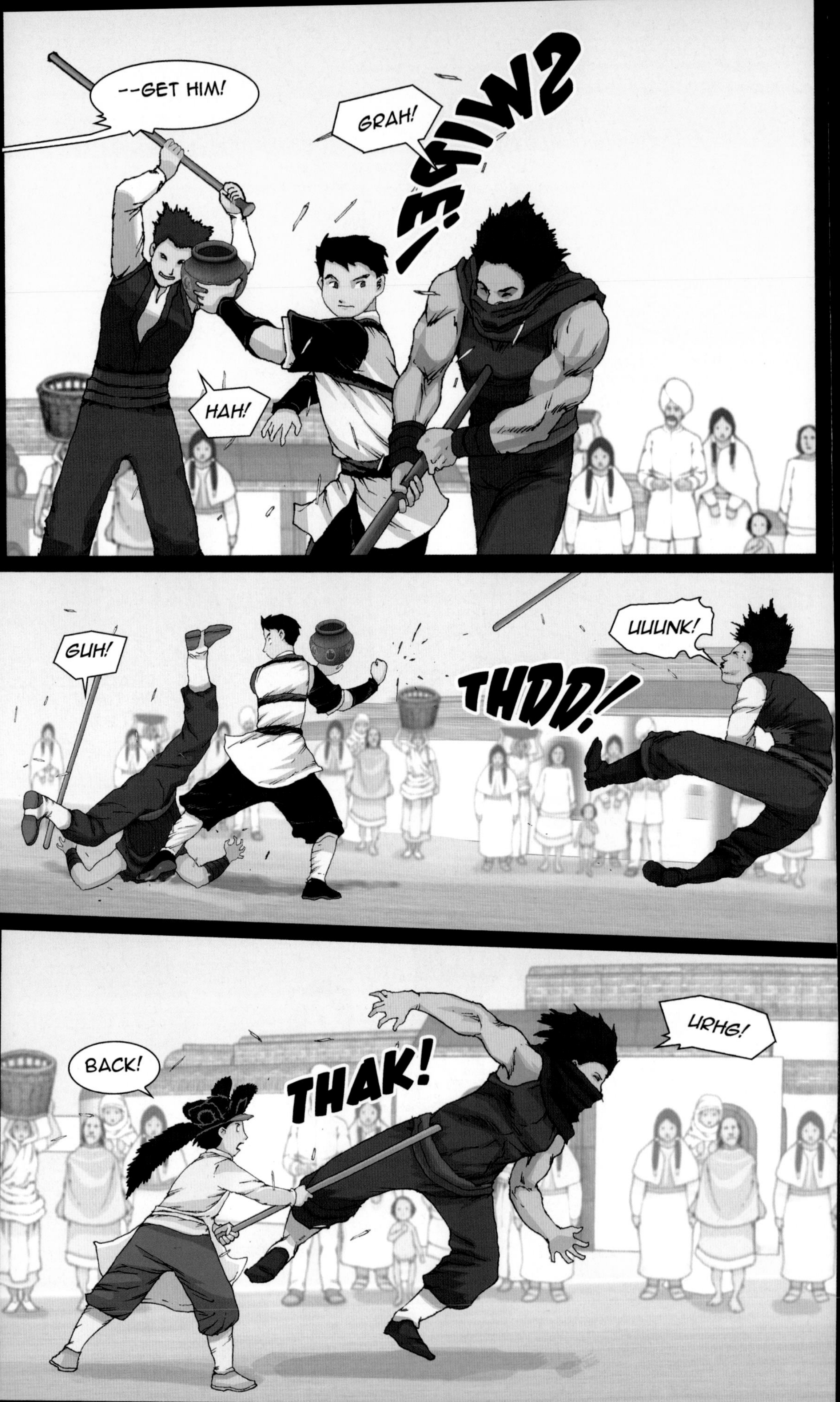
--GET HIM!
GRAH!
SWISH!
HAH!
GUH!
THDD!
UUUNK!
BACK!
THAK!
URHG!

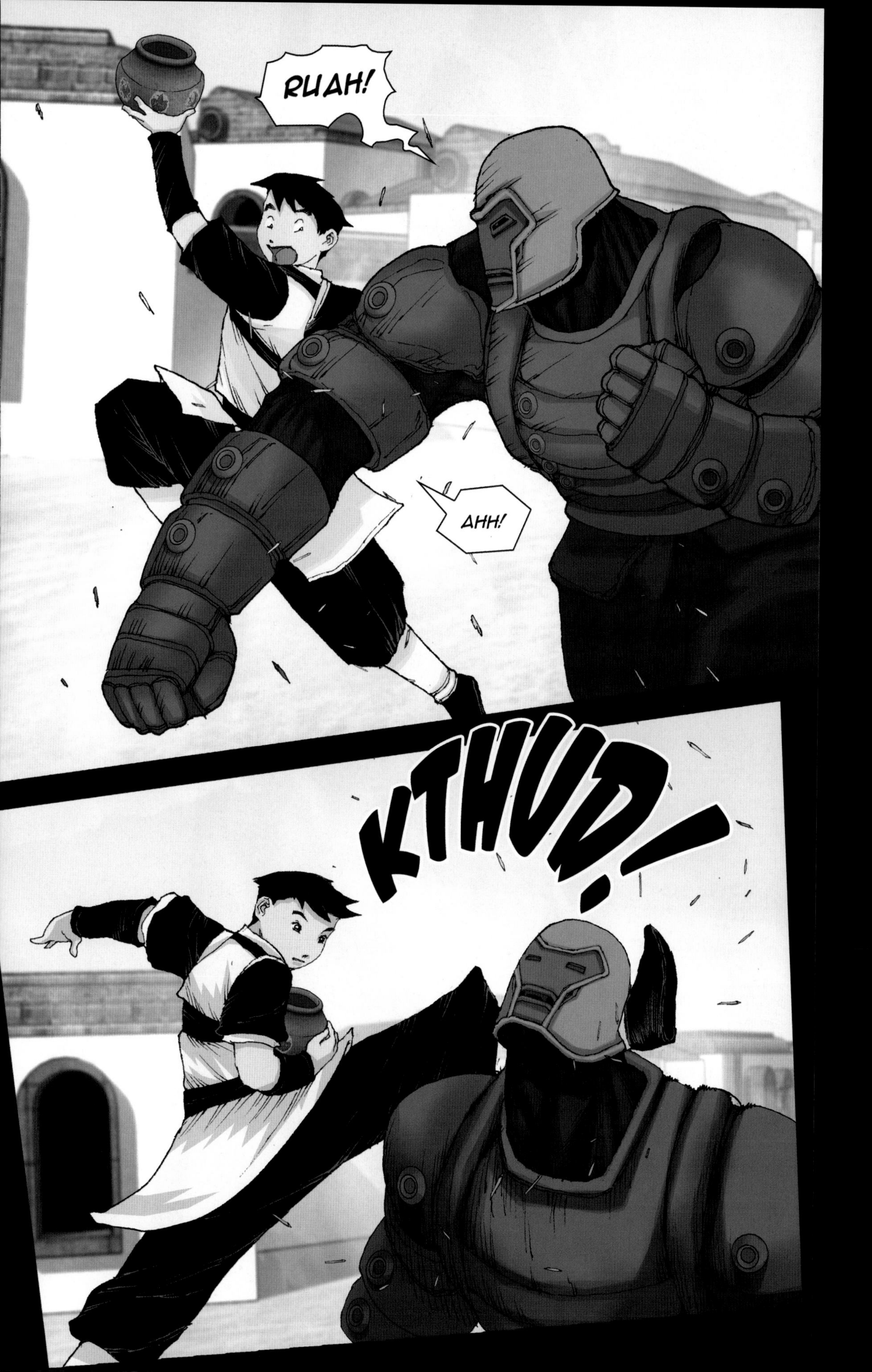
RUAH!
AHH!
KTHUD!

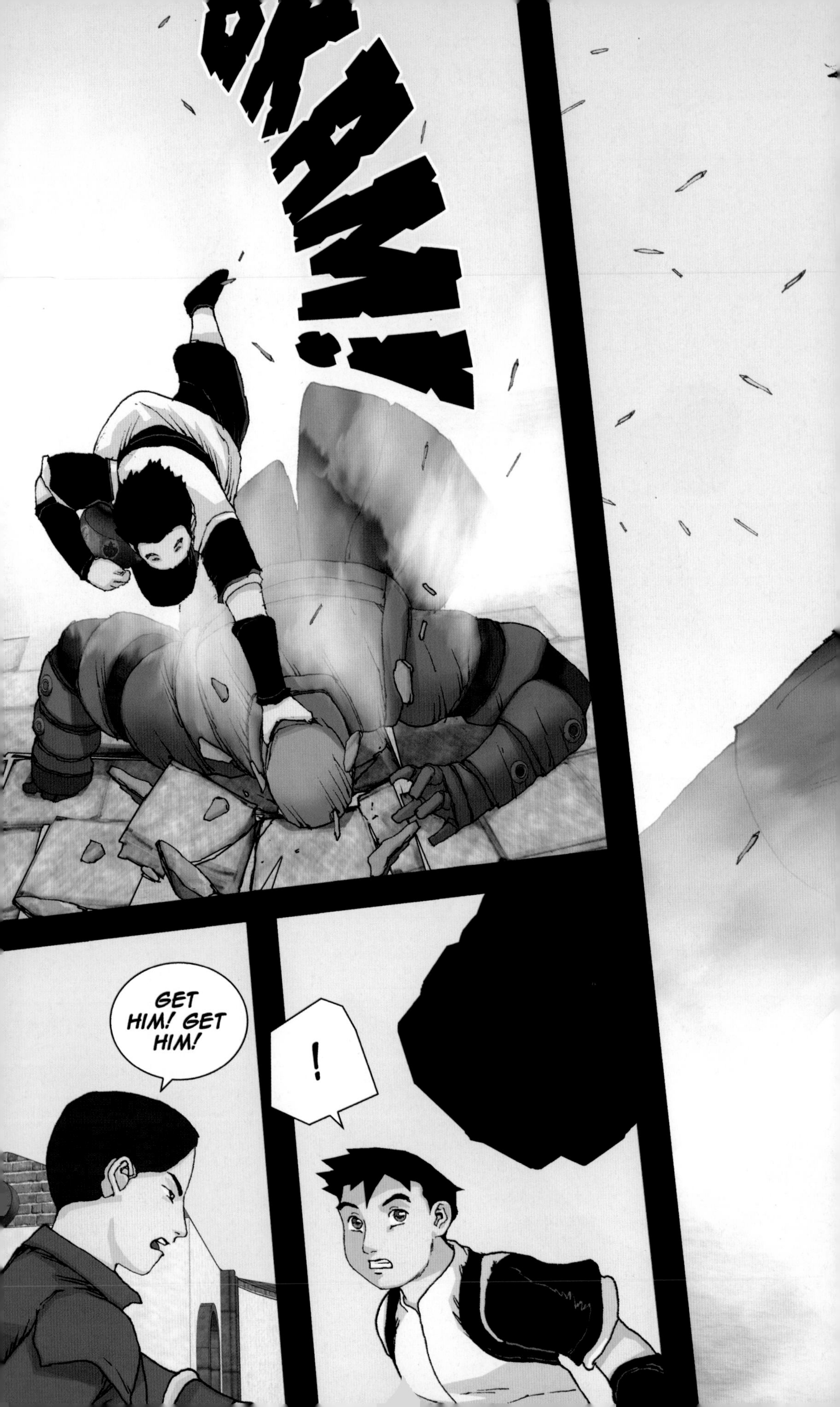
BKRAM!!
GET HIM! GET HIM!
!

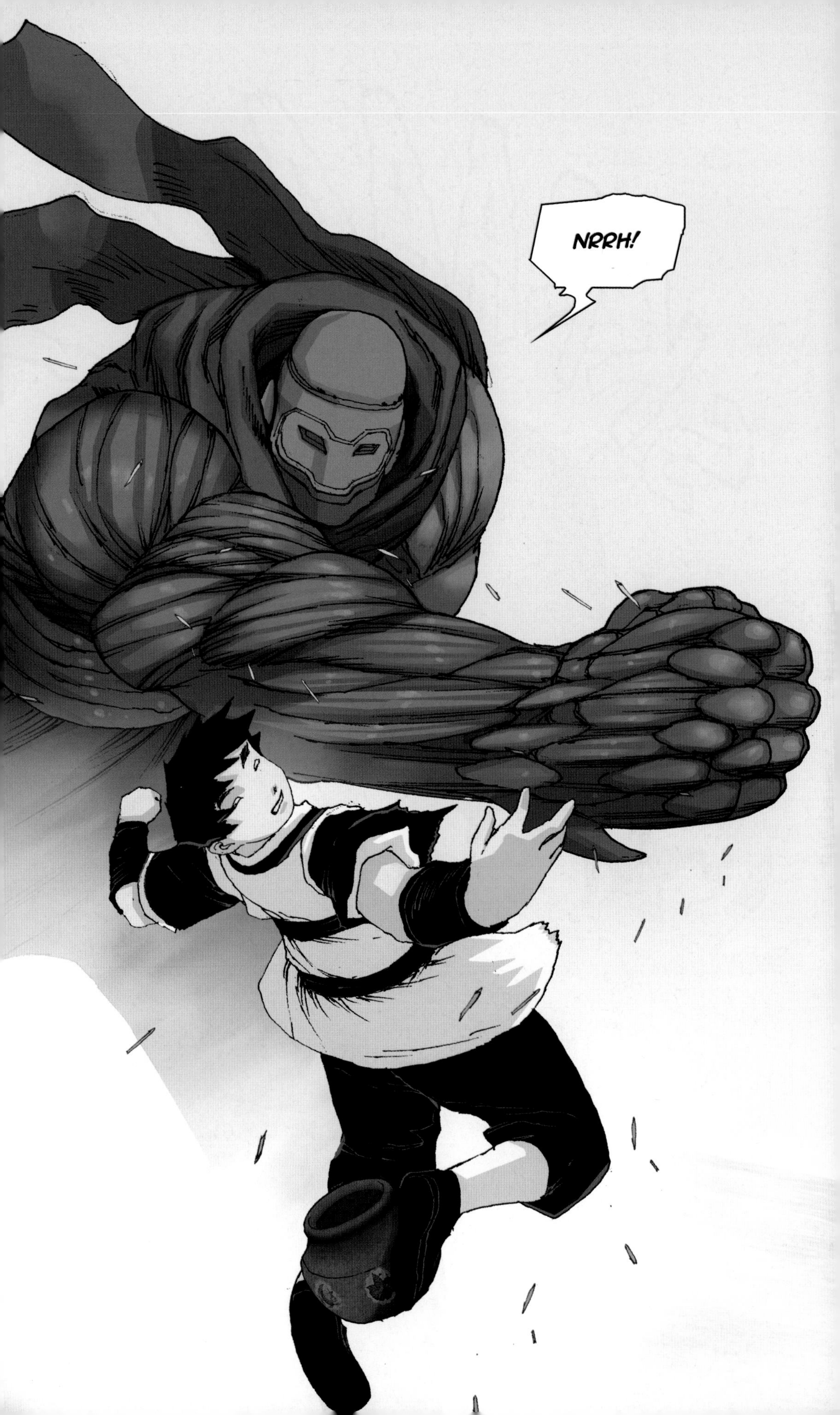
NRRH!

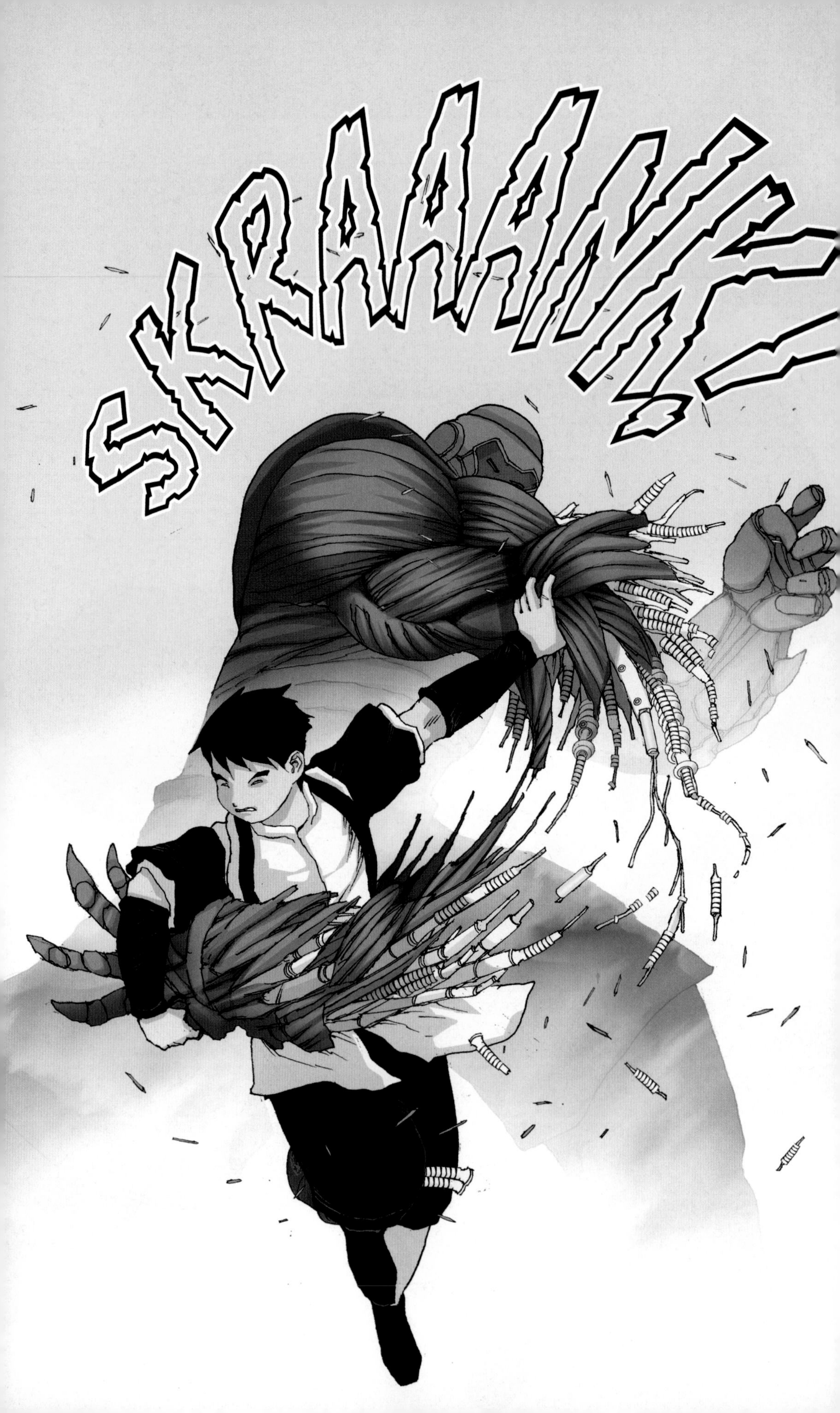
SKRAAANK

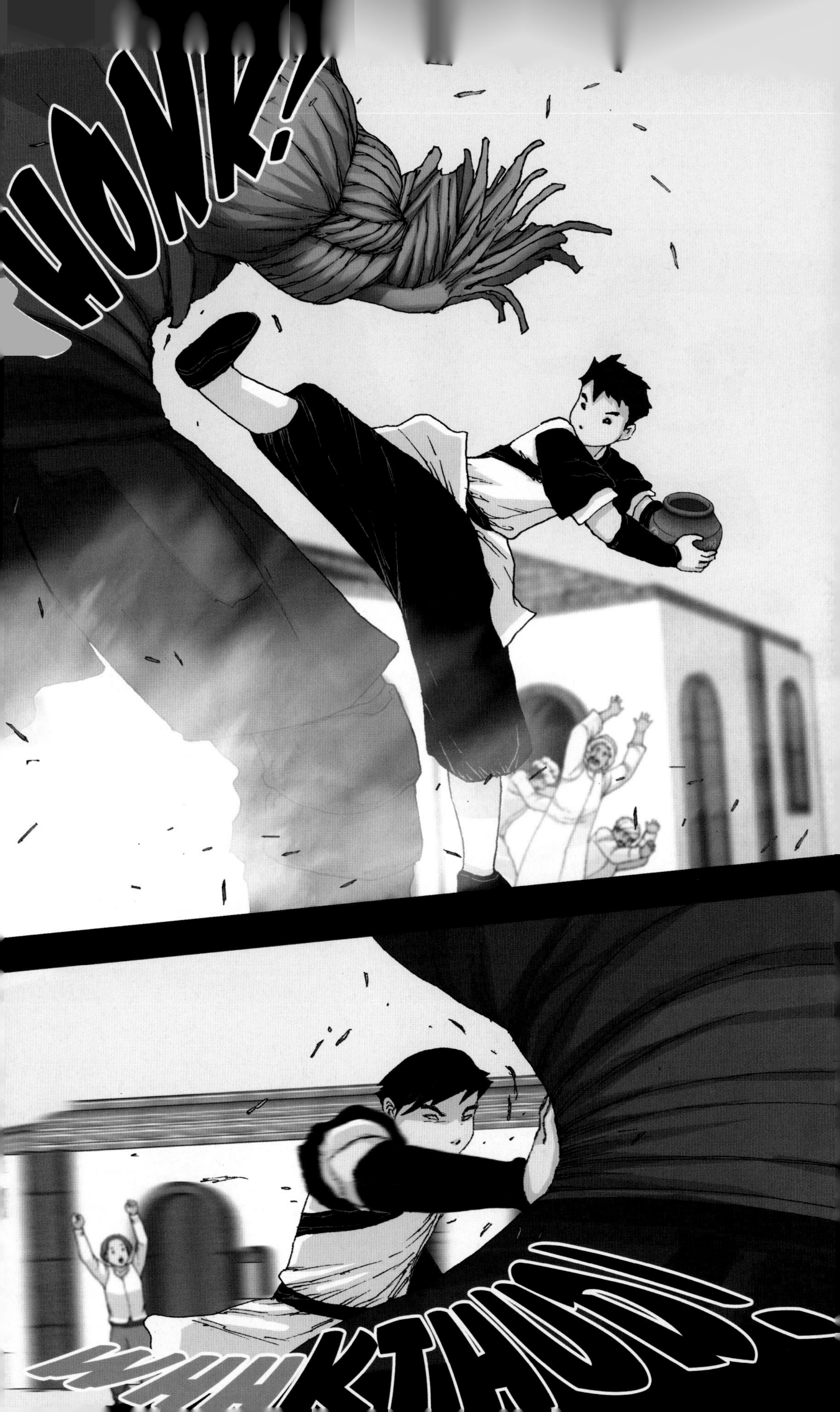
HONK!

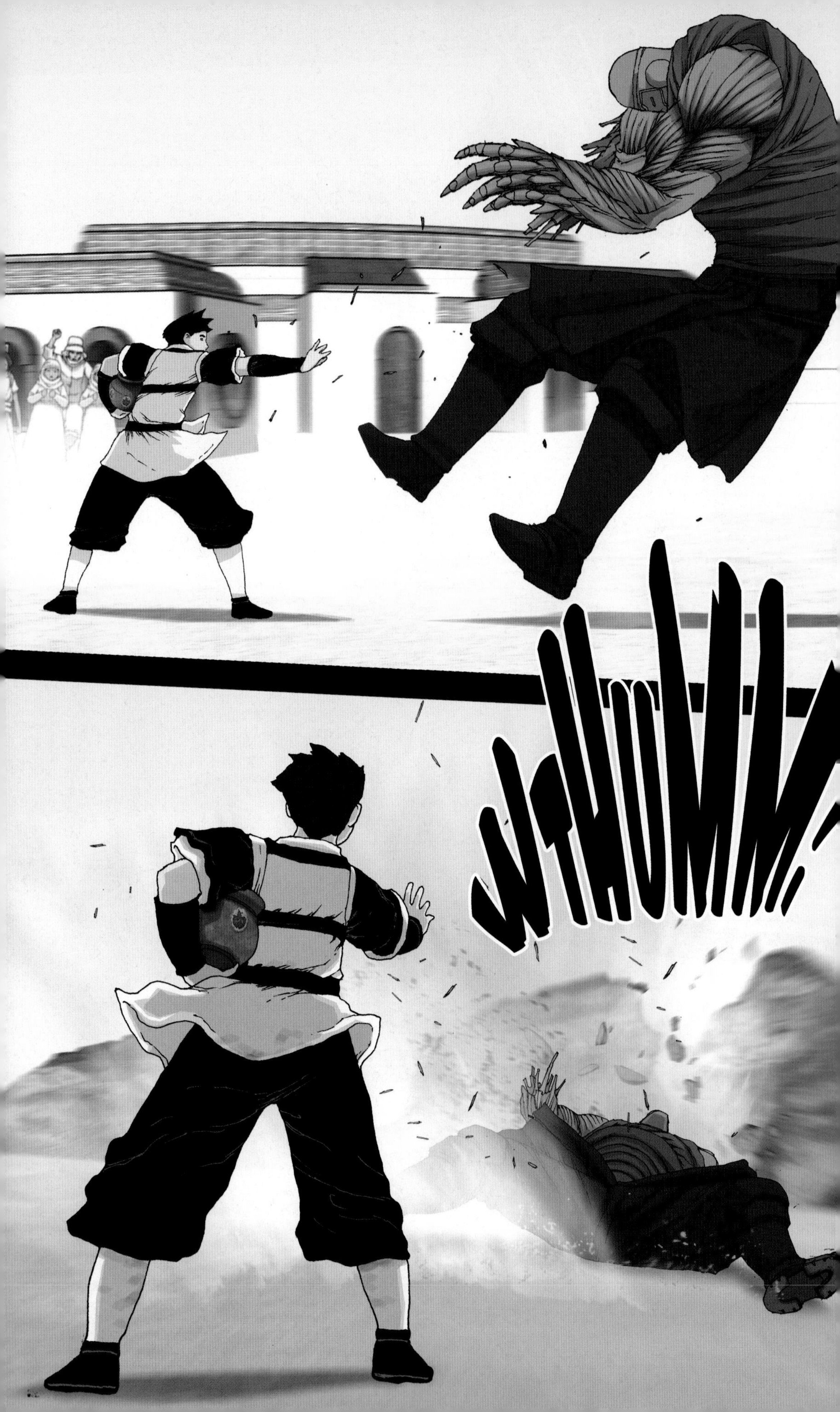
WTHUMM!

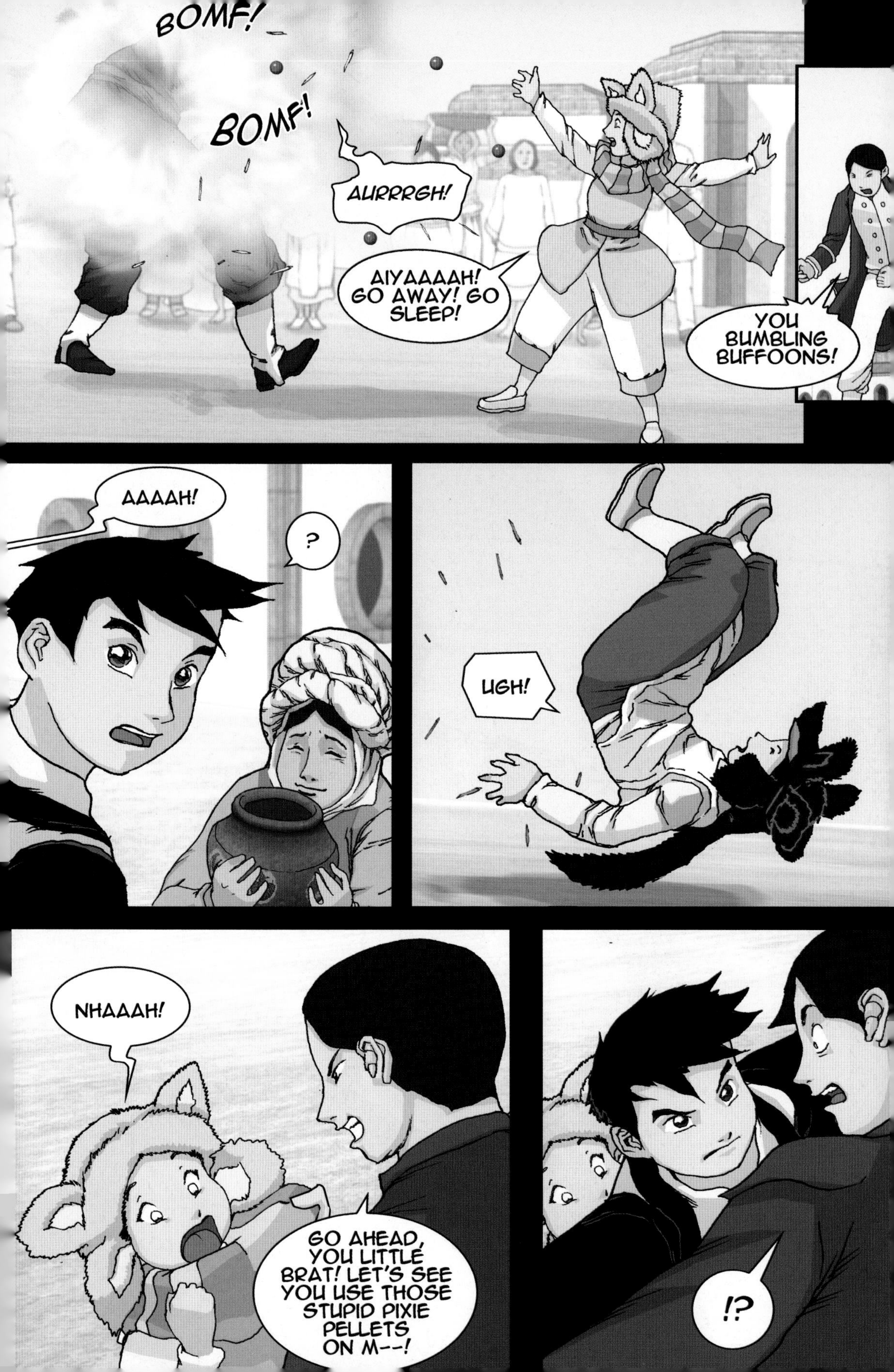
BOMF!
BOMF!
AURRRGH!
AIYAAAAH! GO AWAY! GO SLEEP!
YOU BUMBLING BUFFOONS!
AAAAH!
?
UGH!
NHAAAH!
GO AHEAD, YOU LITTLE BRAT! LET'S SEE YOU USE THOSE STUPID PIXIE PELLETS ON M--!
!?

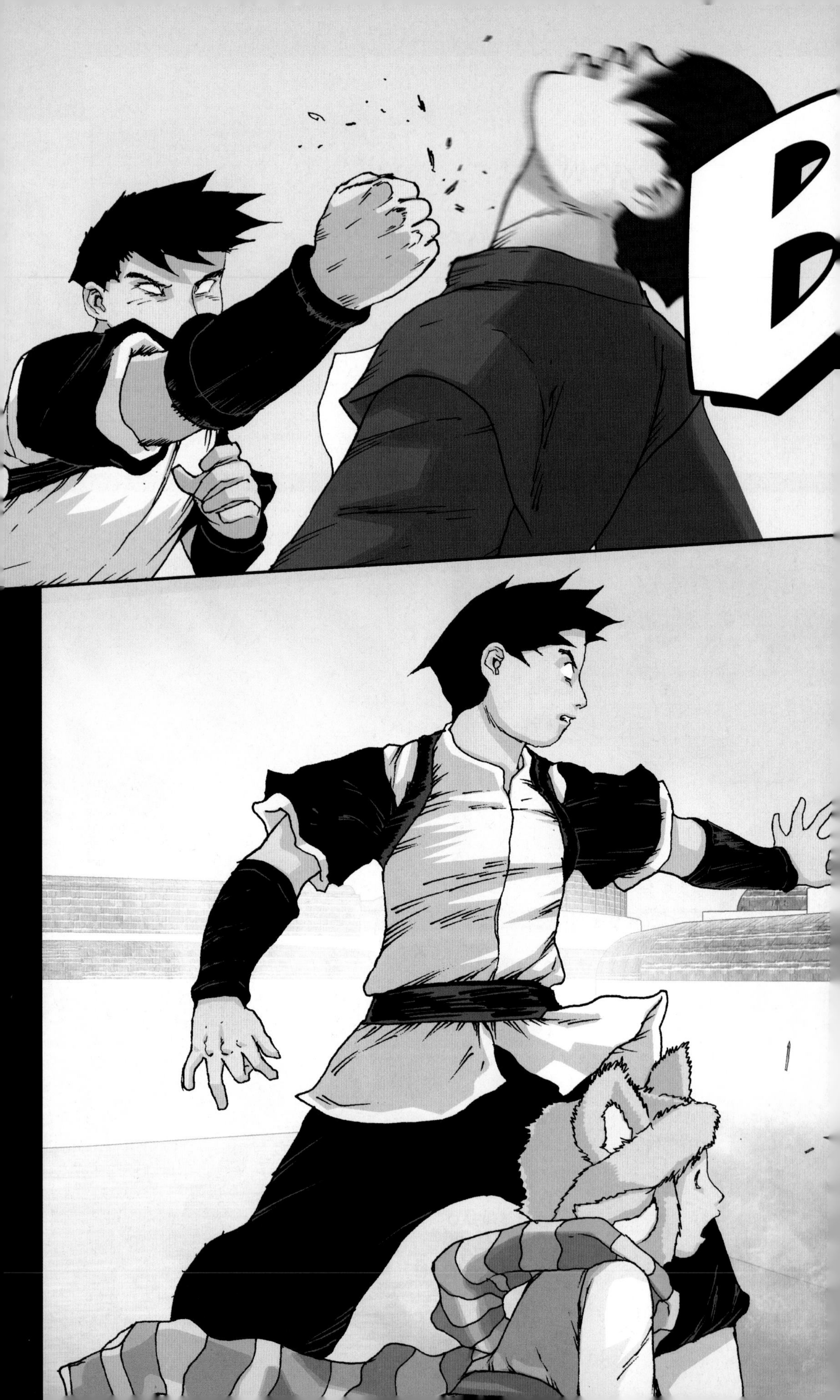
B

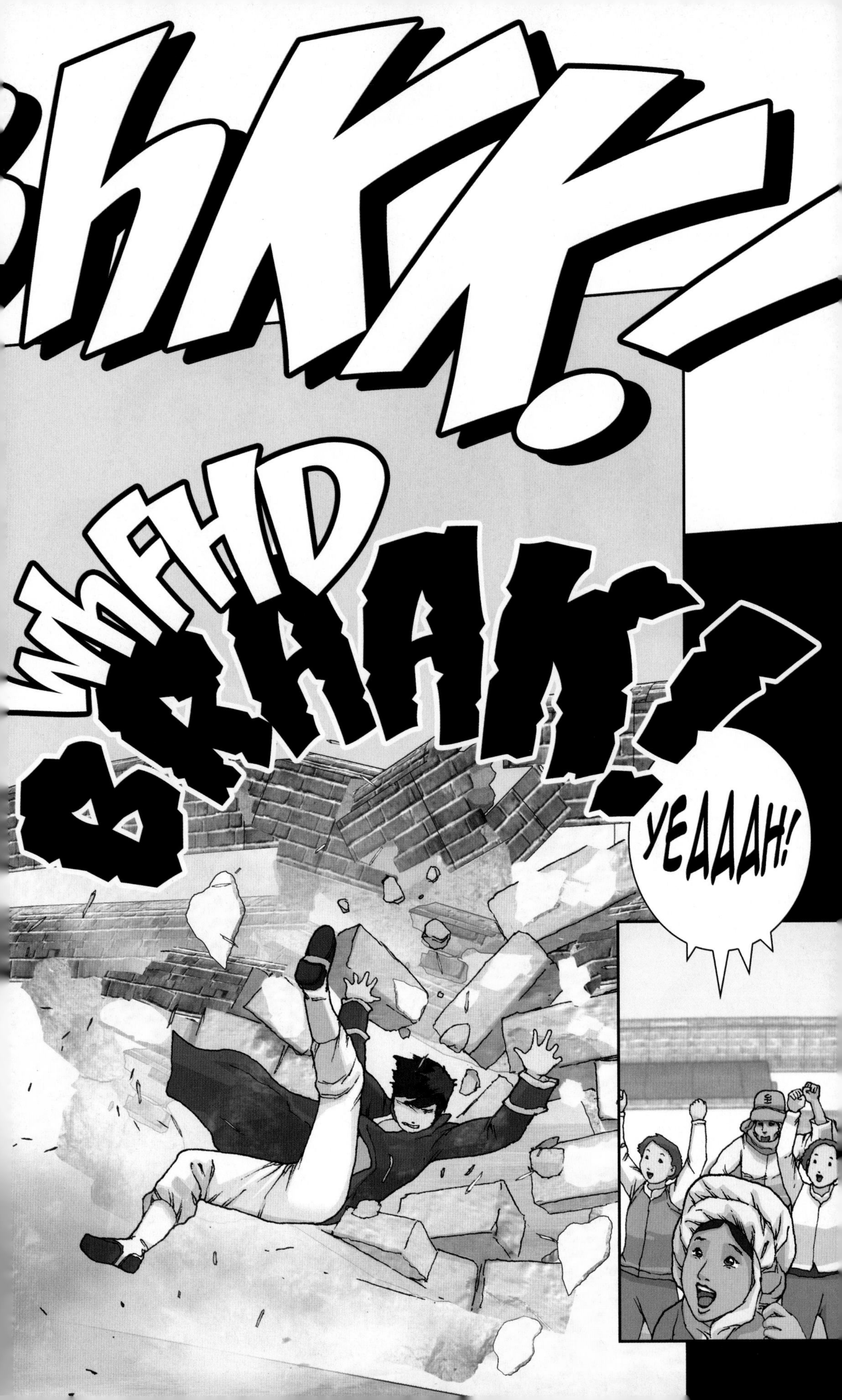
BRAK!
YEAAAH!

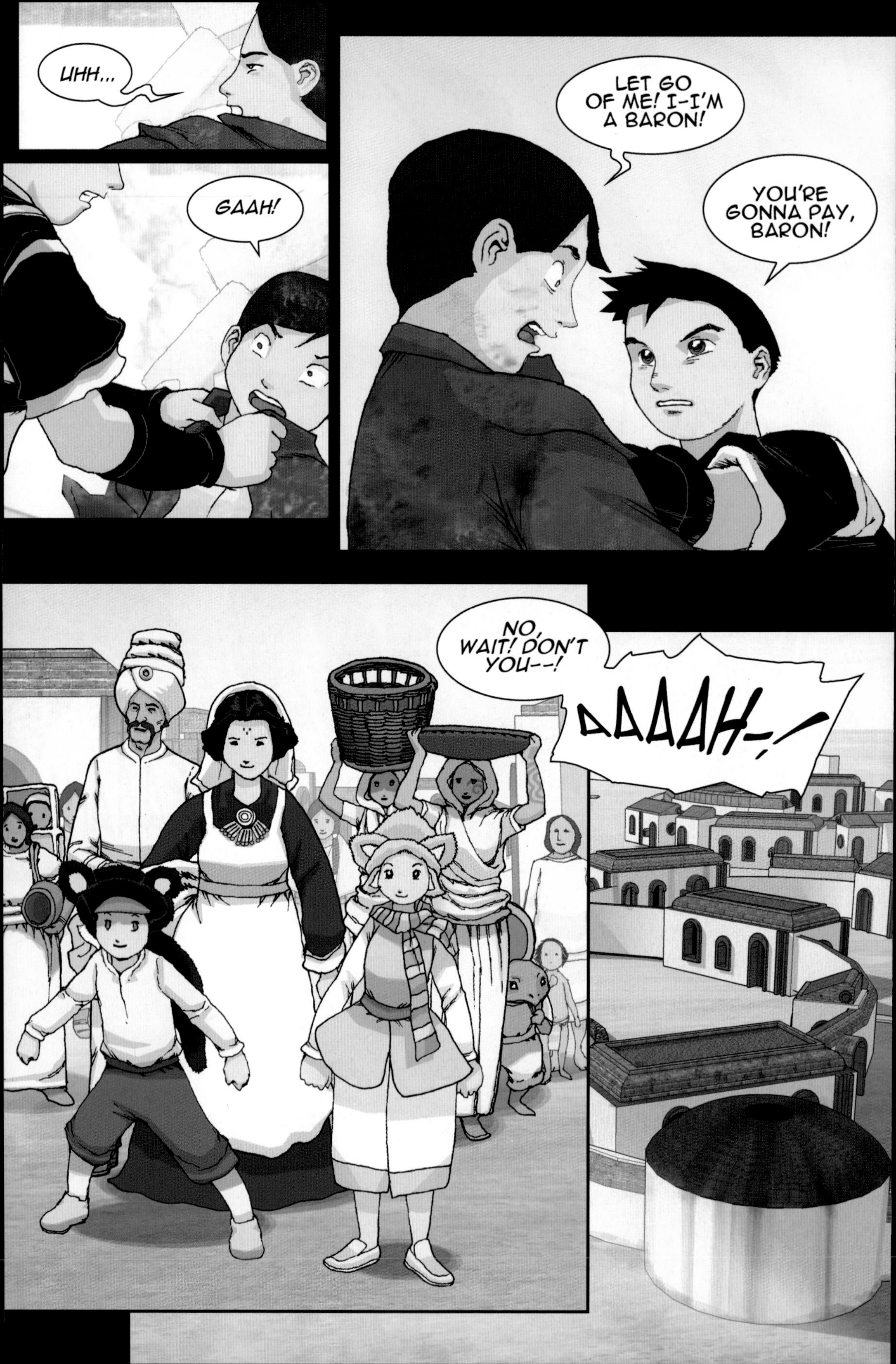
UHH...
GAAH!
LET GO OF ME! I-I'M A BARON!
YOU'RE GONNA PAY, BARON!
NO, WAIT! DON'T YOU--!
AAAAH--!

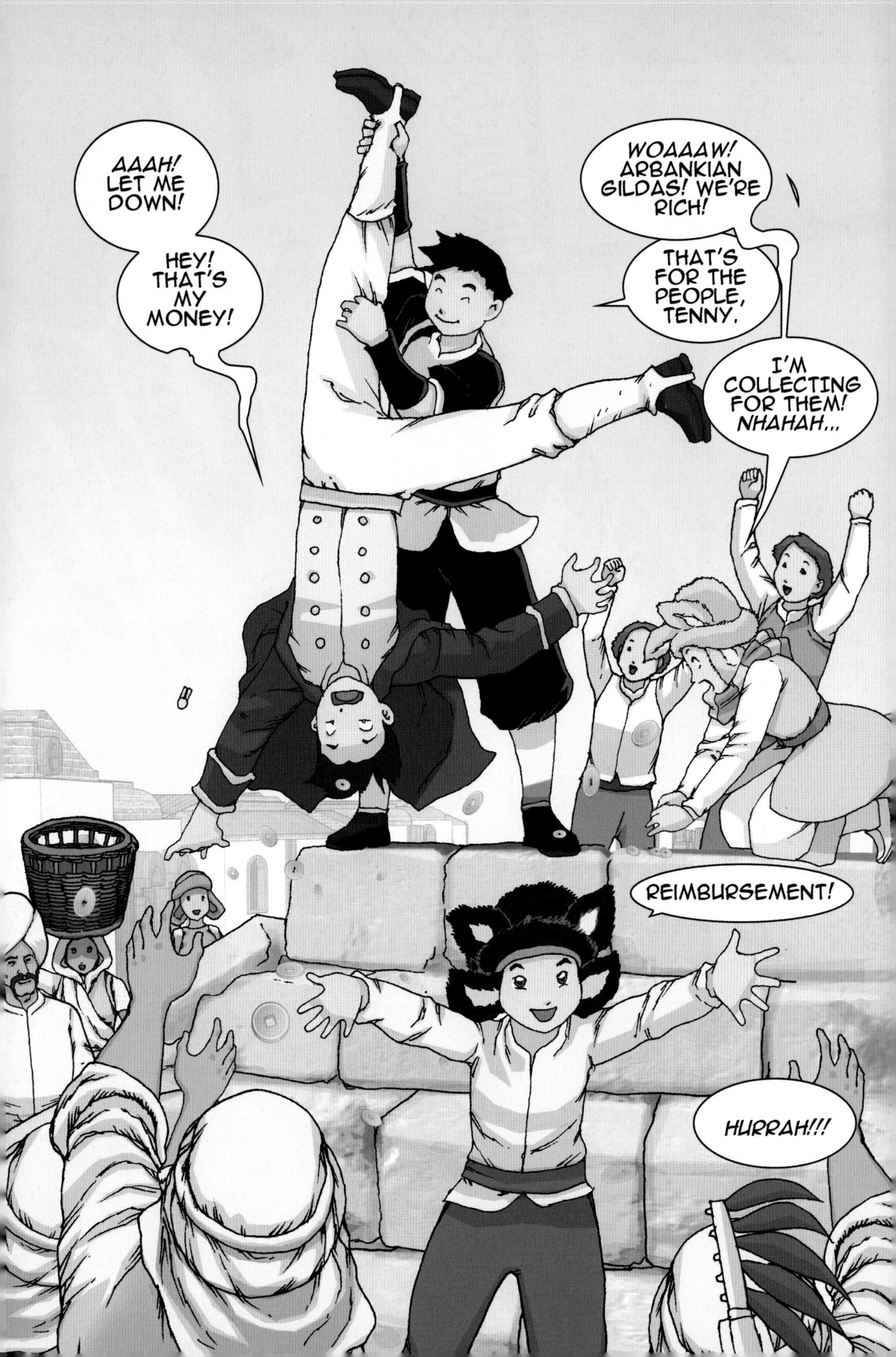
AAAH! LET ME DOWN!
HEY! THAT'S MY MONEY!
WOAAAW! ARBANKIAN GILDAS! WE'RE RICH!
THAT'S FOR THE PEOPLE, TENNY.
I'M COLLECTING FOR THEM! NHAHAH...
REIMBURSEMENT!
HURRAH!!!

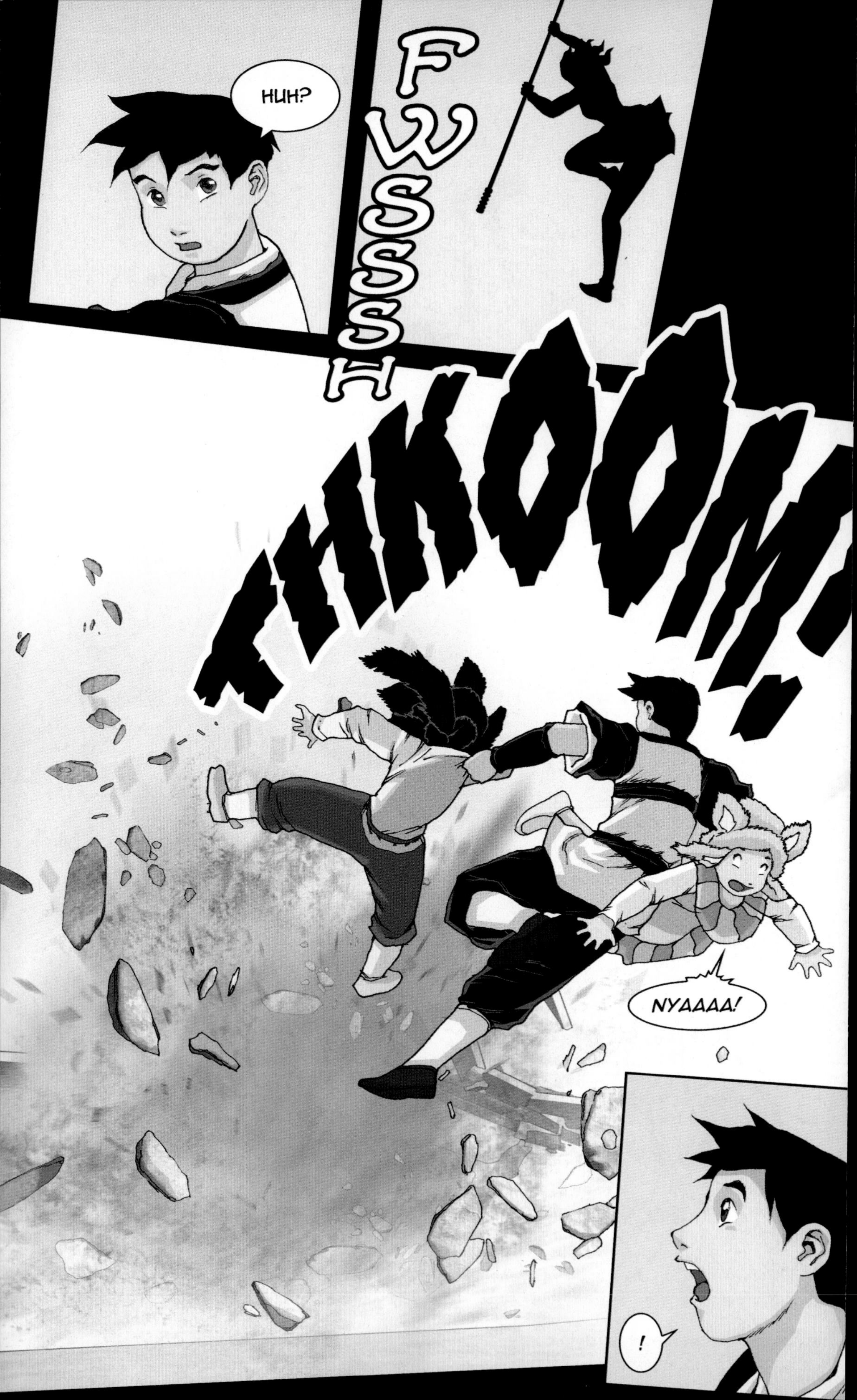
HUH?
FWSSSH
THKOOM!!
NYAAAA!
!

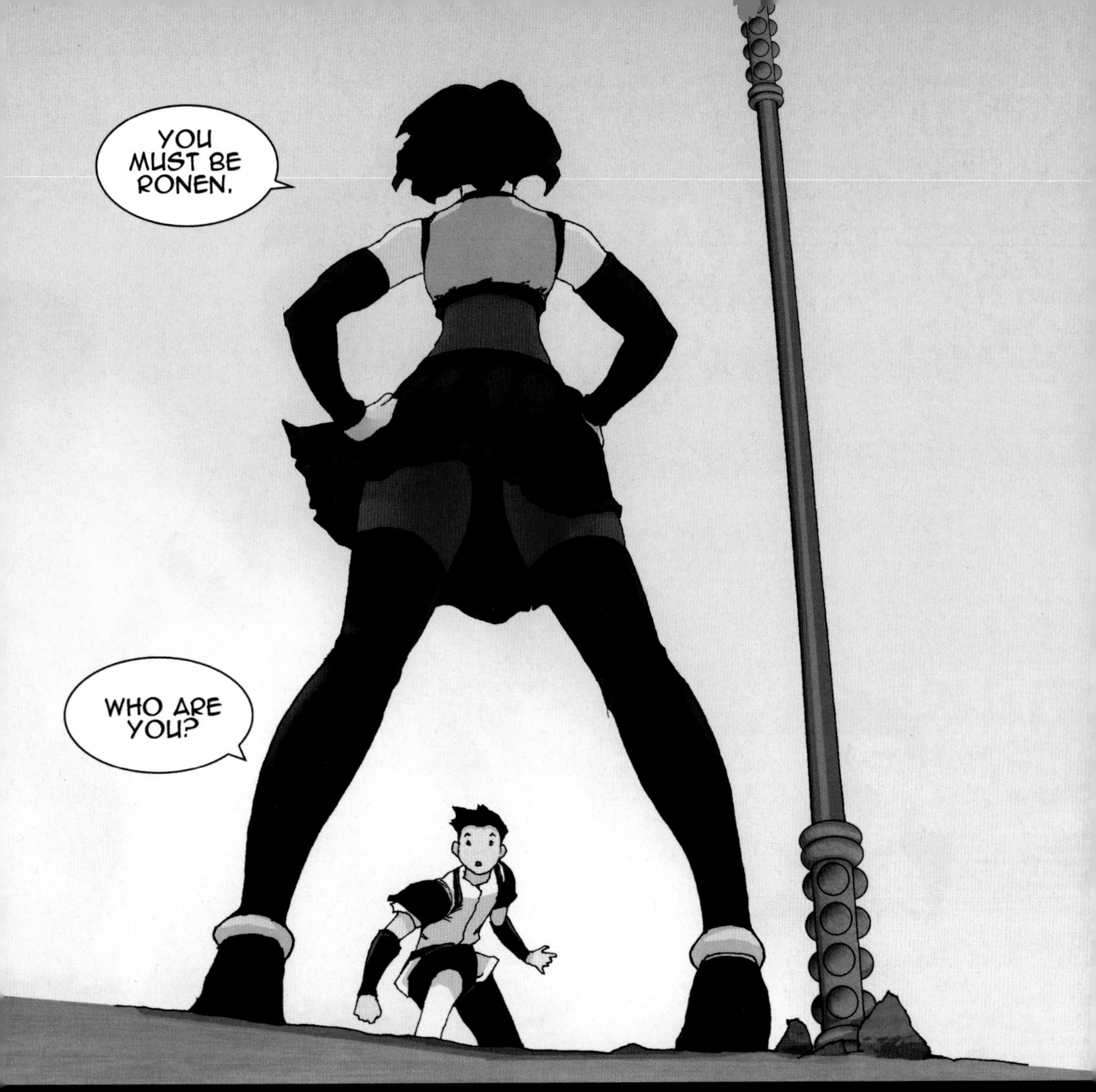
YOU MUST BE RONEN.
WHO ARE YOU?

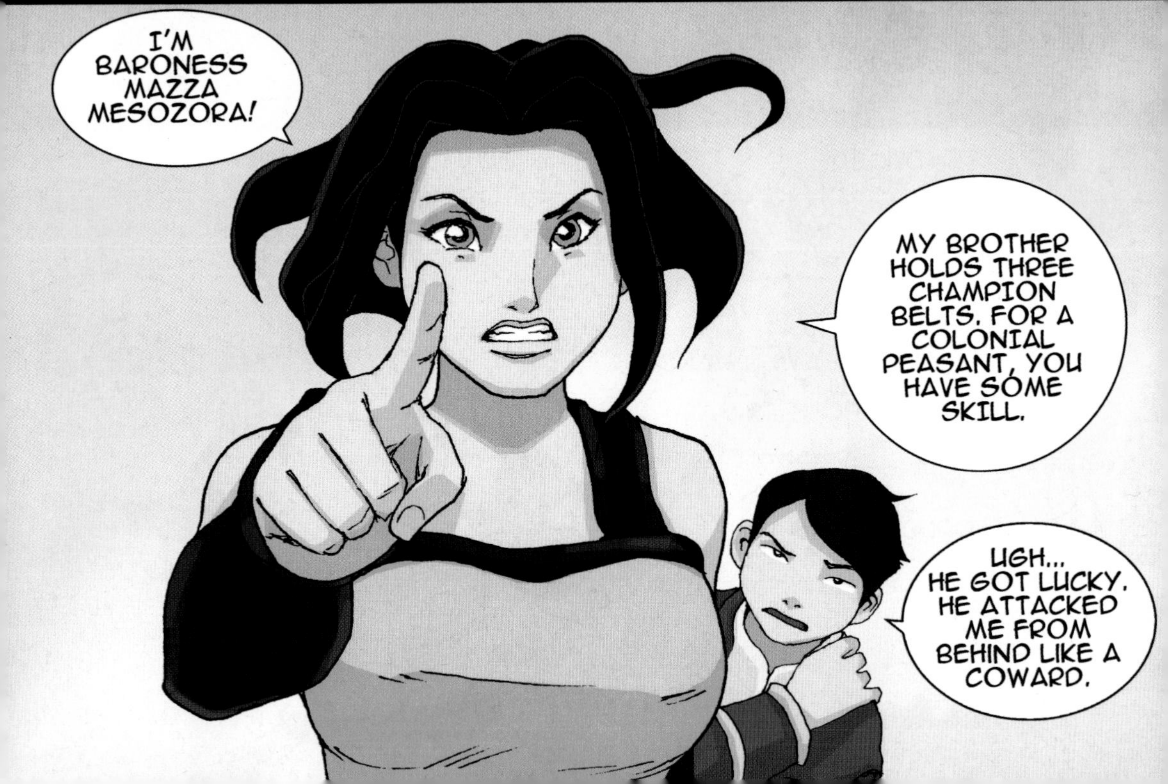
I'M BARONESS MAZZA MESOZORA!
MY BROTHER HOLDS THREE CHAMPION BELTS. FOR A COLONIAL PEASANT, YOU HAVE SOME SKILL.
UGH... HE GOT LUCKY. HE ATTACKED ME FROM BEHIND LIKE A COWARD.

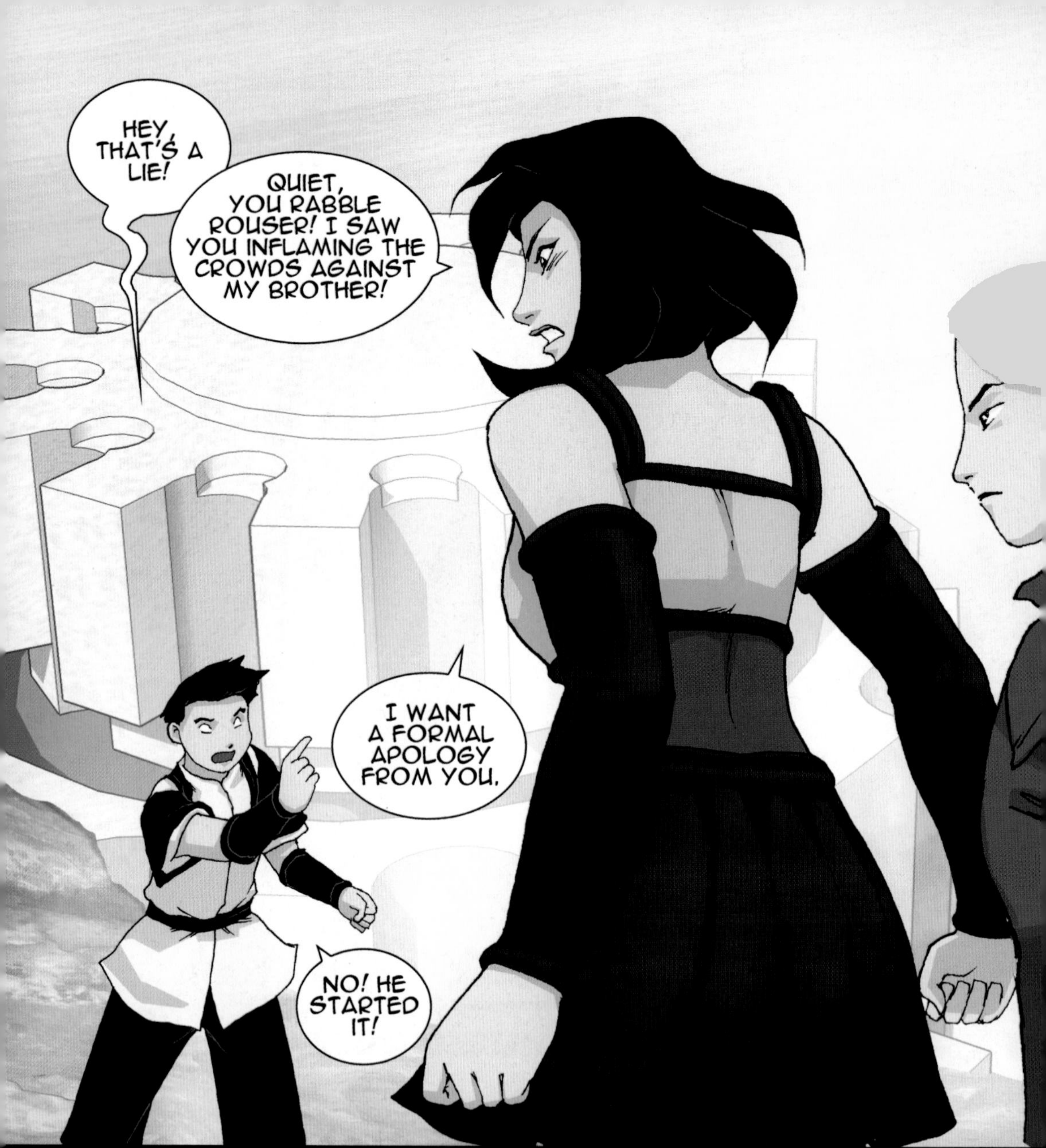
HEY, THAT'S A LIE!
QUIET, YOU RABBLE ROUSER! I SAW YOU INFLAMING THE CROWDS AGAINST MY BROTHER!
I WANT A FORMAL APOLOGY FROM YOU.
NO! HE STARTED IT!
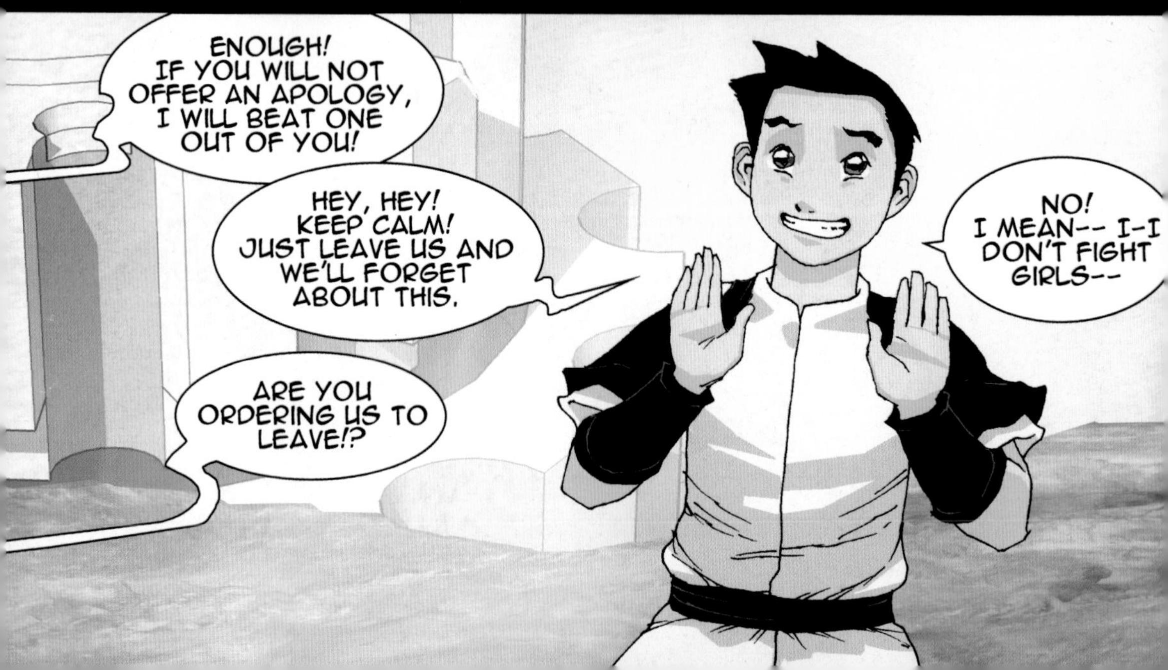
ENOUGH! IF YOU WILL NOT OFFER AN APOLOGY, I WILL BEAT ONE OUT OF YOU!
HEY, HEY! KEEP CALM! JUST LEAVE US AND WE'LL FORGET ABOUT THIS.
NO! I MEAN-- I-I DON'T FIGHT GIRLS--
ARE YOU ORDERING US TO LEAVE!?

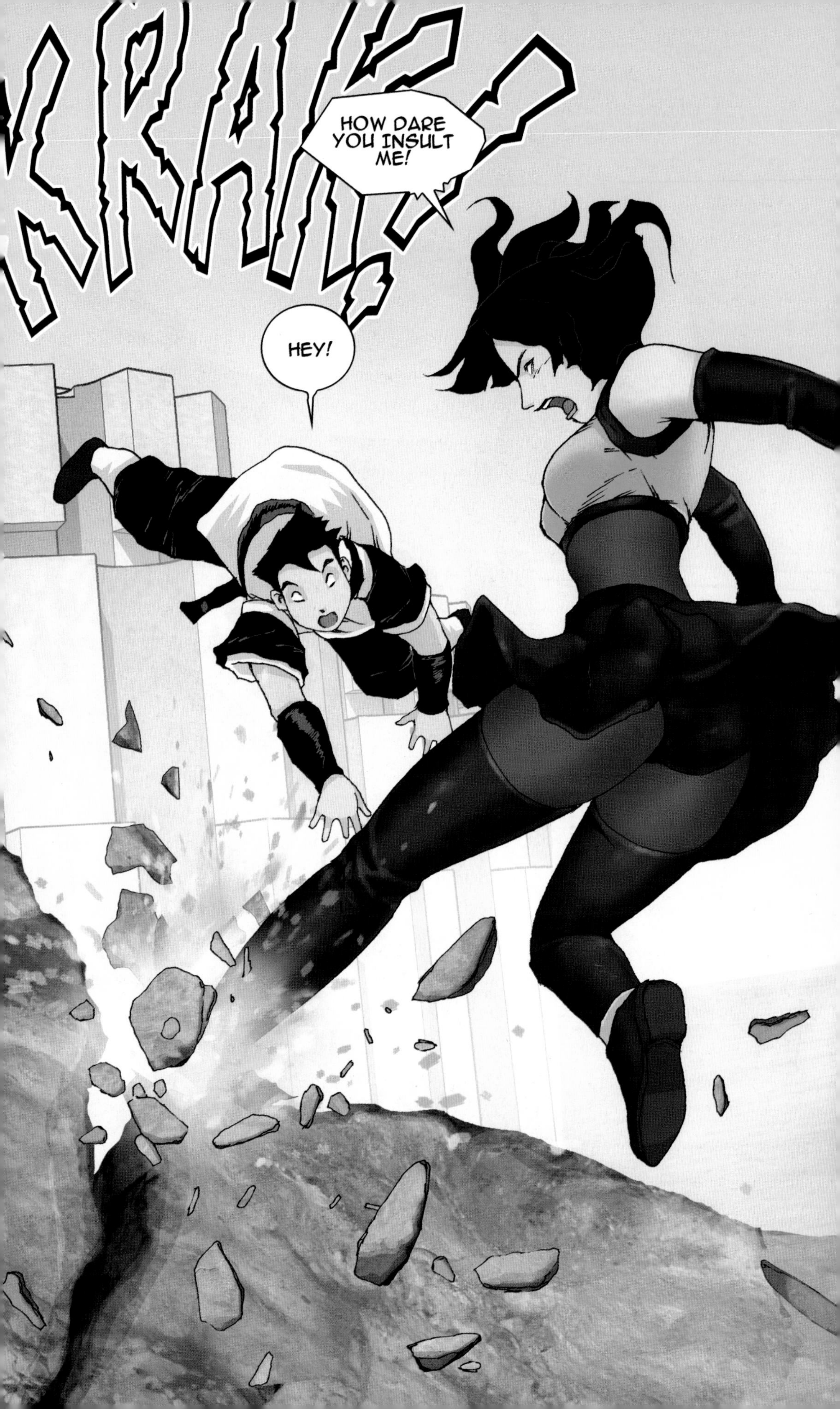
KRAK!
HOW DARE YOU INSULT ME!
HEY!

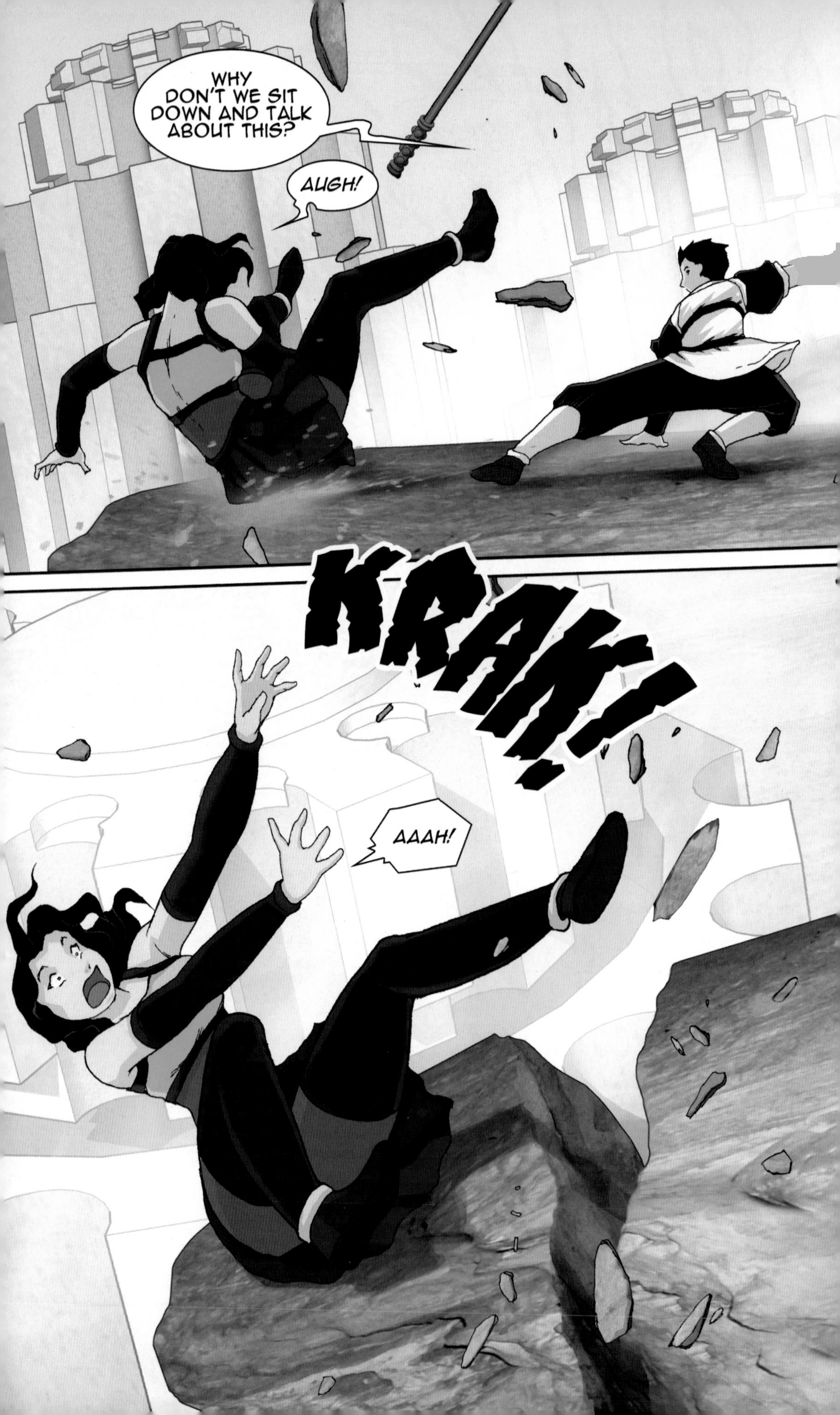
WHY DON'T WE SIT DOWN AND TALK ABOUT THIS?
AUGH!
KRAK!!
AAAH!

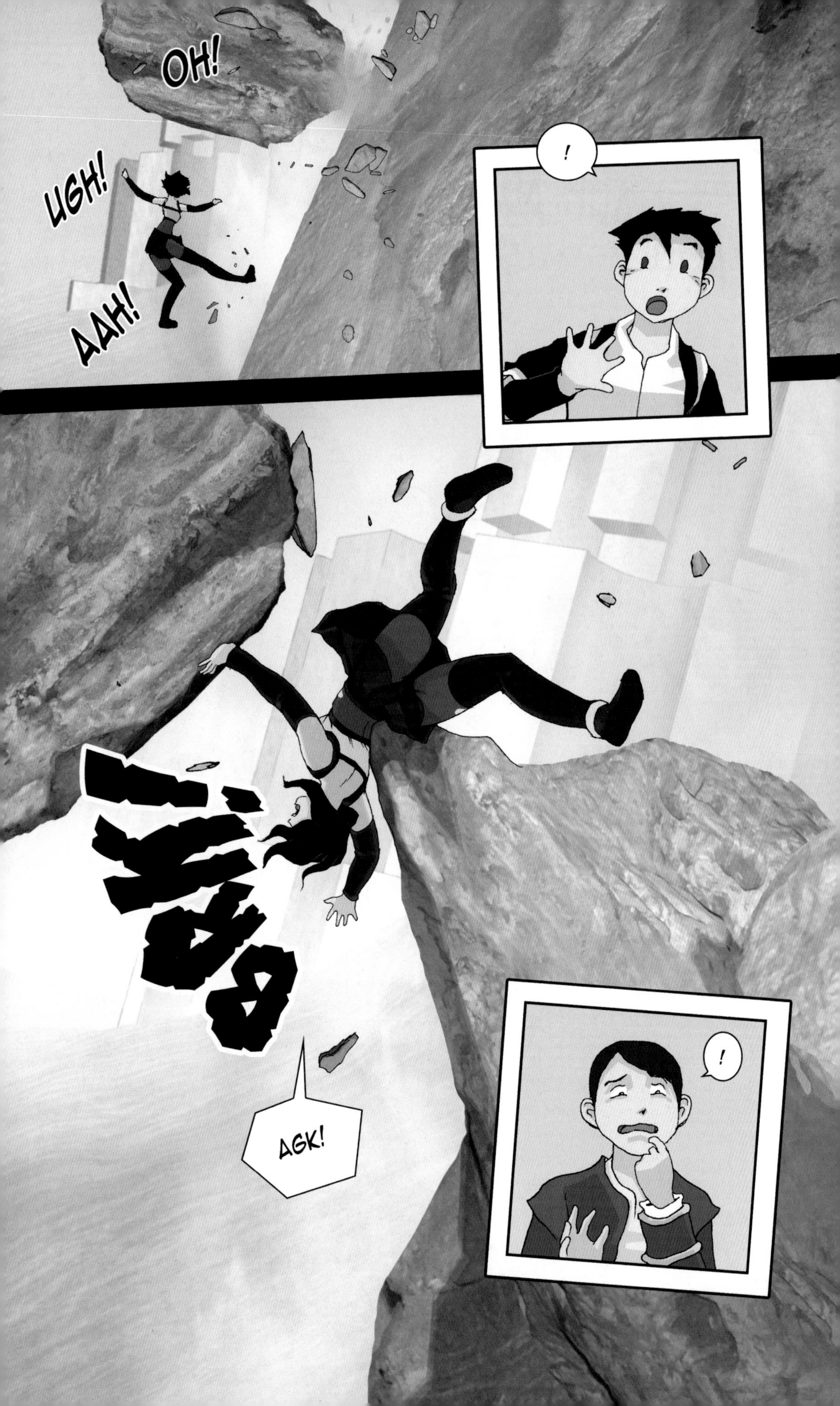
OH!
UGH!
AAH!
!
BAM!!
AGK!
!

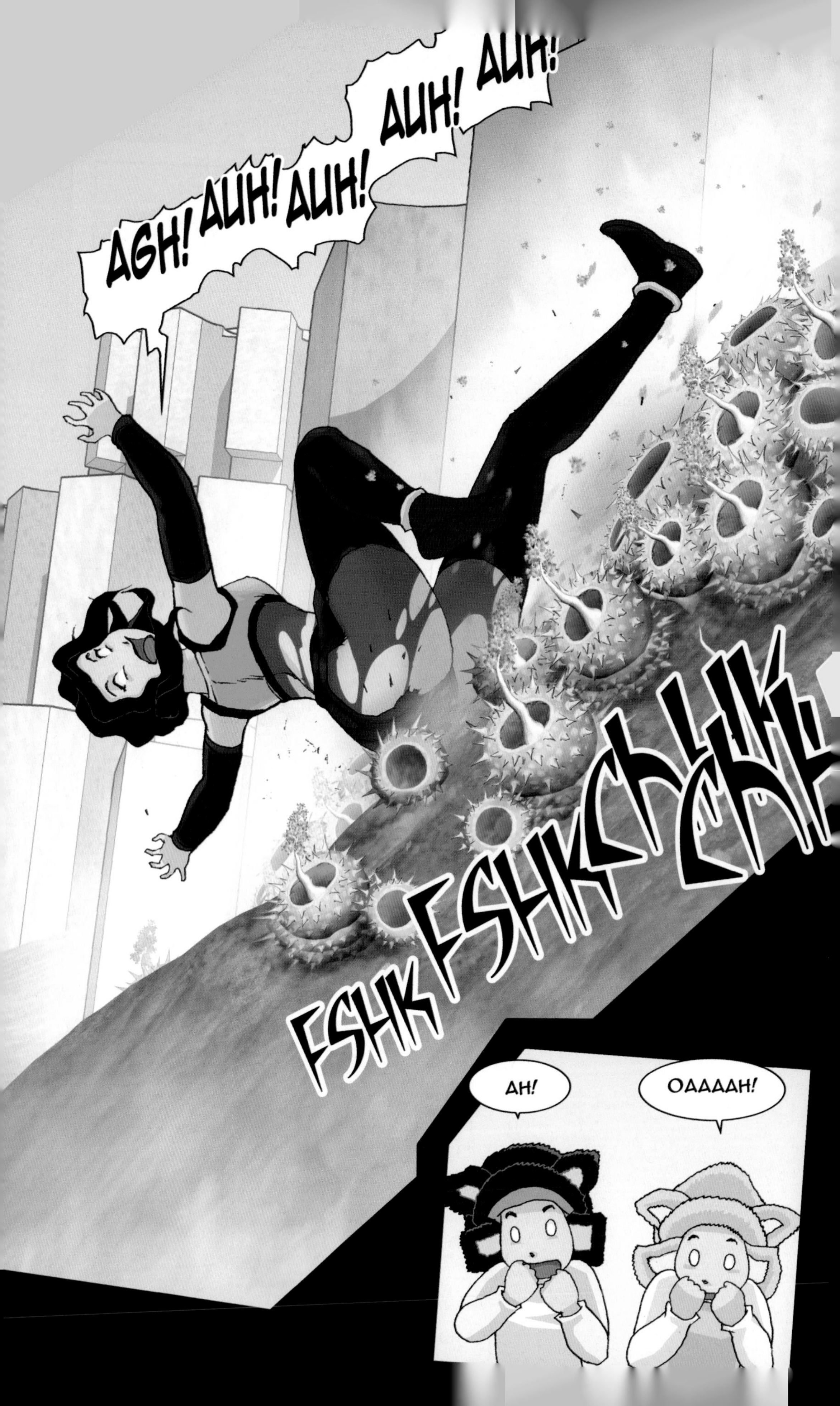
AGH! AUH! AUH! AUH! AUH!
FSHK FSHK FSHK FSHK
AH!
OAAAAH!

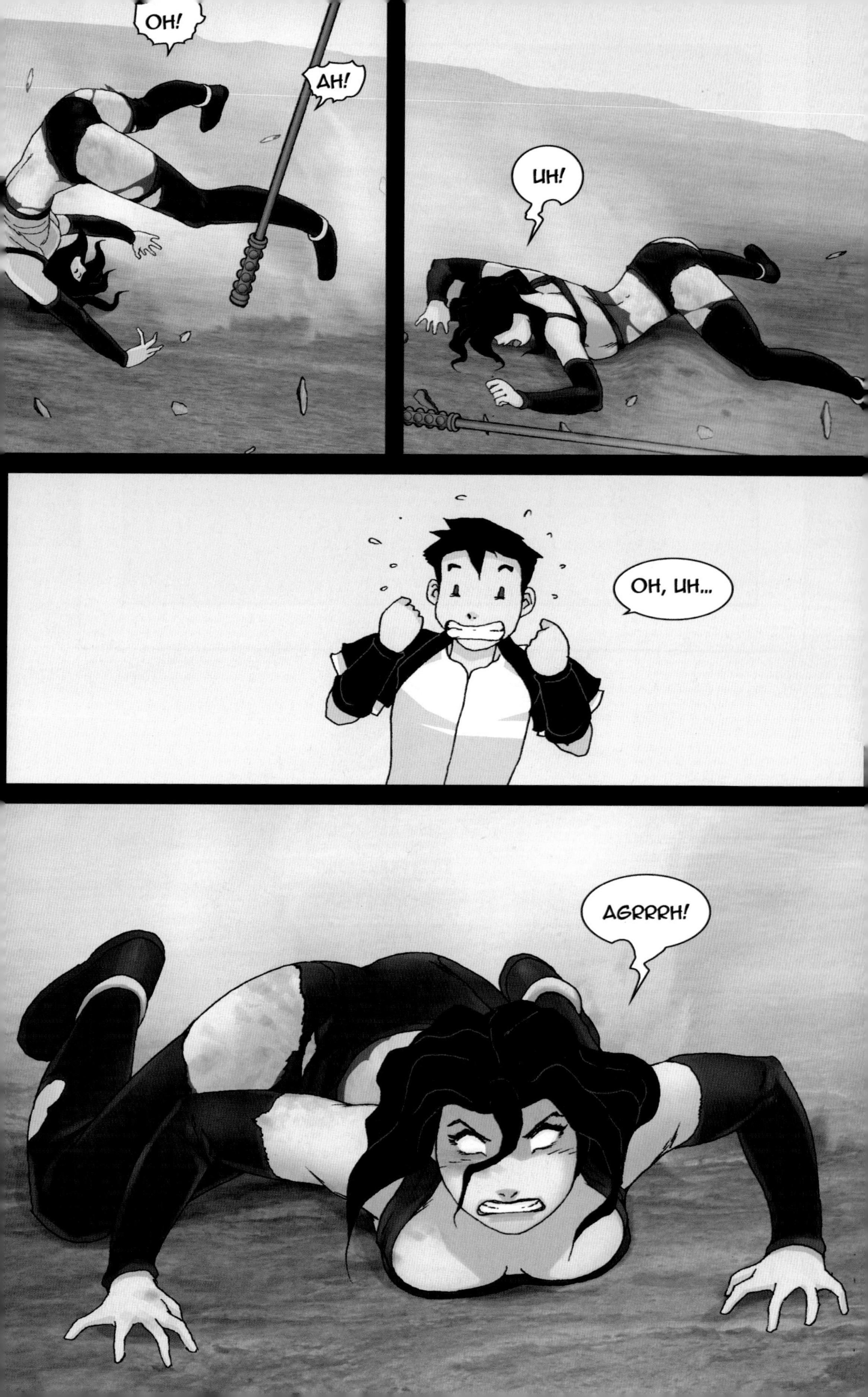
OH!
AH!
UH!
OH, UH...
AGRRRH!

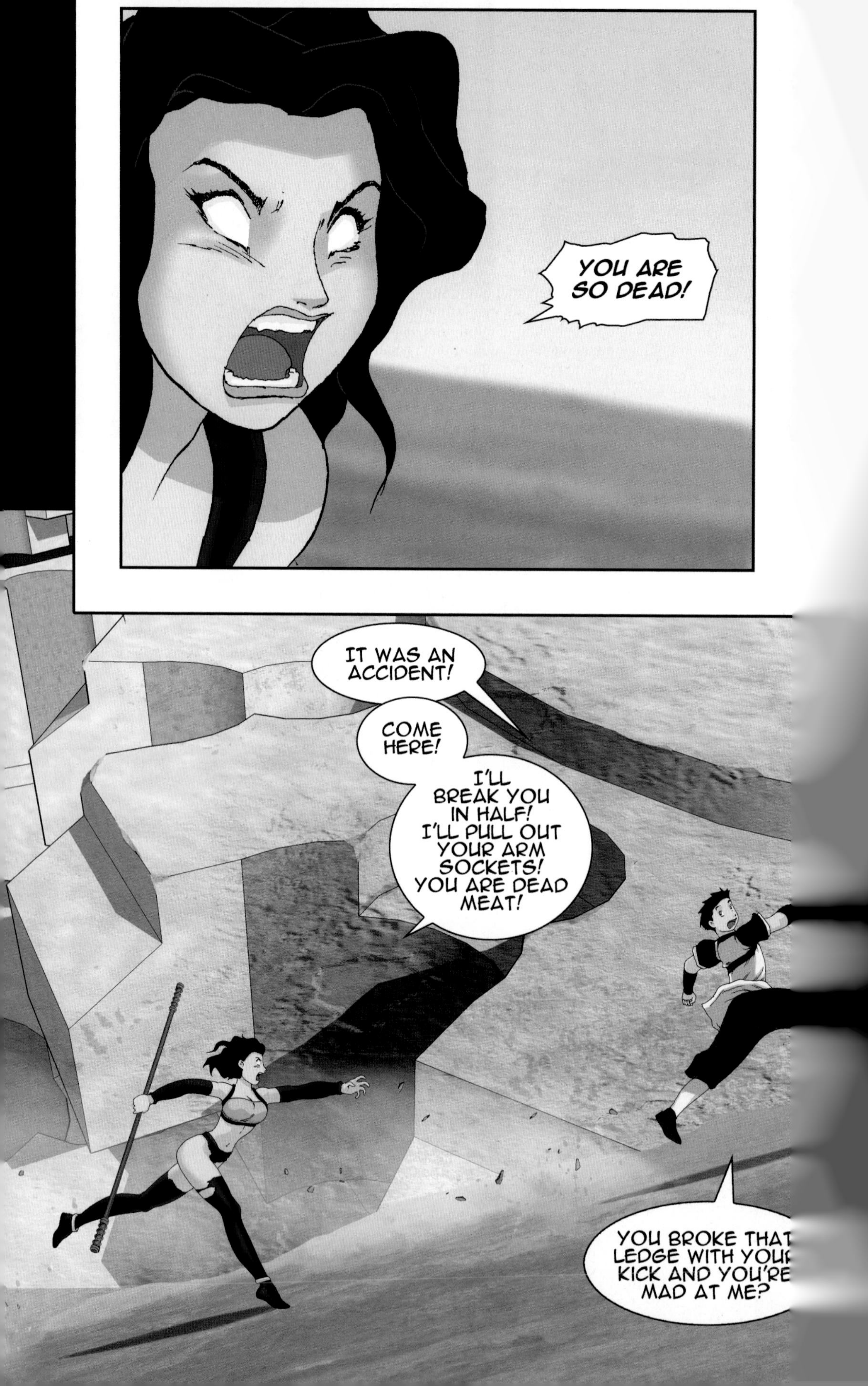
YOU ARE SO DEAD!
IT WAS AN ACCIDENT!
COME HERE!
I'LL BREAK YOU IN HALF! I'LL PULL OUT YOUR ARM SOCKETS! YOU ARE DEAD MEAT!
YOU BROKE THAT LEDGE WITH YOUR KICK AND YOU'RE MAD AT ME?

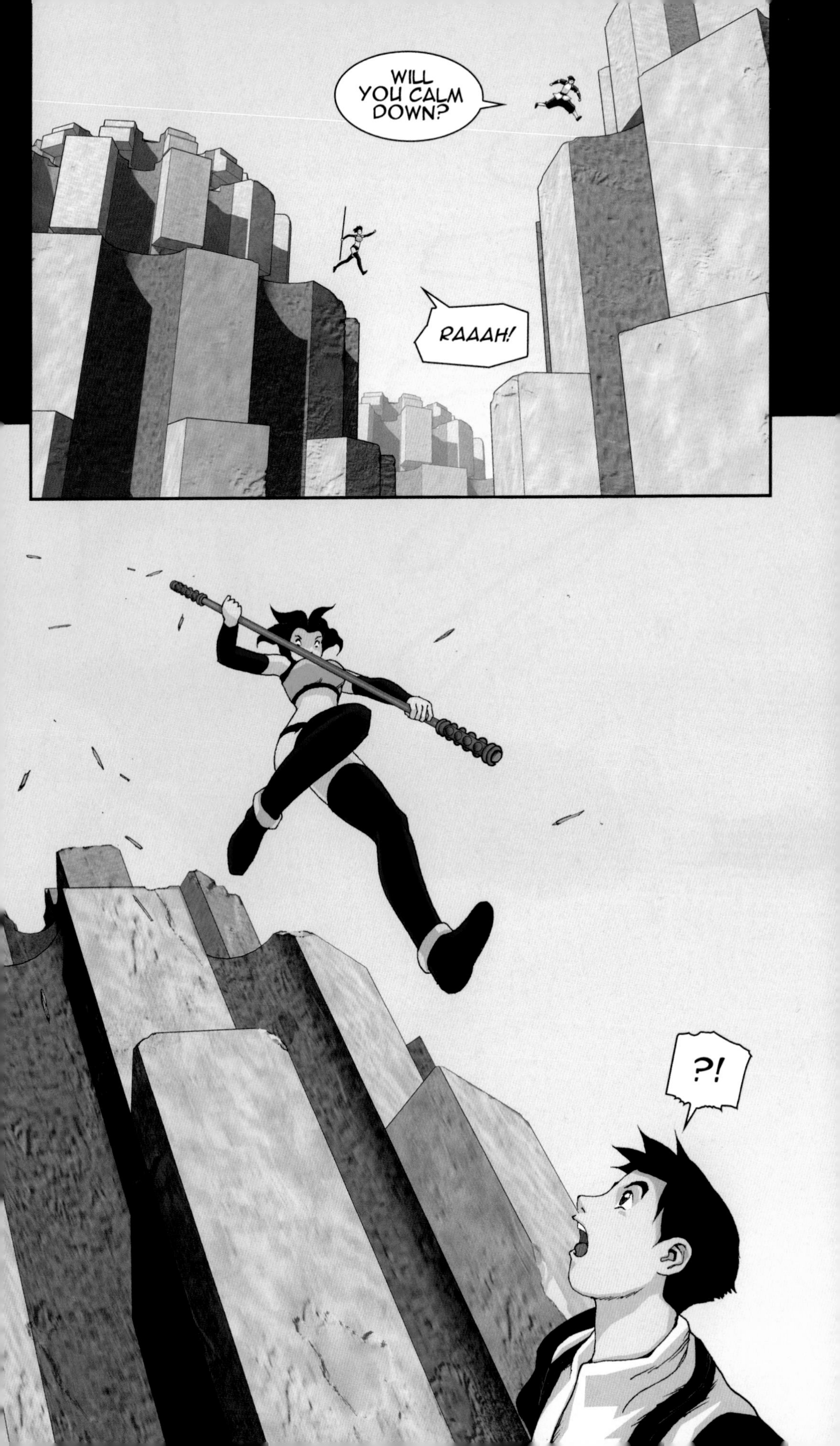
WILL YOU CALM DOWN?
RAAAH!
?!

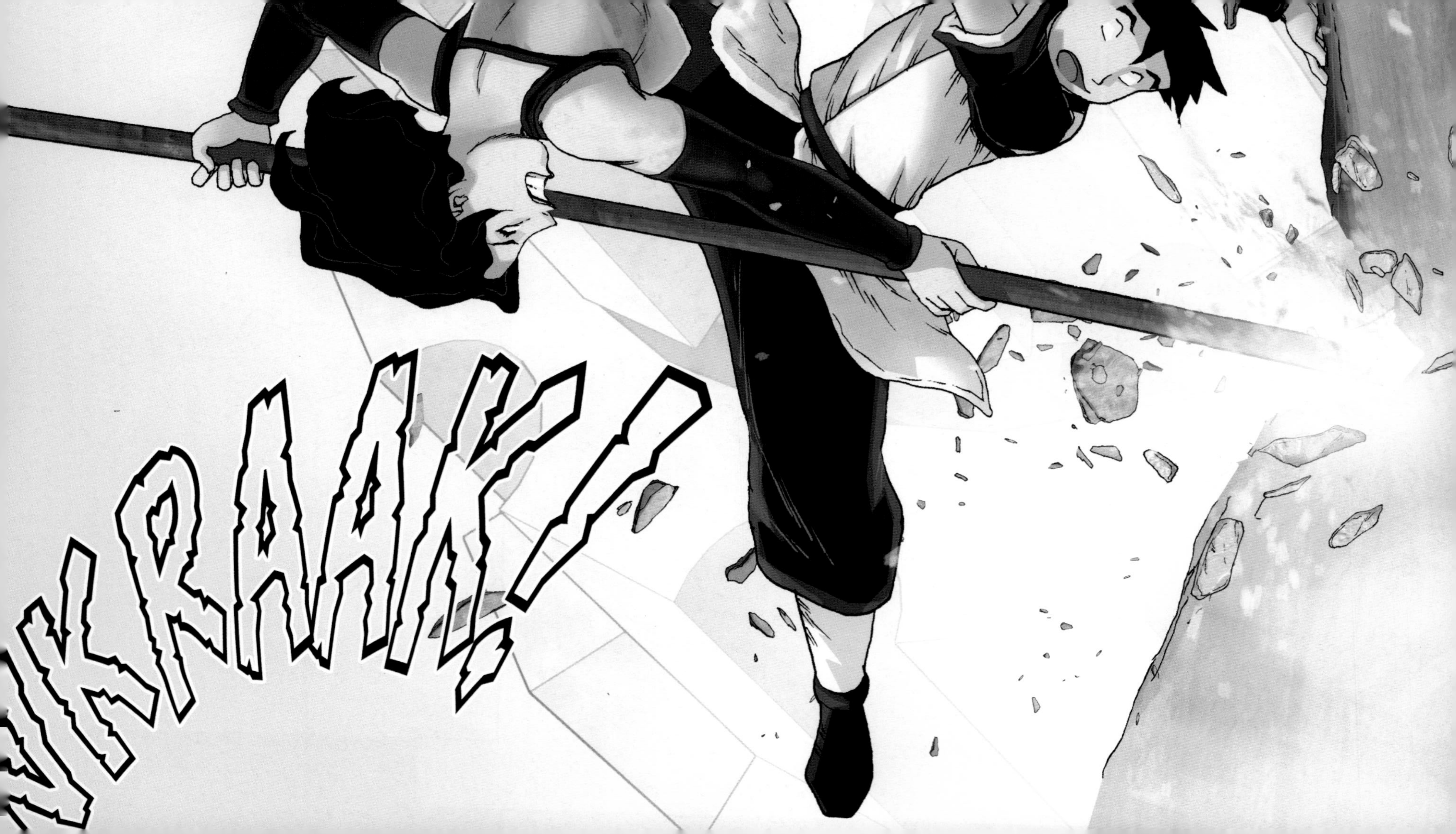
KRAAK!

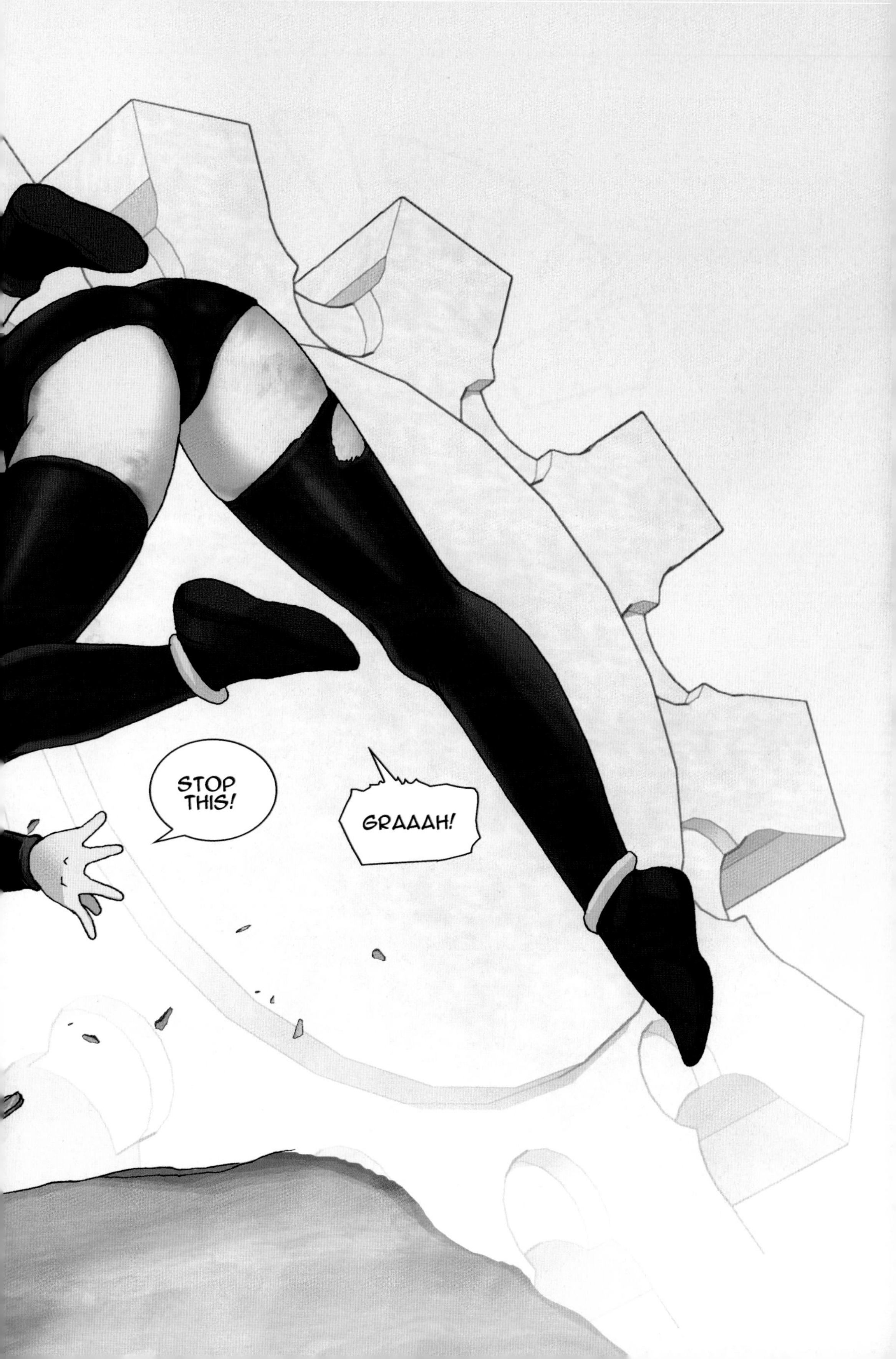
STOP THIS!
GRAAAH!

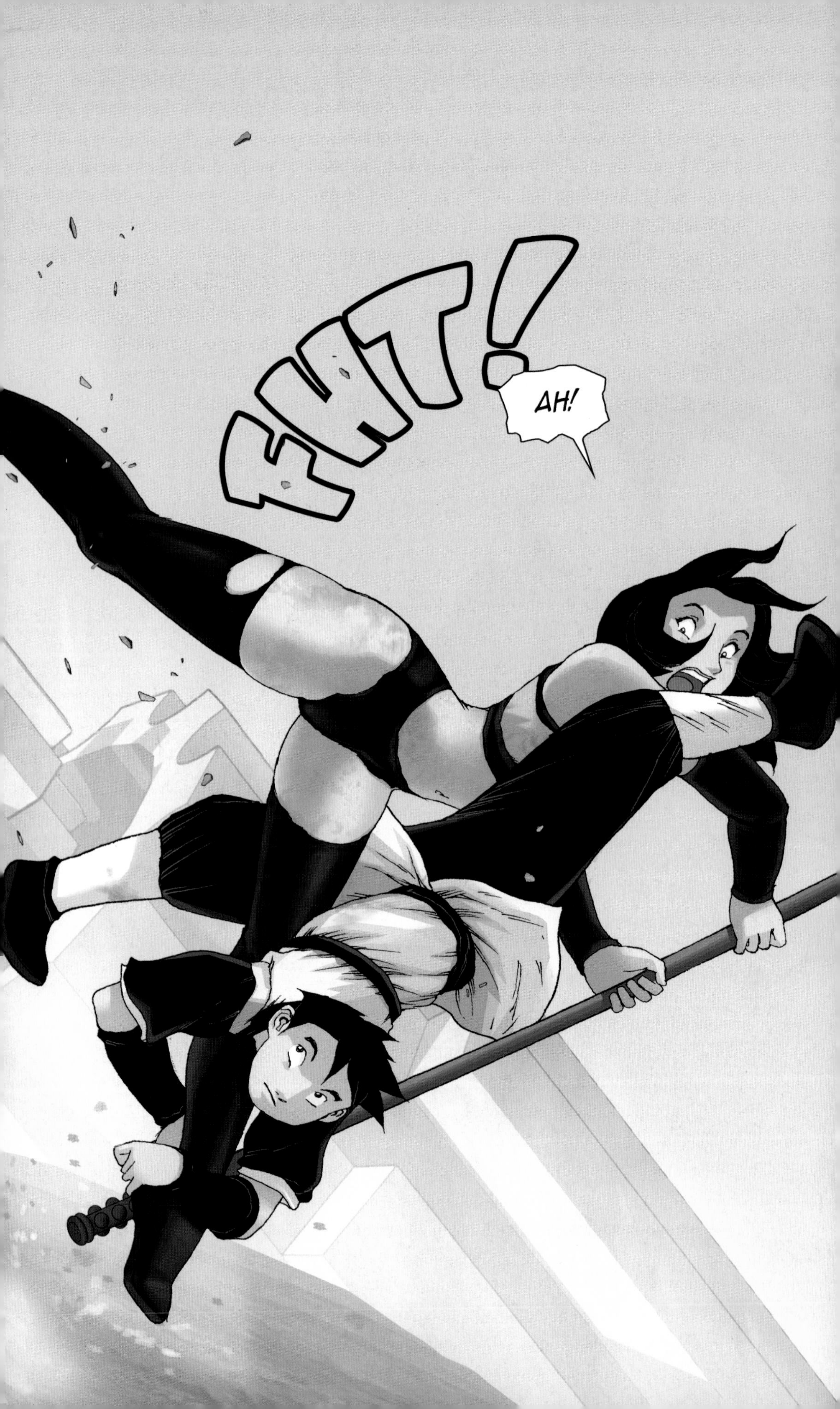
FHT!
AH!

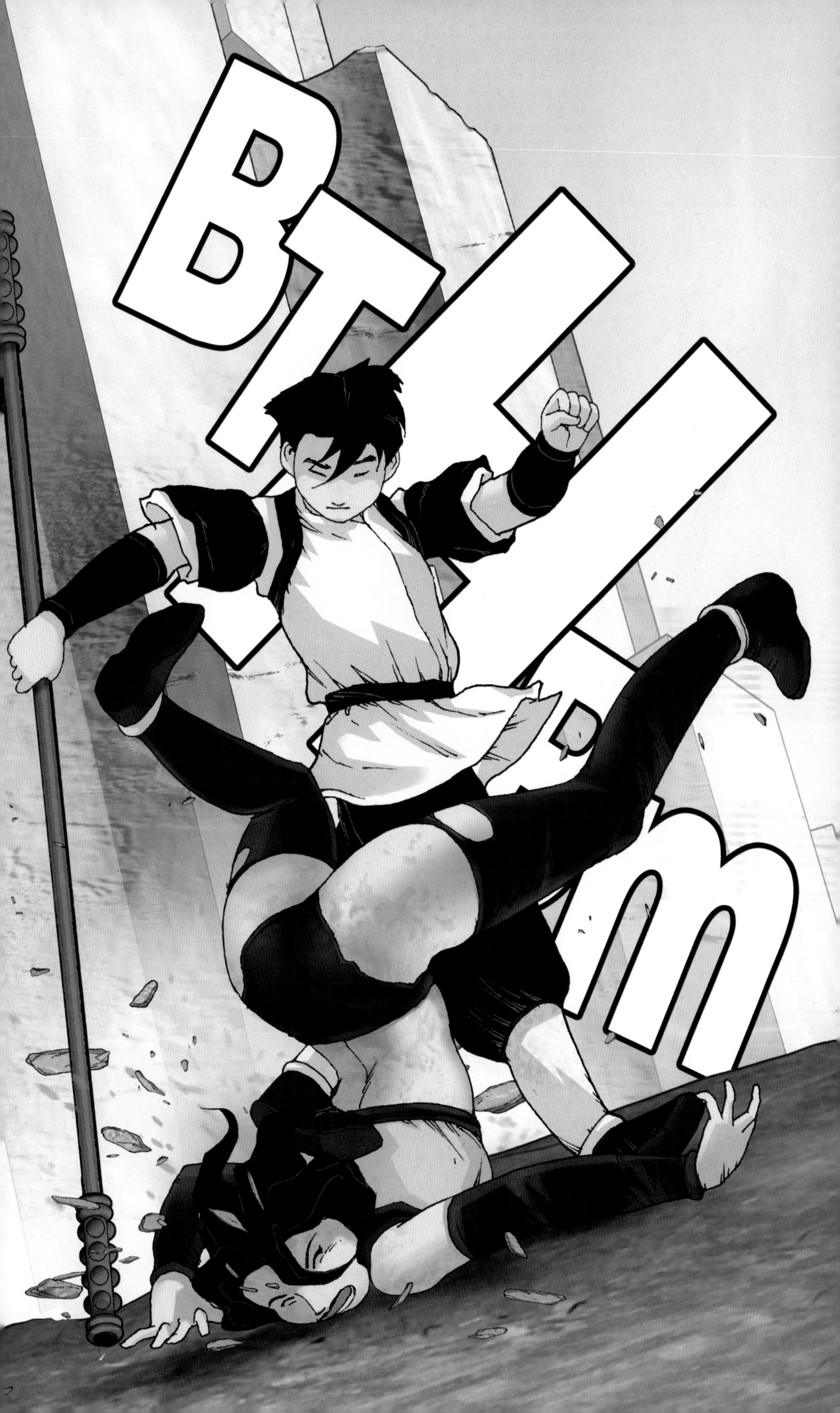

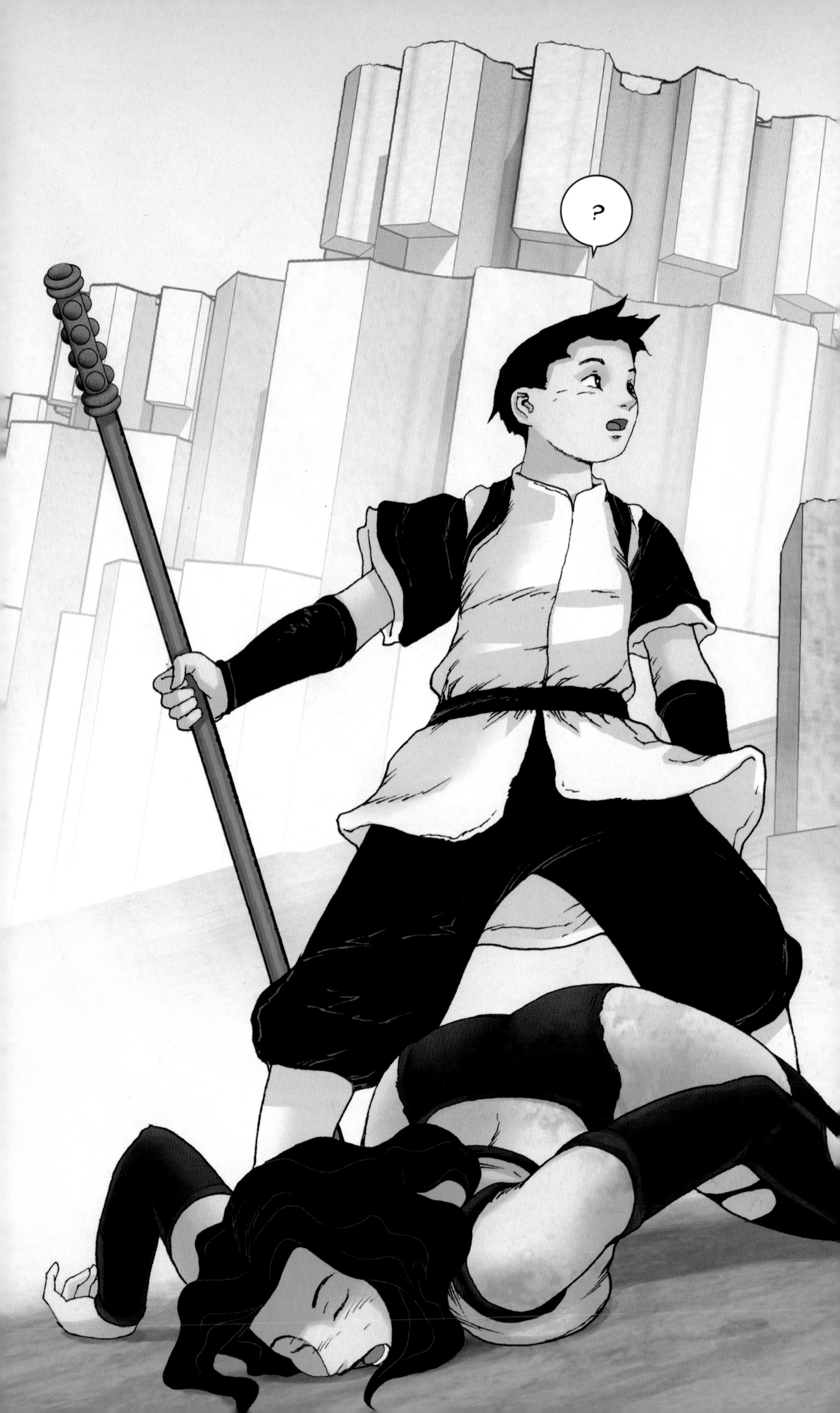
?

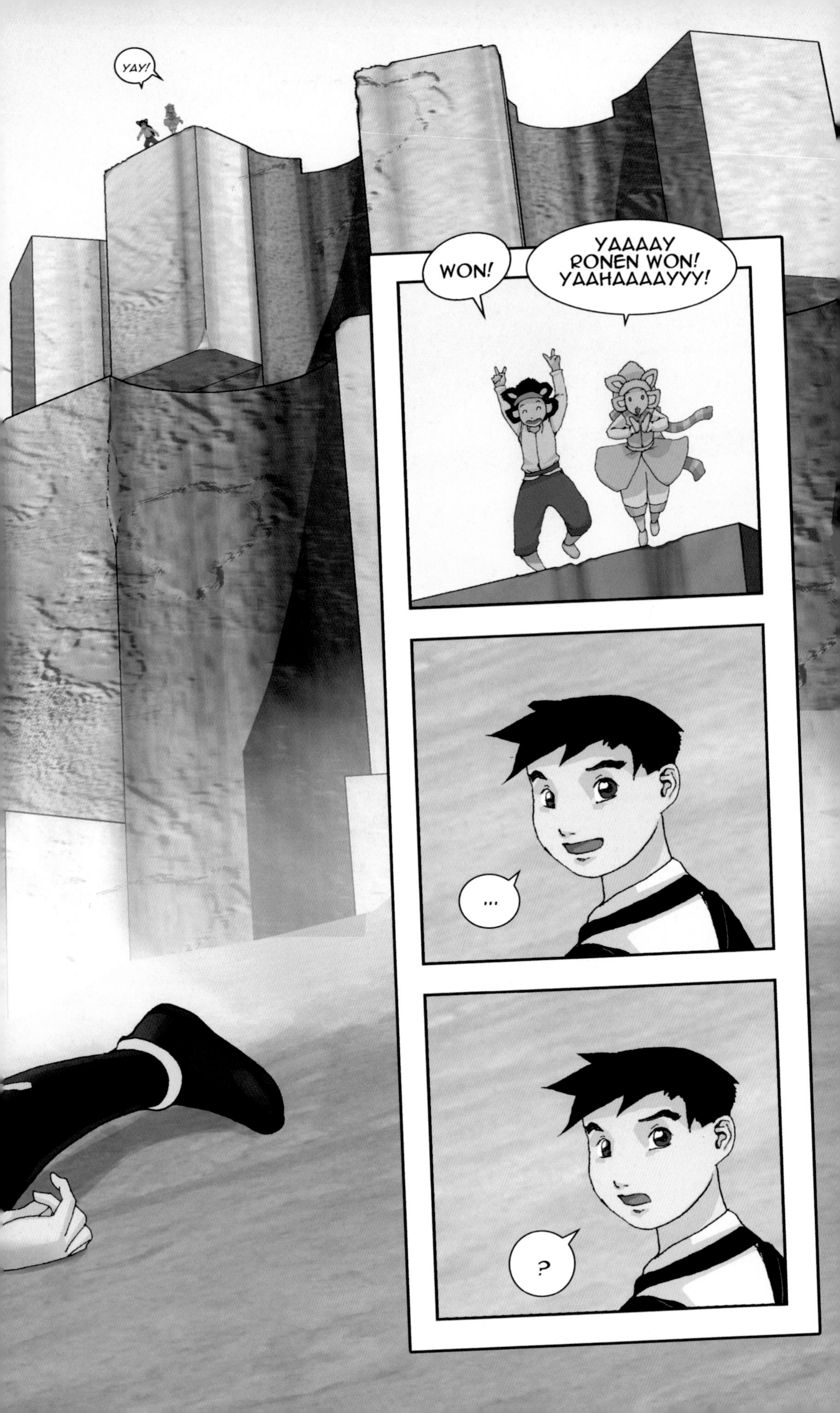
YAY!
WON!
YAAAAY RONEN WON! YAAHAAAAYYY!
...
?

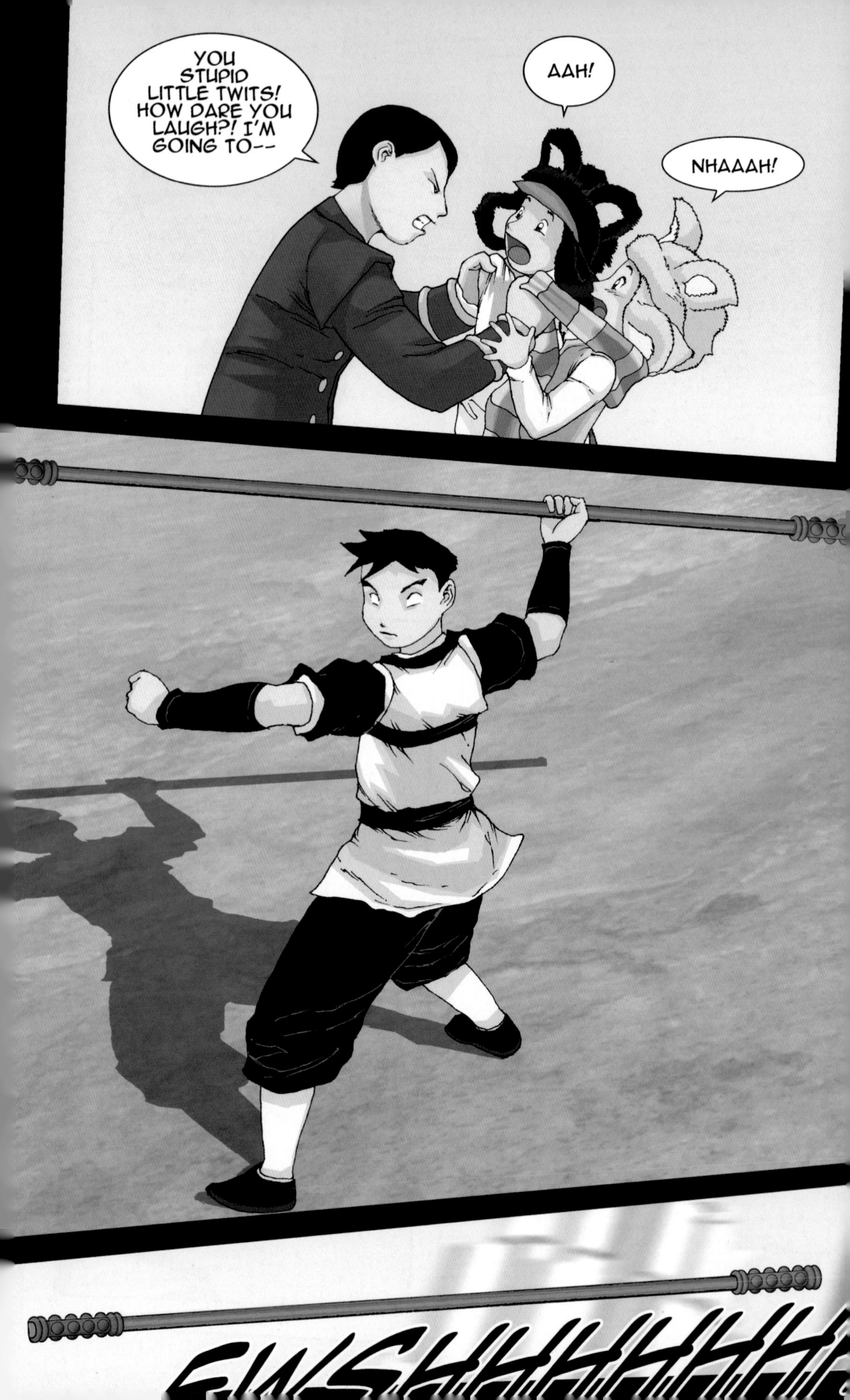
YOU STUPID LITTLE TWITS! HOW DARE YOU LAUGH?! I'M GOING TO--
AAH!
NHAAAH!

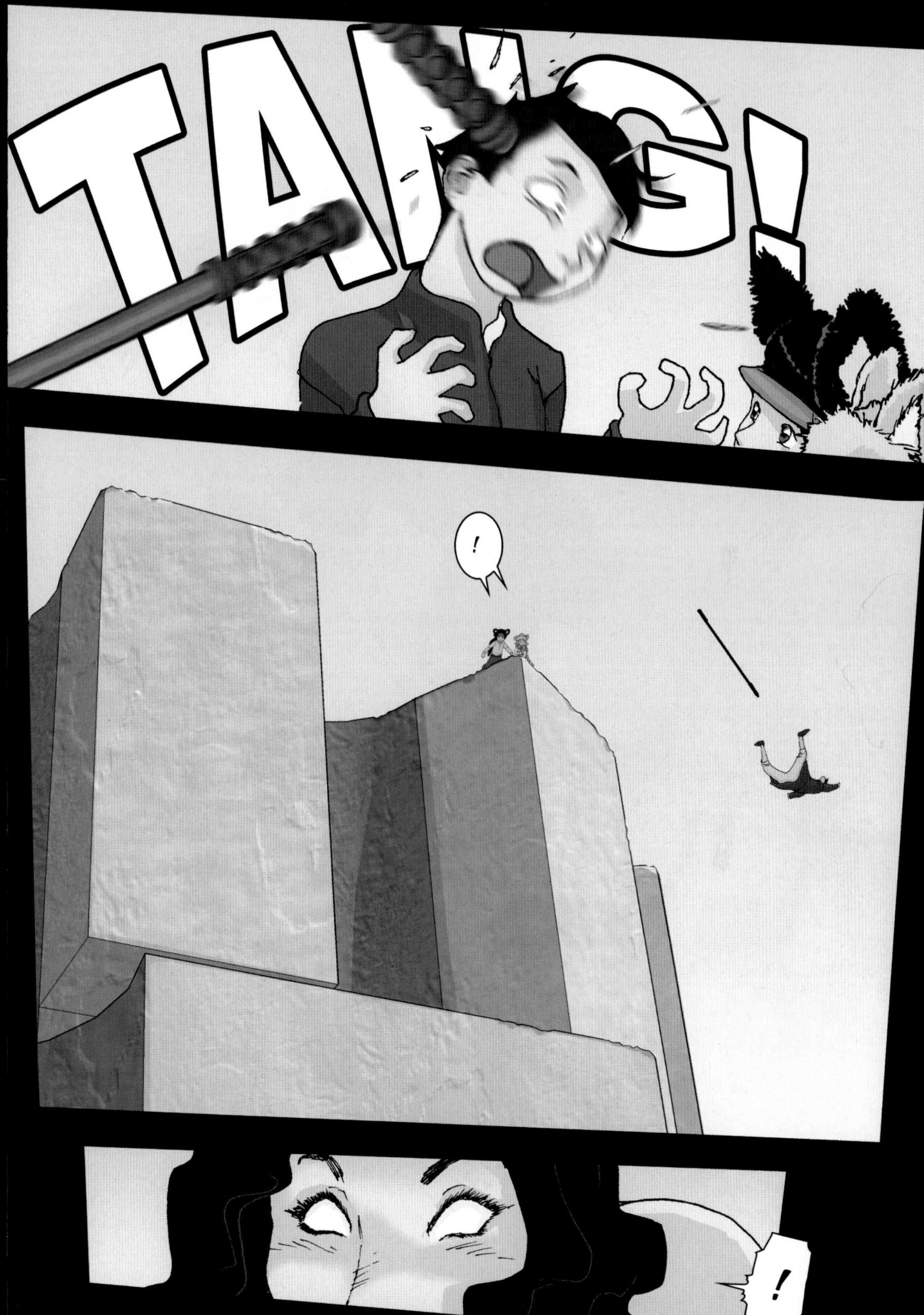
TANG!
!
!

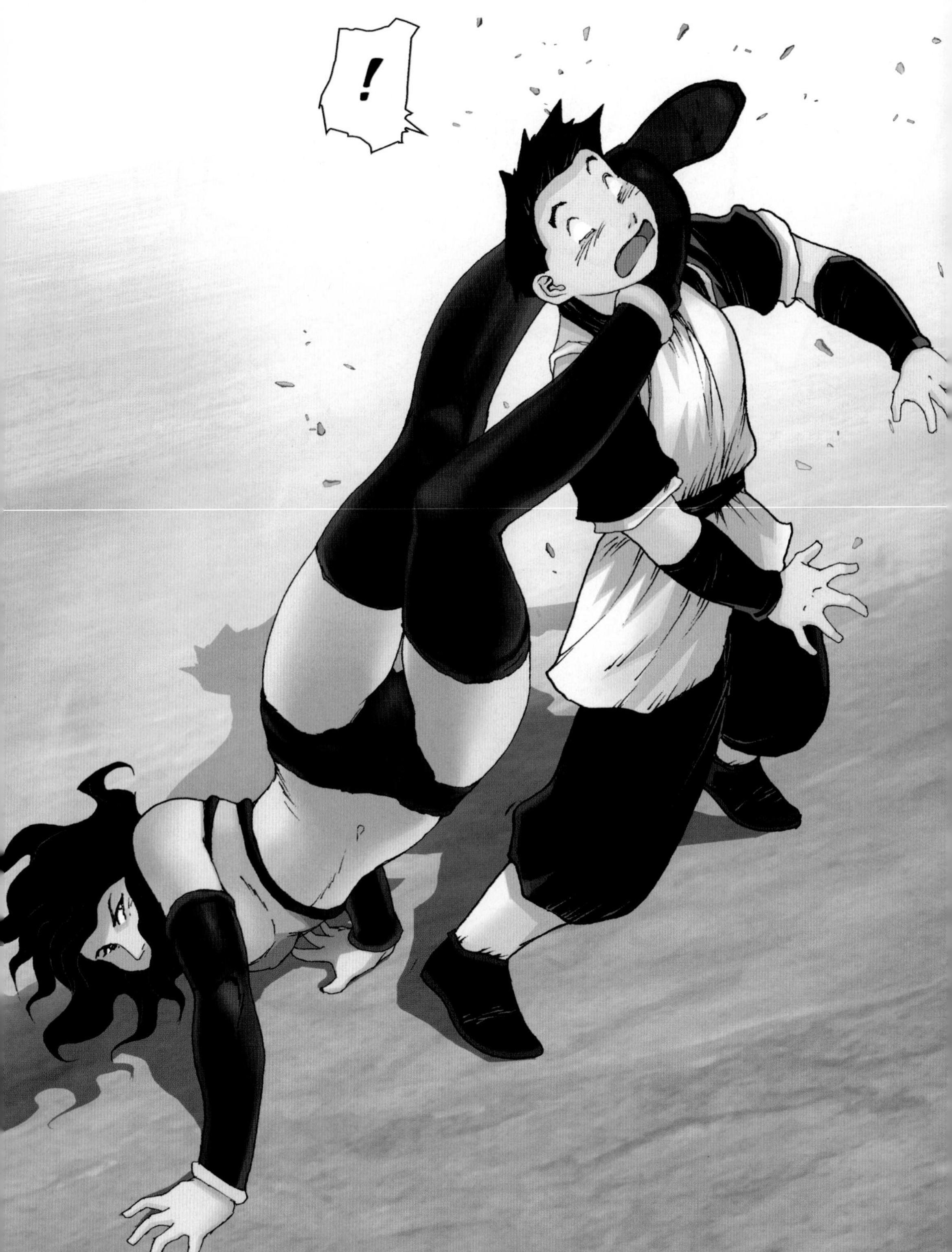
!

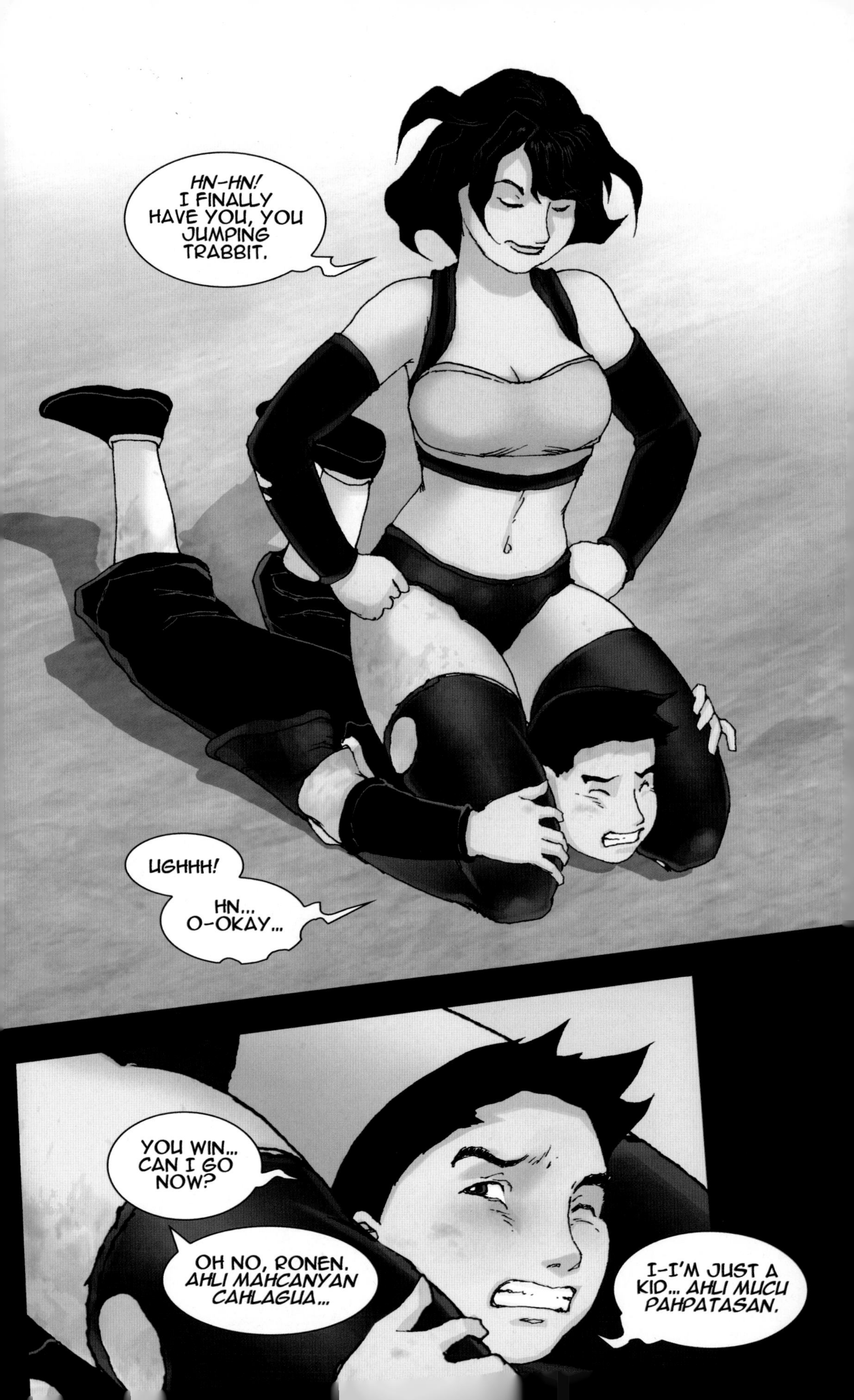
HN-HN! I FINALLY HAVE YOU, YOU JUMPING TRABBIT.
UGHHH!
HN... O-OKAY...
YOU WIN... CAN I GO NOW?
OH NO, RONEN. AHLI MAHCANYAN CAHLAGUA...
I-I'M JUST A KID... AHLI MUCU PAHPATASAN.

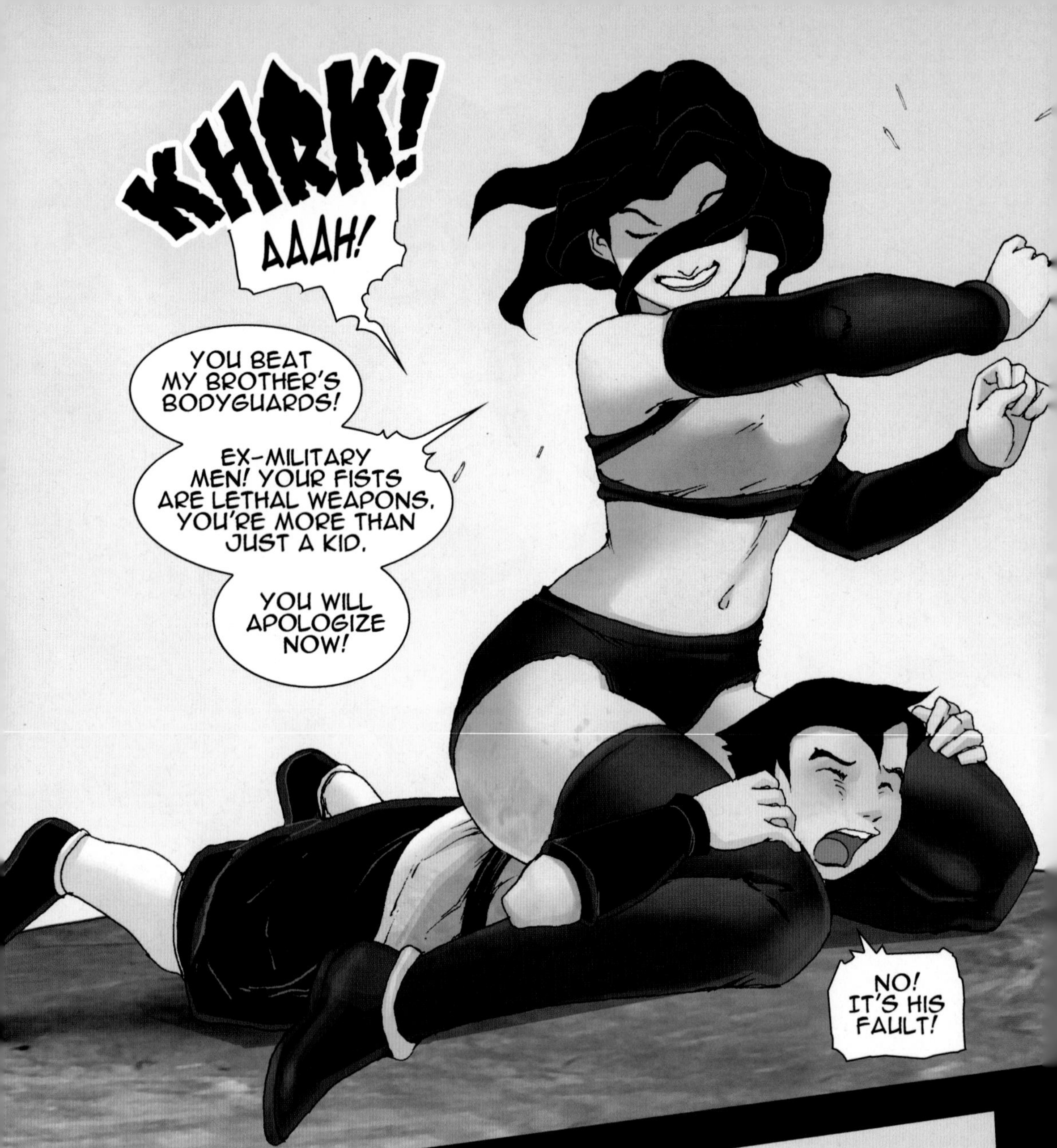
KHRK!
AAAH!
YOU BEAT MY BROTHER'S BODYGUARDS!
EX-MILITARY MEN! YOUR FISTS ARE LETHAL WEAPONS. YOU'RE MORE THAN JUST A KID.
YOU WILL APOLOGIZE NOW!
NO! IT'S HIS FAULT!

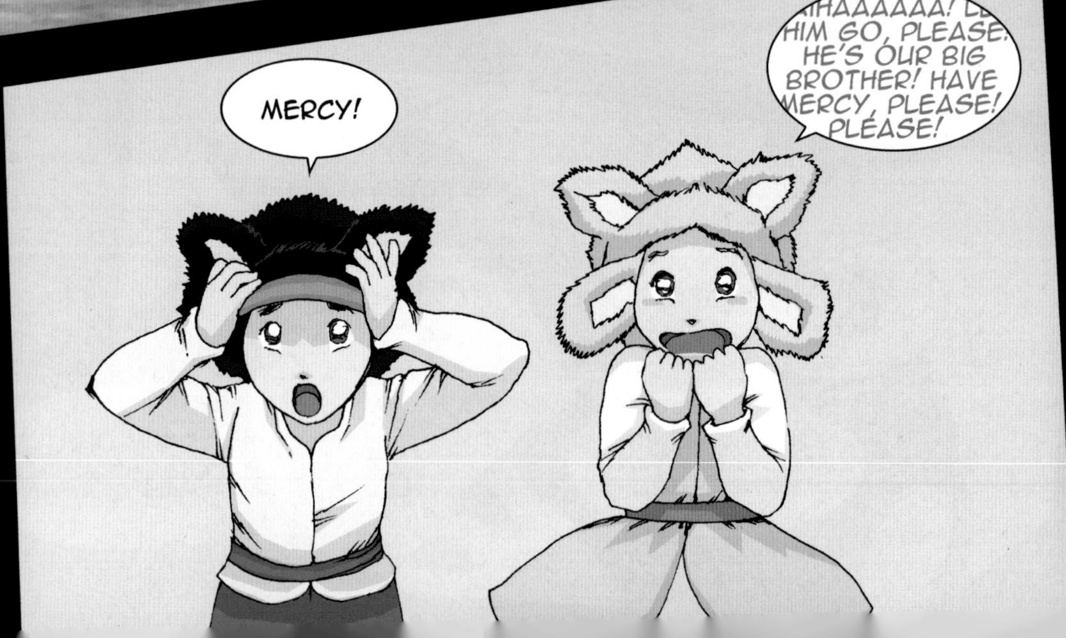
MERCY!
HIM GO, PLEASE! HE'S OUR BIG BROTHER! HAVE MERCY, PLEASE! PLEASE!

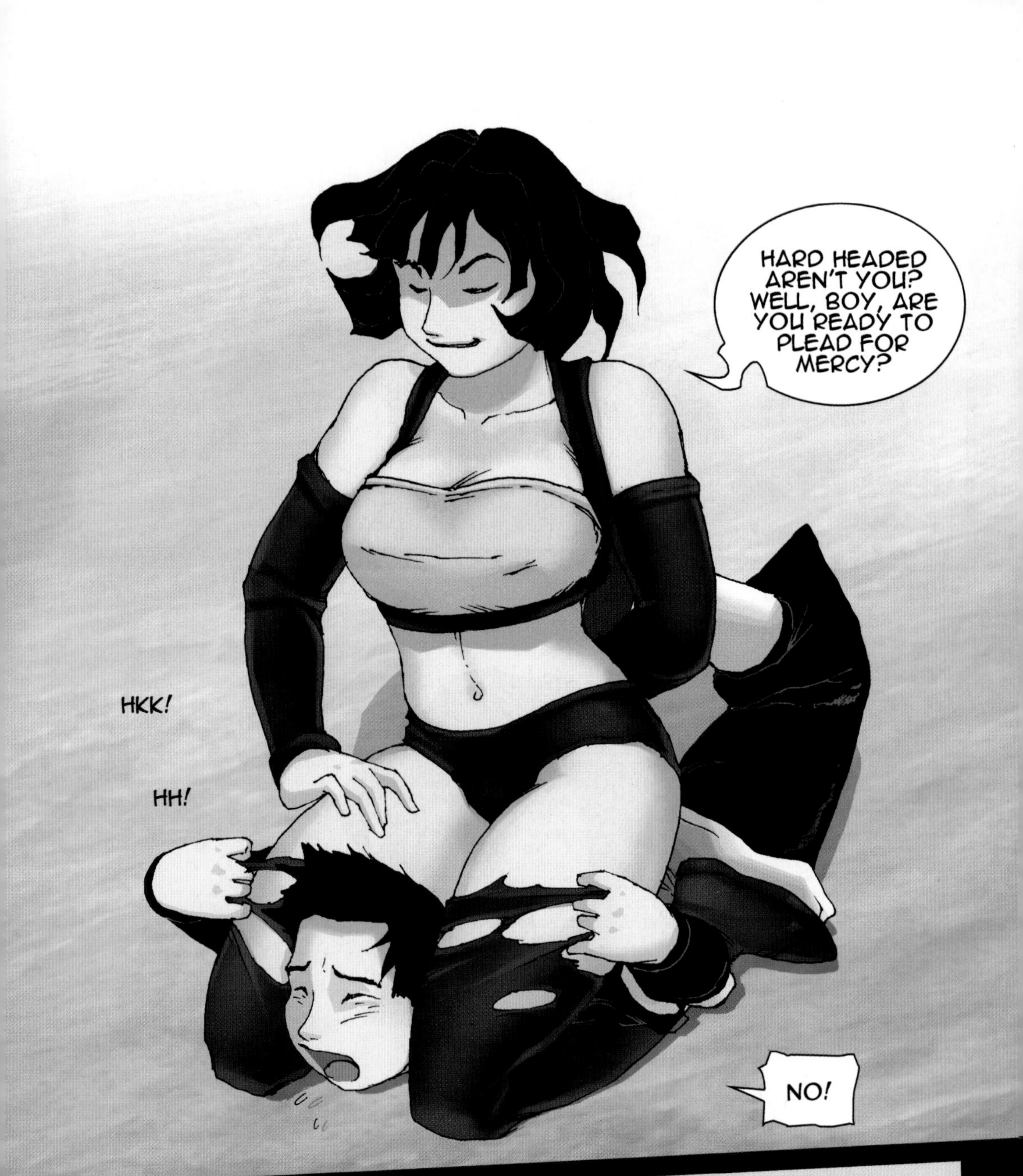
HARD HEADED AREN'T YOU? WELL, BOY, ARE YOU READY TO PLEAD FOR MERCY?
HKK!
HH!
NO!

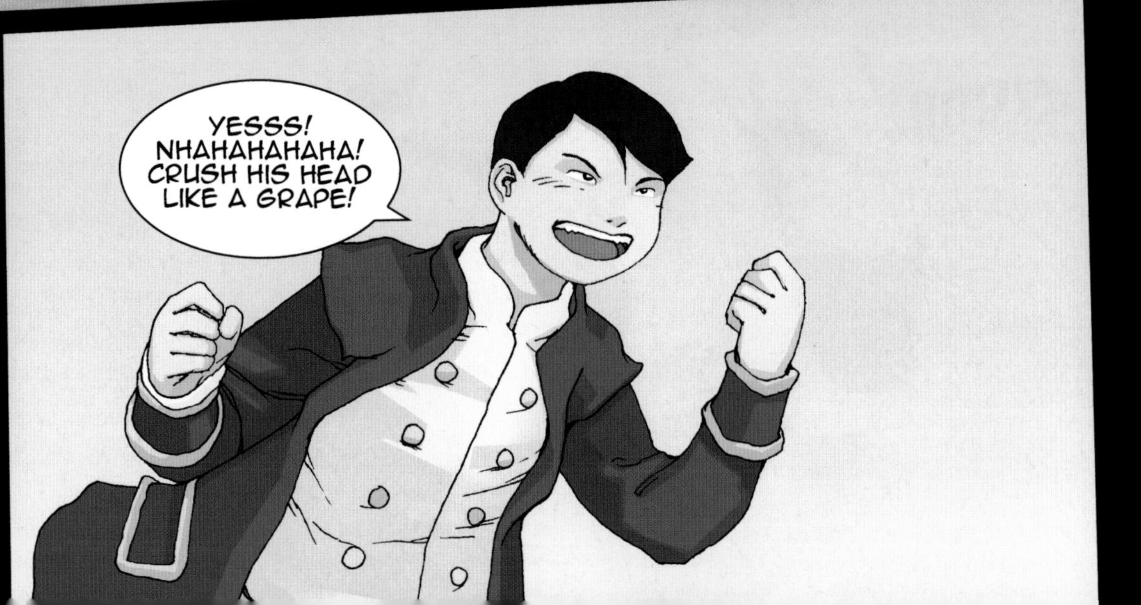
YESSS! NHAHAHAHAHA! CRUSH HIS HEAD LIKE A GRAPE!

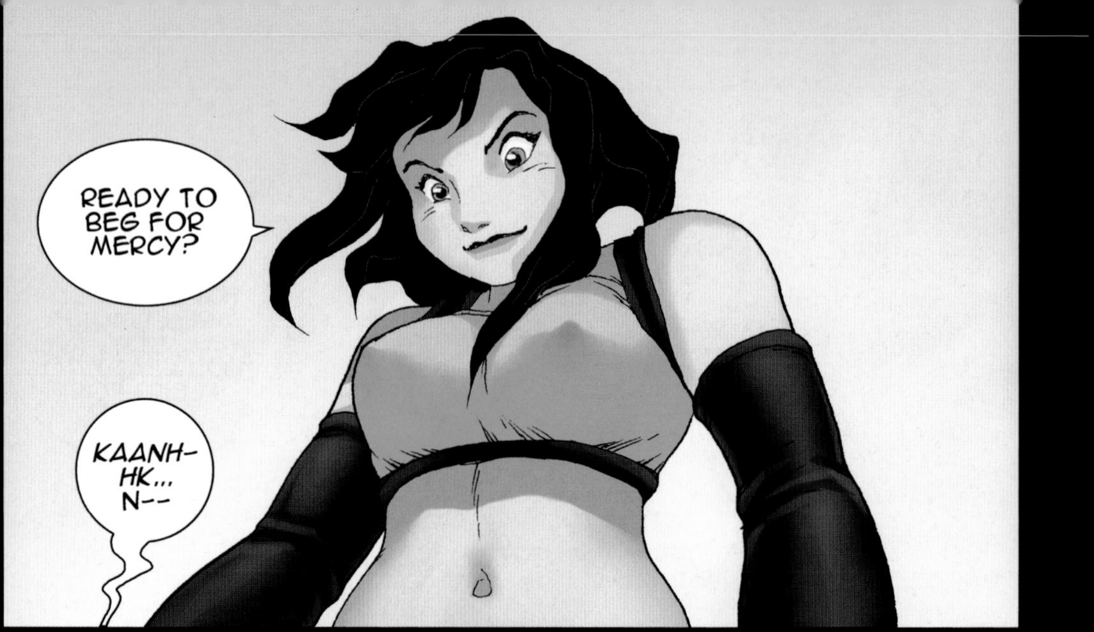
READY TO BEG FOR MERCY?
KAANH-HK... N--

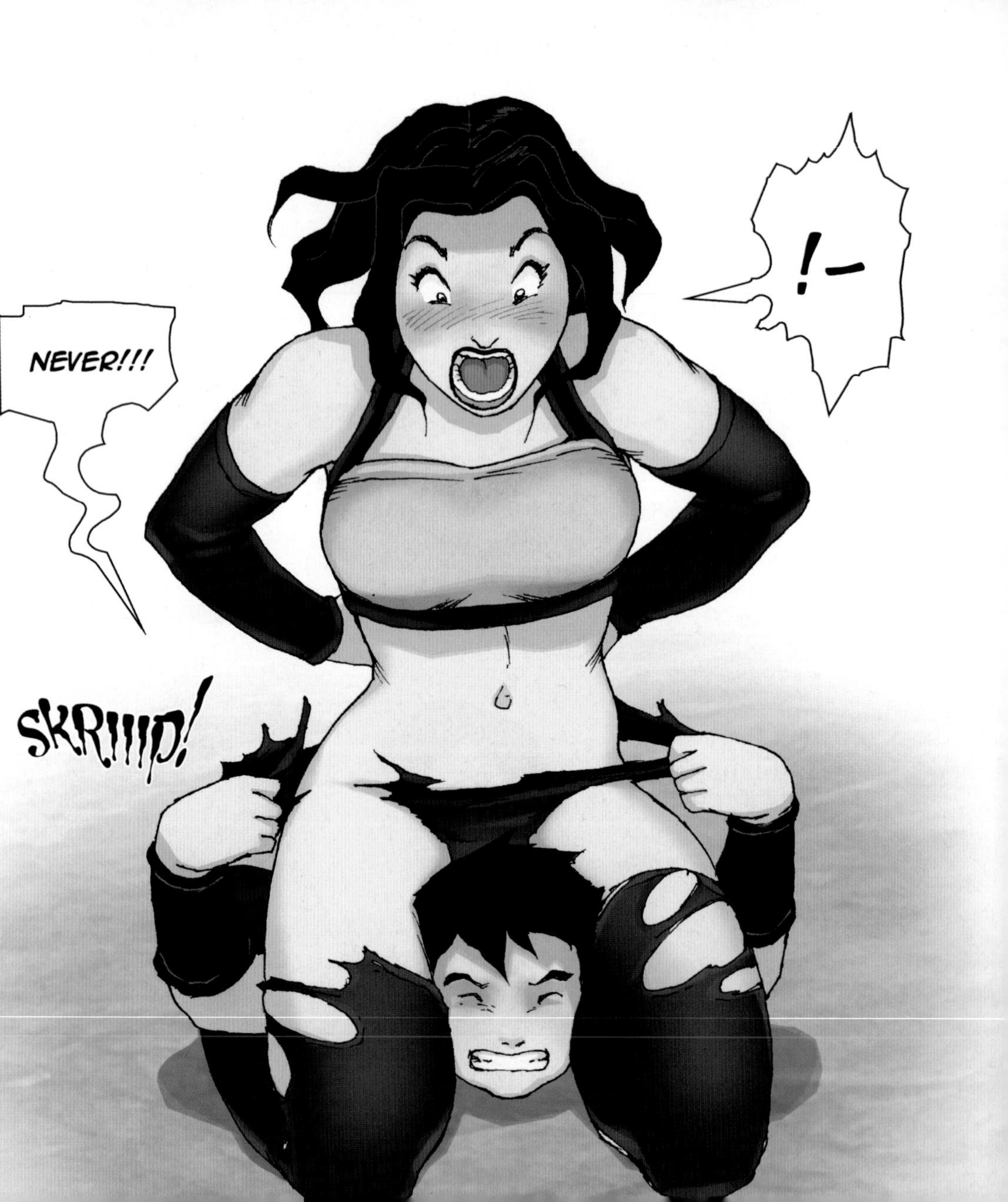
!-
NEVER!!!
SKRIIIP!

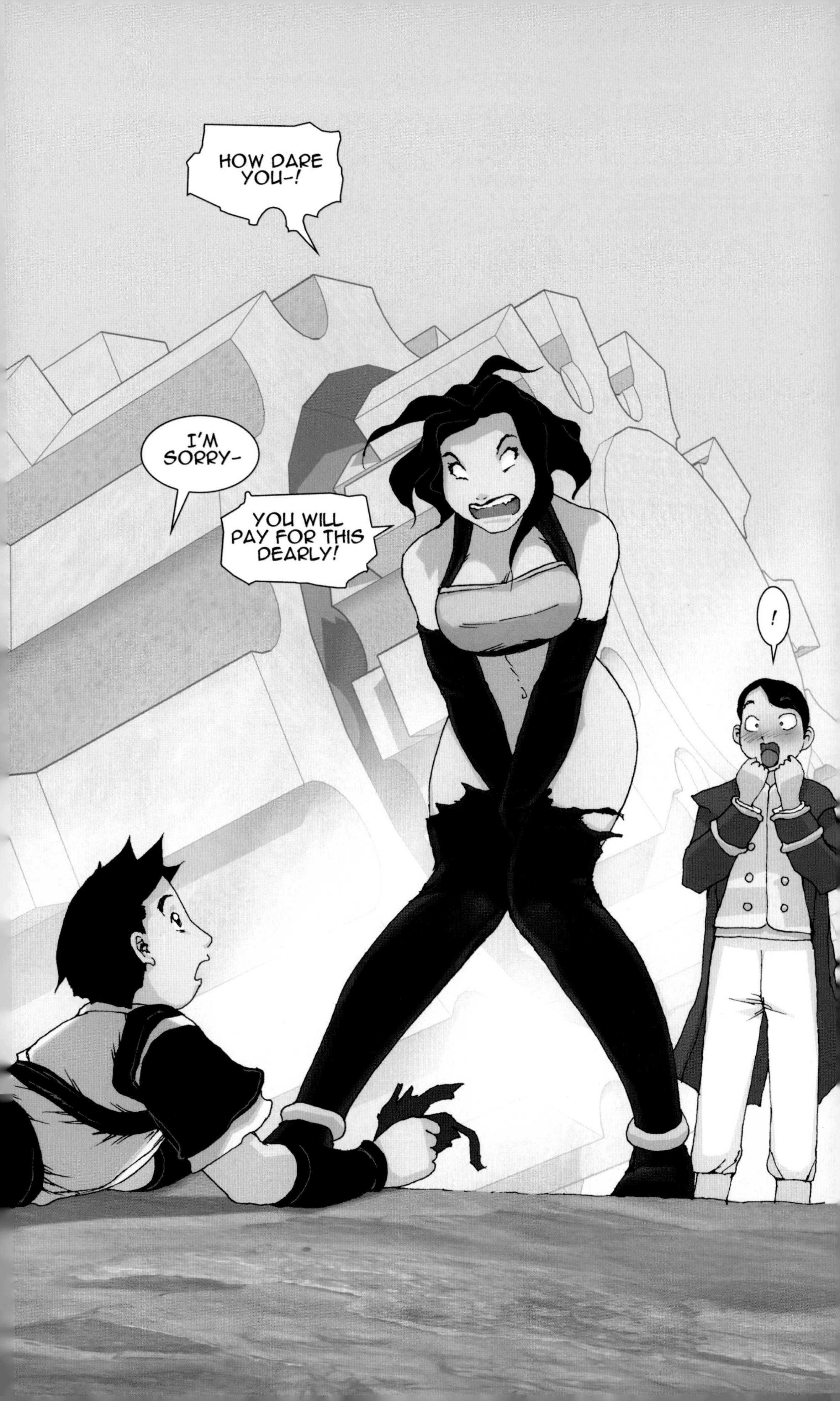
HOW DARE YOU-!
I'M SORRY-
YOU WILL PAY FOR THIS DEARLY!
!

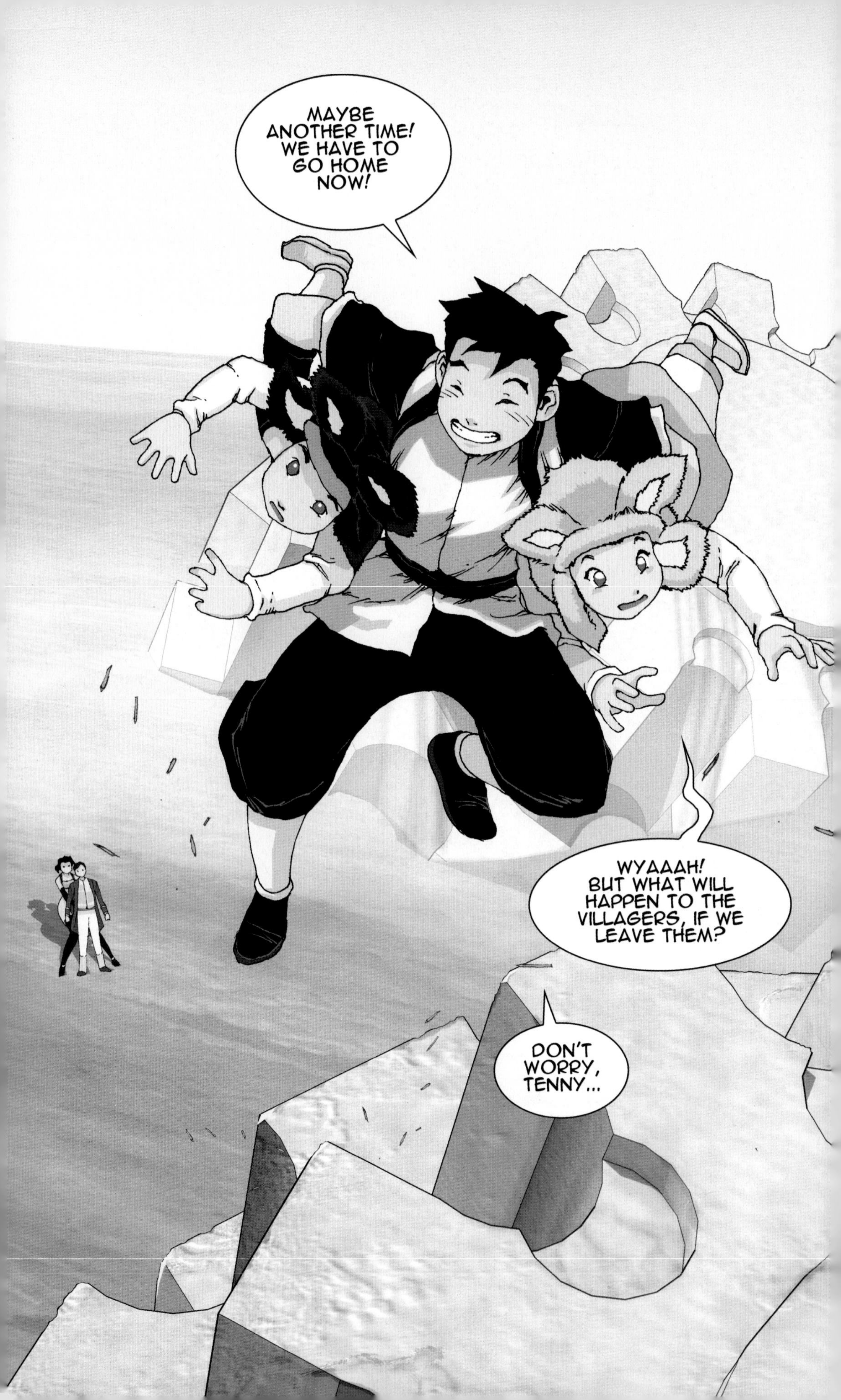
MAYBE ANOTHER TIME! WE HAVE TO GO HOME NOW!
WYAAAH! BUT WHAT WILL HAPPEN TO THE VILLAGERS, IF WE LEAVE THEM?
DON'T WORRY, TENNY...

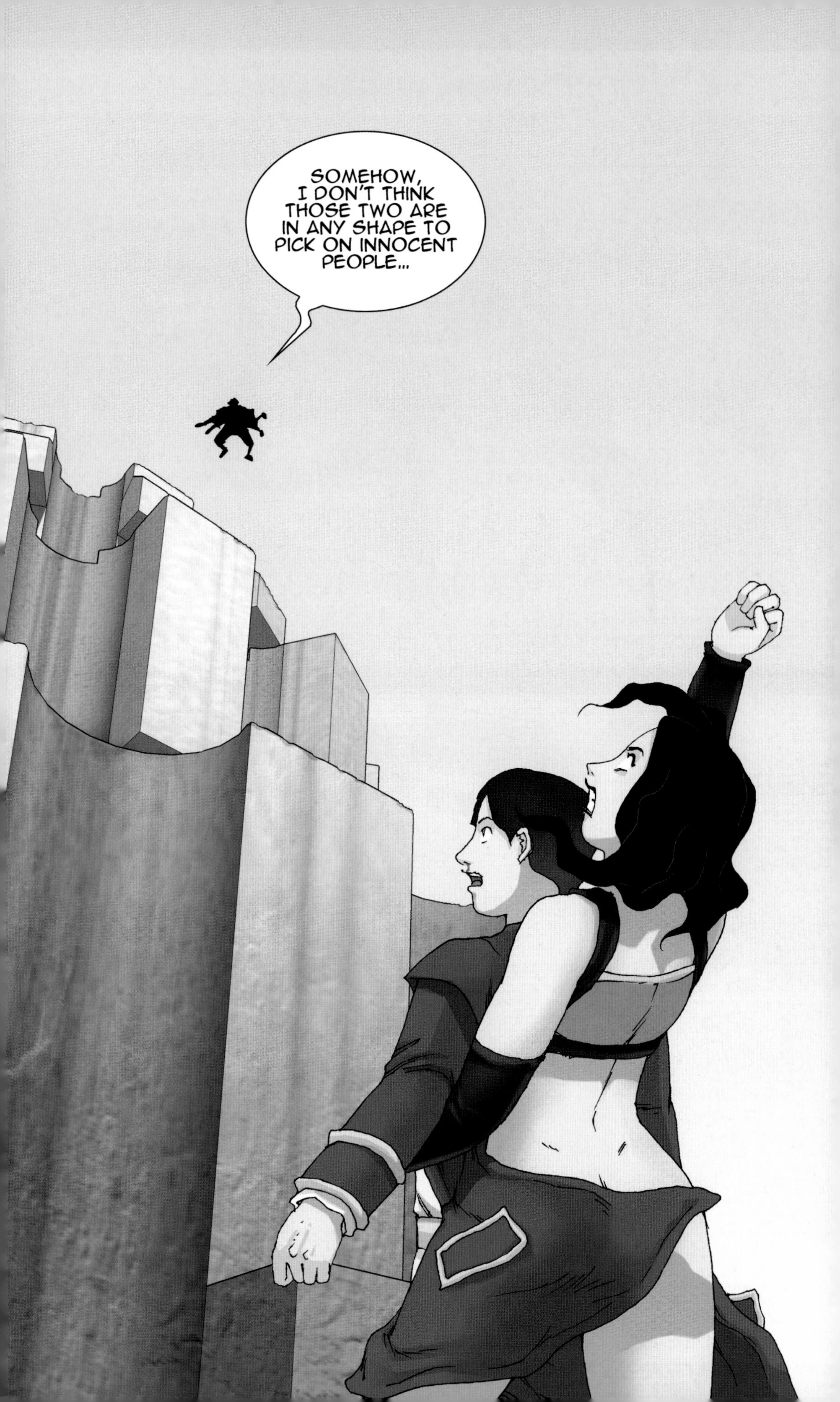
SOMEHOW, I DON'T THINK THOSE TWO ARE IN ANY SHAPE TO PICK ON INNOCENT PEOPLE...

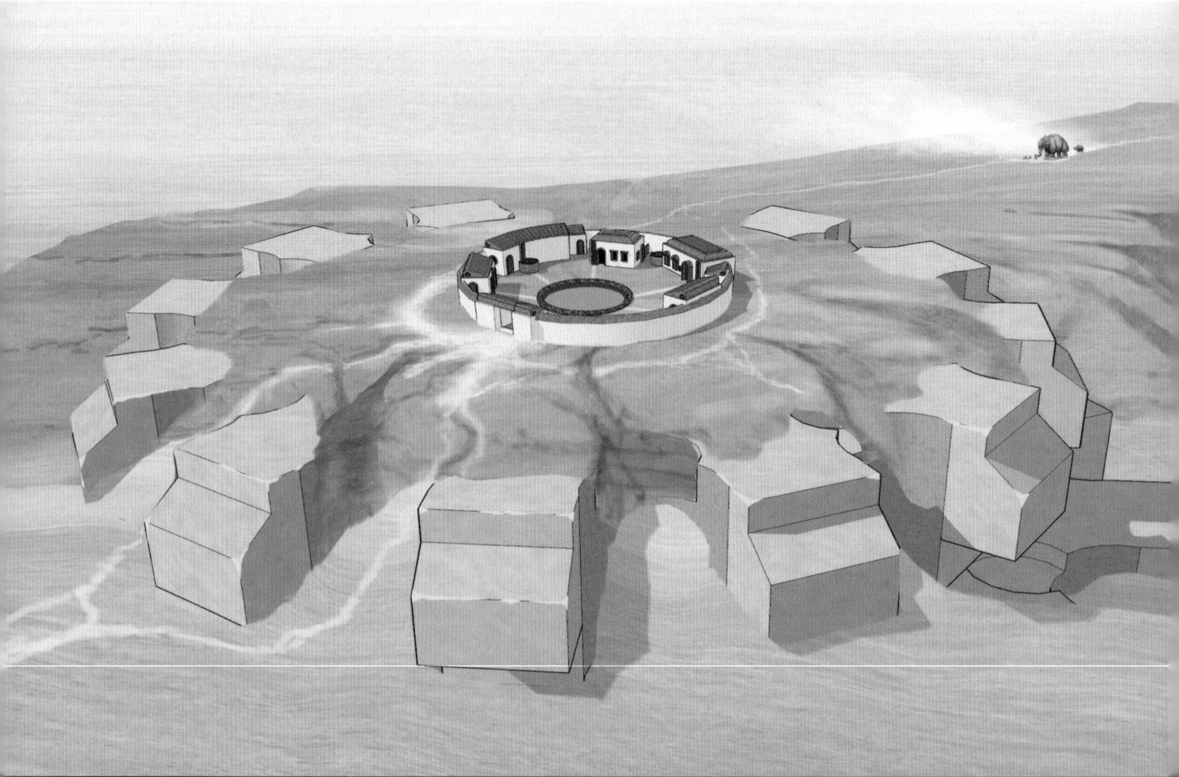

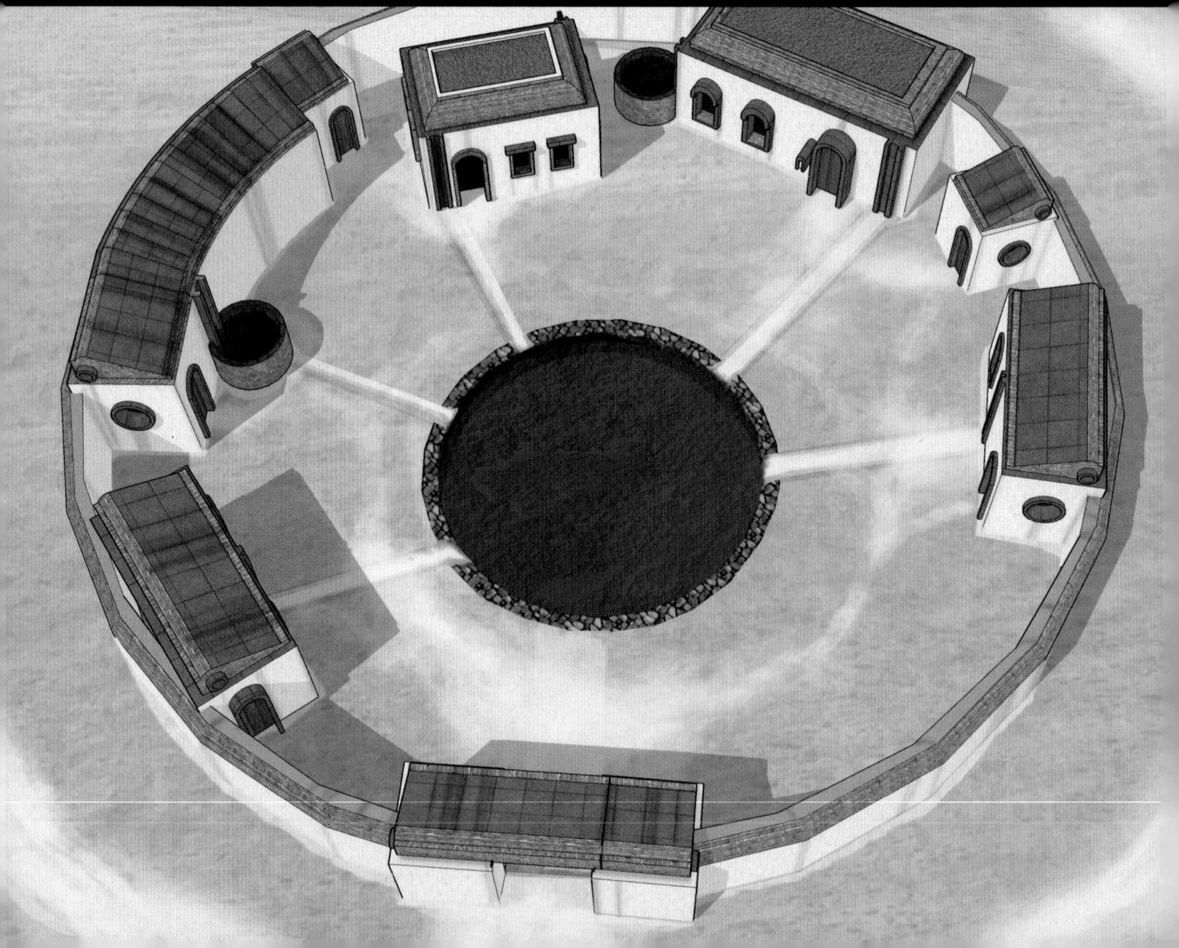

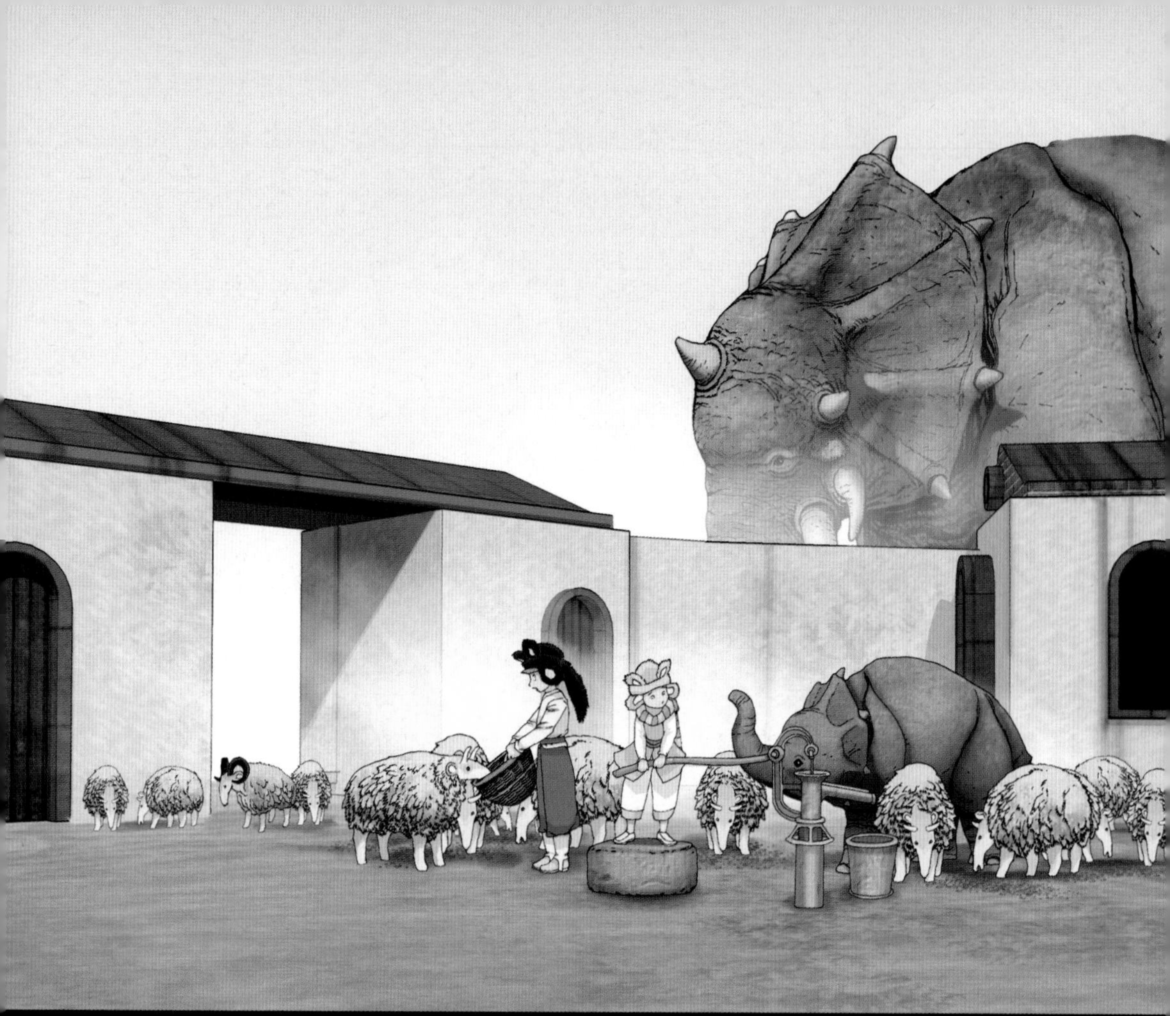

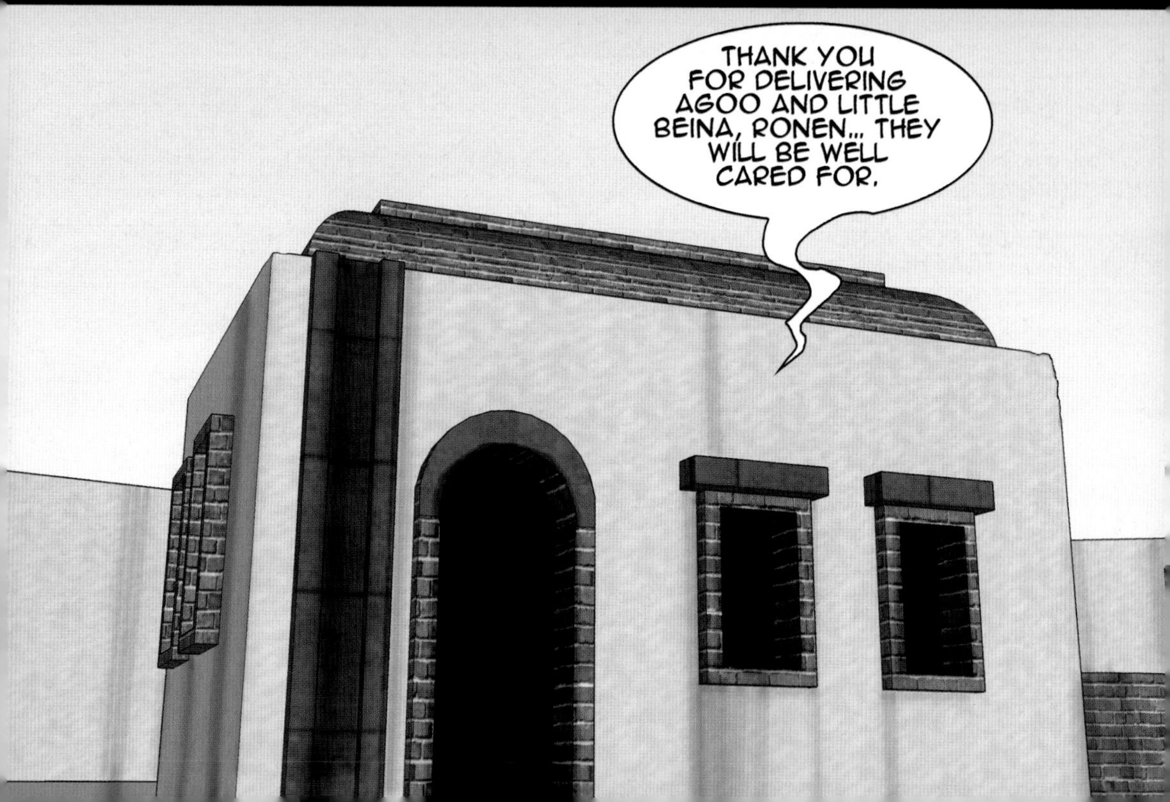
THANK YOU FOR DELIVERING AGOO AND LITTLE BEINA, RONEN... THEY WILL BE WELL CARED FOR.

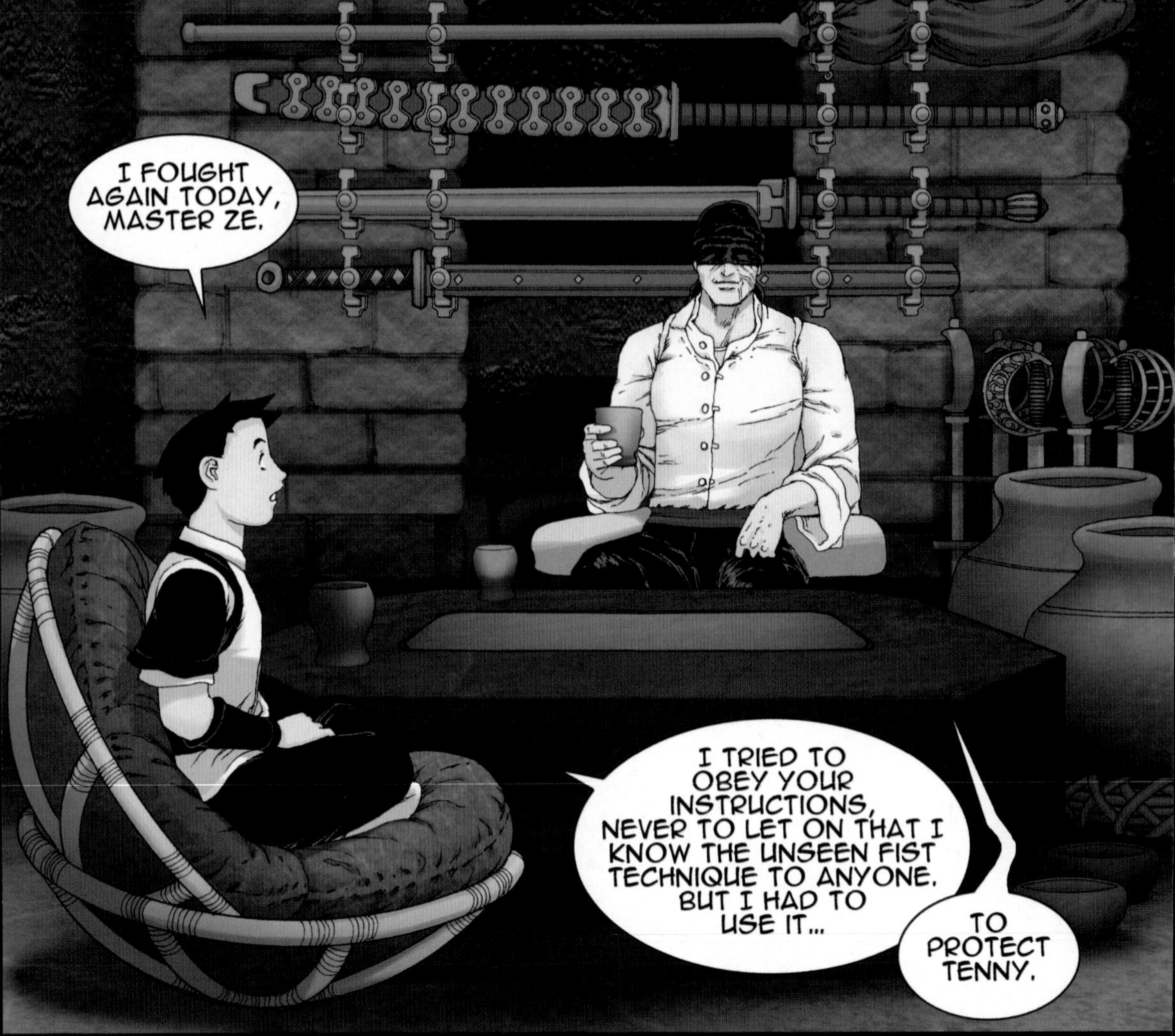
I FOUGHT AGAIN TODAY, MASTER ZE.
I TRIED TO OBEY YOUR INSTRUCTIONS, NEVER TO LET ON THAT I KNOW THE UNSEEN FIST TECHNIQUE TO ANYONE. BUT I HAD TO USE IT...
TO PROTECT TENNY.

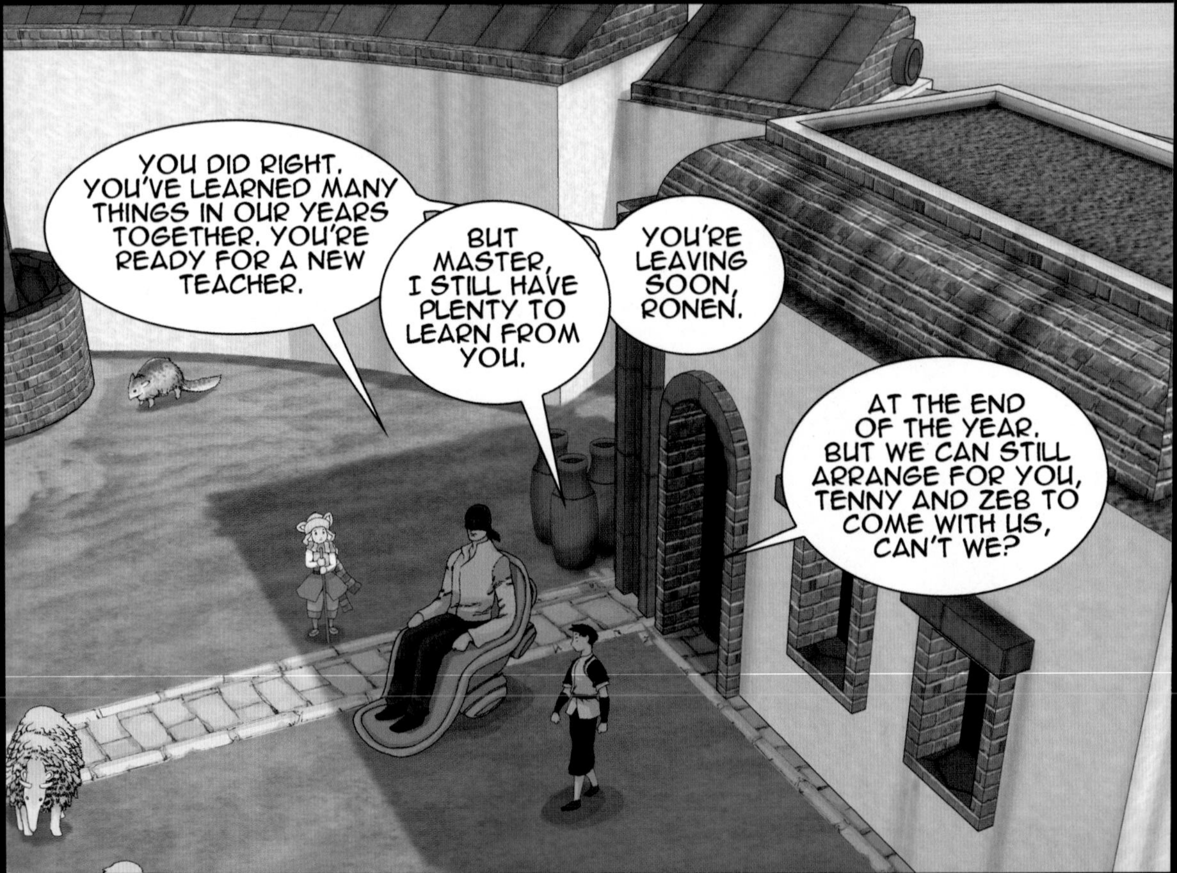
YOU DID RIGHT. YOU'VE LEARNED MANY THINGS IN OUR YEARS TOGETHER. YOU'RE READY FOR A NEW TEACHER.
BUT MASTER, I STILL HAVE PLENTY TO LEARN FROM YOU.
YOU'RE LEAVING SOON, RONEN.
AT THE END OF THE YEAR. BUT WE CAN STILL ARRANGE FOR YOU, TENNY AND ZEB TO COME WITH US, CAN'T WE?

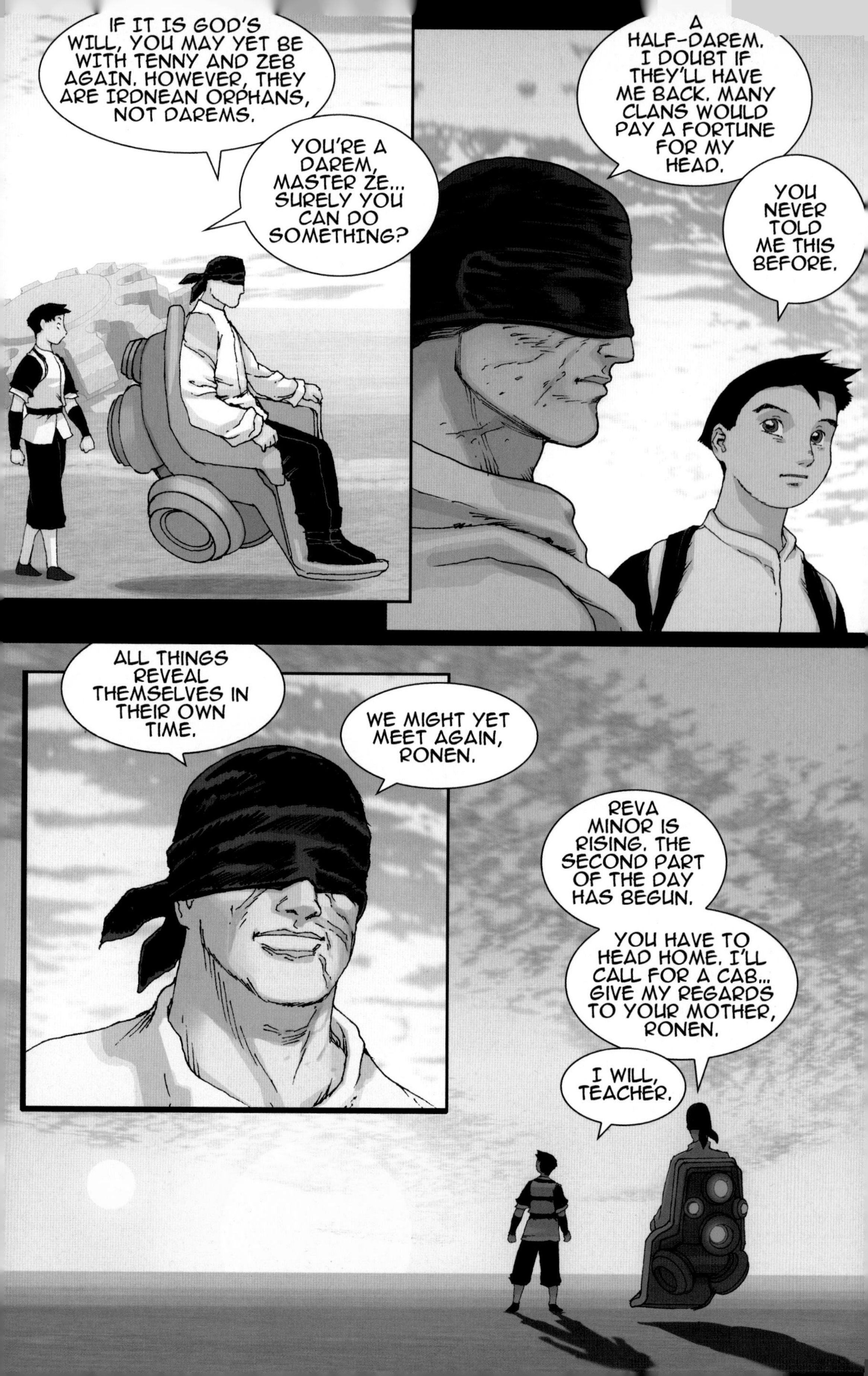
IF IT IS GOD'S WILL, YOU MAY YET BE WITH TENNY AND ZEB AGAIN. HOWEVER, THEY ARE IRONEAN ORPHANS, NOT DAREMS.
YOU'RE A DAREM, MASTER ZE... SURELY YOU CAN DO SOMETHING?
A HALF-DAREM. I DOUBT IF THEY'LL HAVE ME BACK. MANY CLANS WOULD PAY A FORTUNE FOR MY HEAD.
YOU NEVER TOLD ME THIS BEFORE.
ALL THINGS REVEAL THEMSELVES IN THEIR OWN TIME.
WE MIGHT YET MEET AGAIN, RONEN.
REVA MINOR IS RISING. THE SECOND PART OF THE DAY HAS BEGUN.
YOU HAVE TO HEAD HOME. I'LL CALL FOR A CAB... GIVE MY REGARDS TO YOUR MOTHER, RONEN.
I WILL, TEACHER.

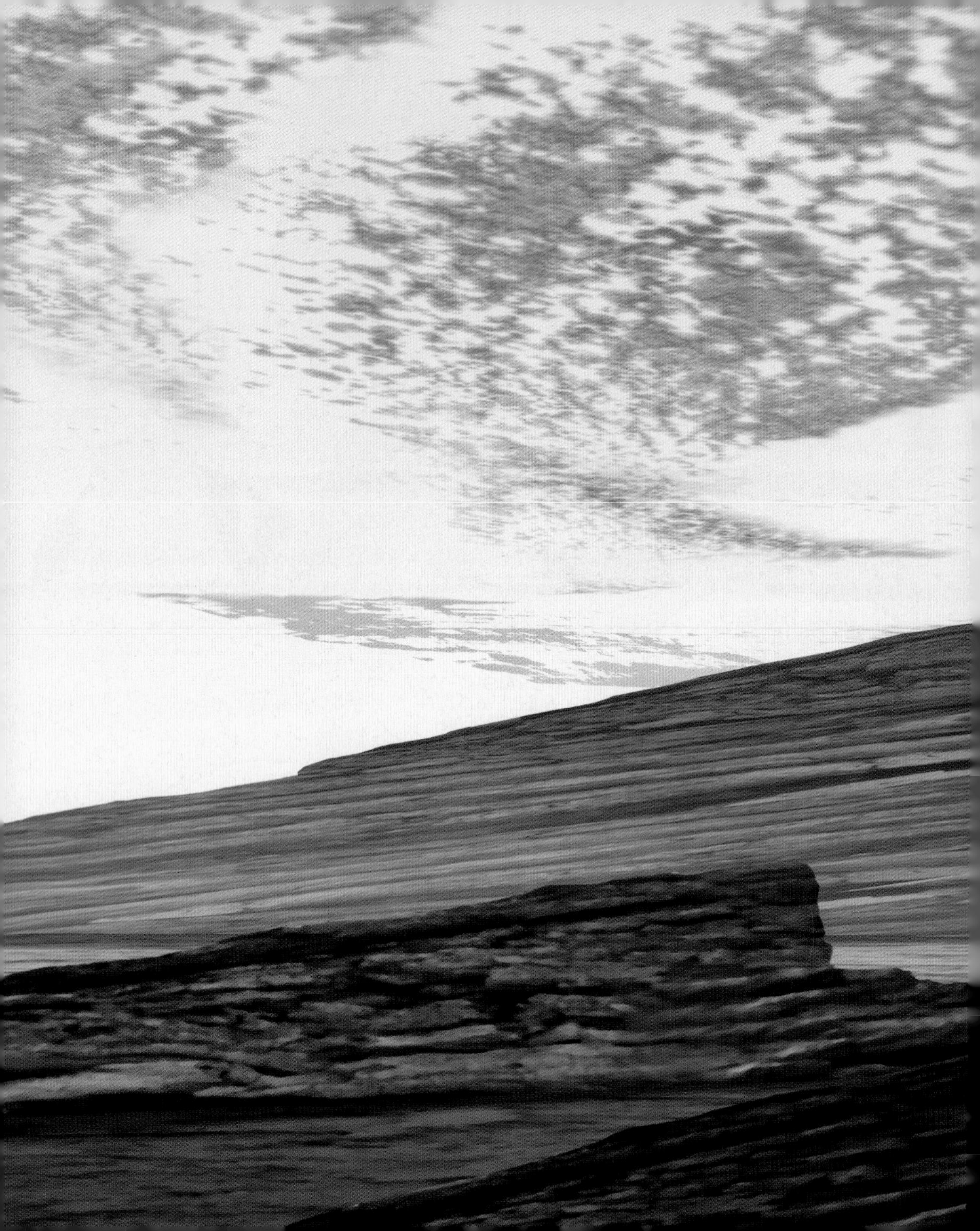

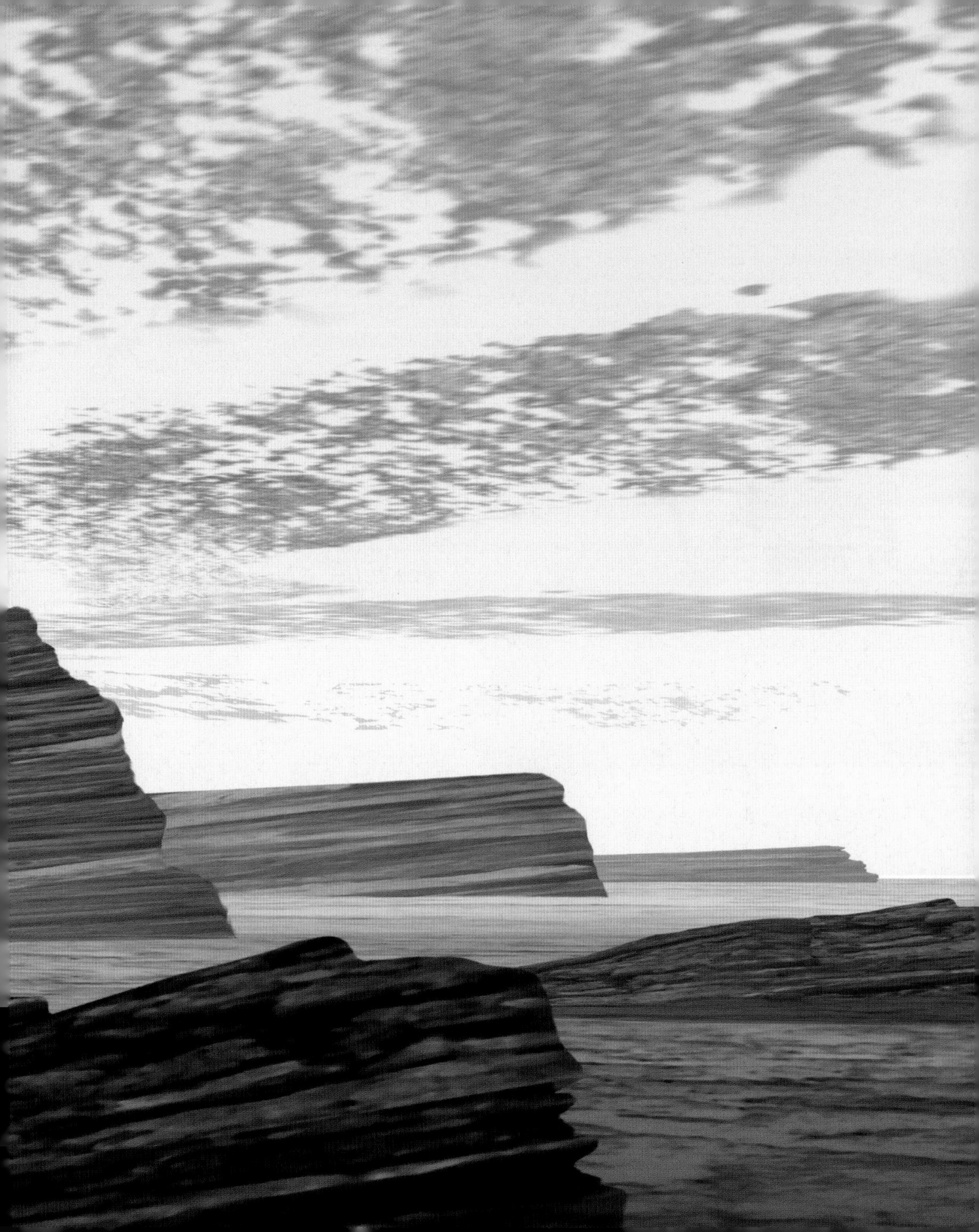

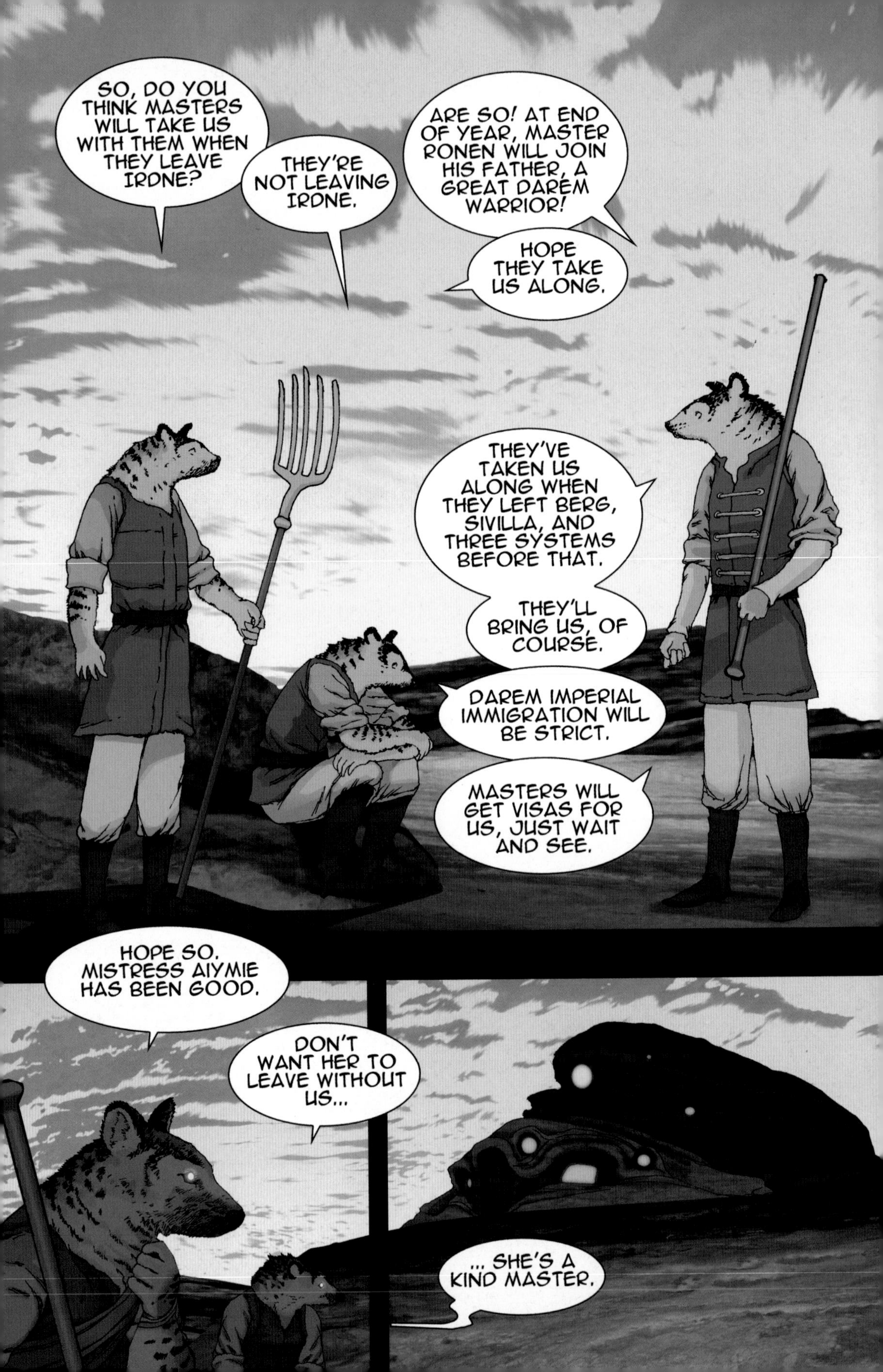
SO, DO YOU THINK MASTERS WILL TAKE US WITH THEM WHEN THEY LEAVE IRDNE?
THEY'RE NOT LEAVING IRDNE.
ARE SO! AT END OF YEAR, MASTER RONEN WILL JOIN HIS FATHER, A GREAT DAREM WARRIOR!
HOPE THEY TAKE US ALONG.
THEY'VE TAKEN US ALONG WHEN THEY LEFT BERG, SIVILLA, AND THREE SYSTEMS BEFORE THAT.
THEY'LL BRING US, OF COURSE.
DAREM IMPERIAL IMMIGRATION WILL BE STRICT.
MASTERS WILL GET VISAS FOR US, JUST WAIT AND SEE.
HOPE SO. MISTRESS AIYMIE HAS BEEN GOOD.
DON'T WANT HER TO LEAVE WITHOUT US...
... SHE'S A KIND MASTER.

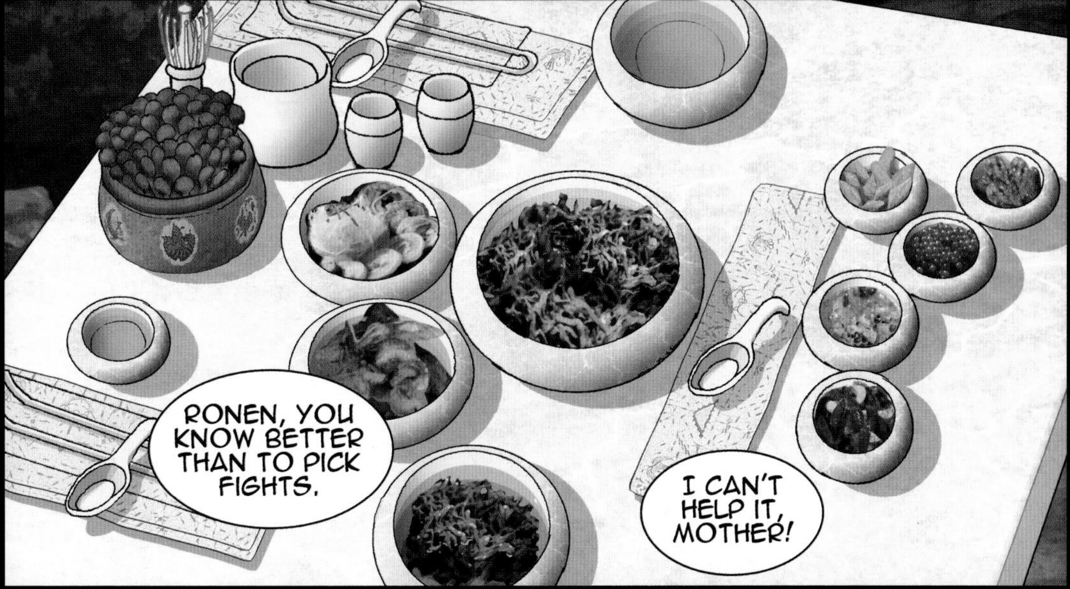
RONEN, YOU KNOW BETTER THAN TO PICK FIGHTS.
I CAN'T HELP IT, MOTHER!

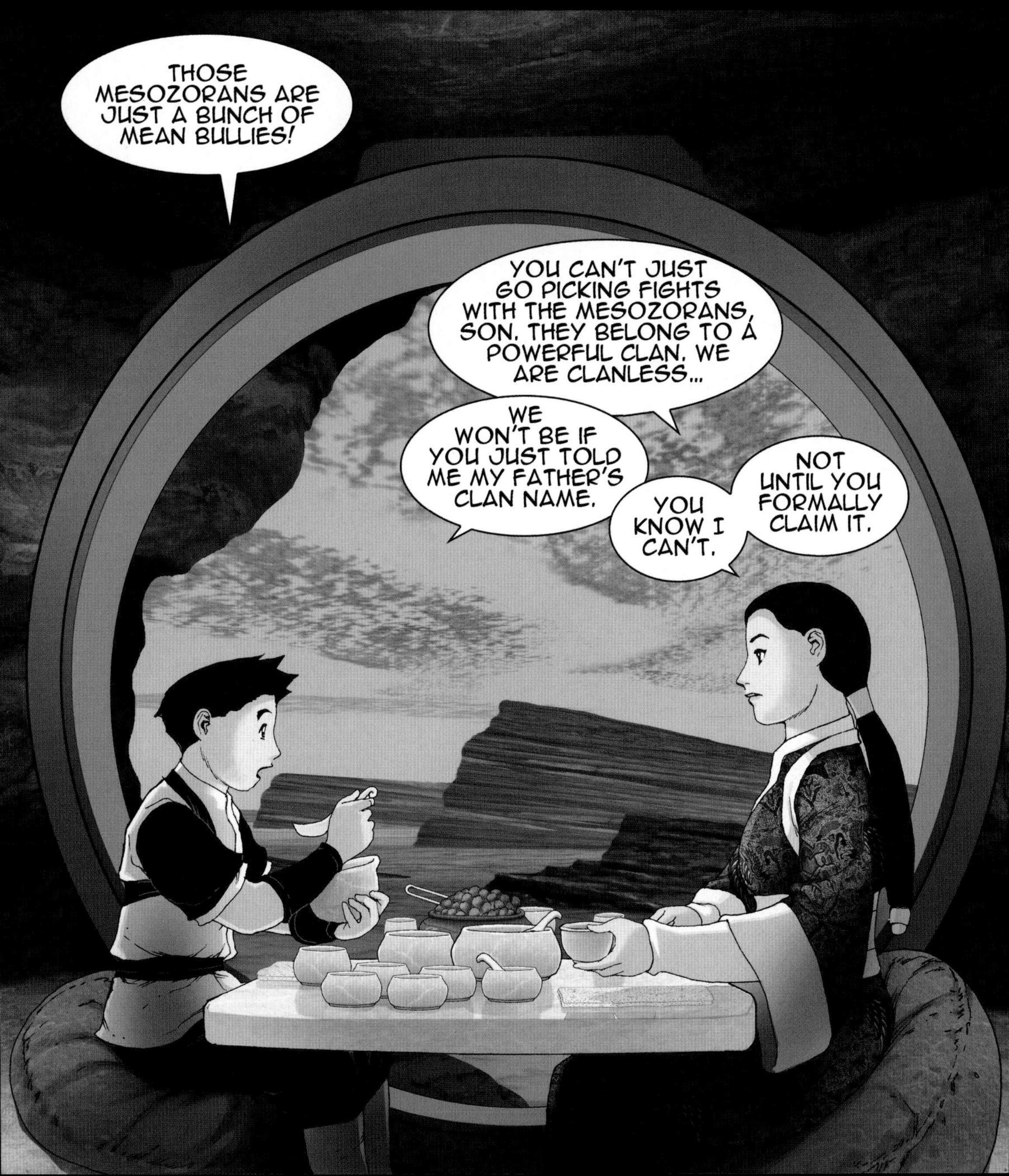
THOSE MESOZORANS ARE JUST A BUNCH OF MEAN BULLIES!
YOU CAN'T JUST GO PICKING FIGHTS WITH THE MESOZORANS, SON. THEY BELONG TO A POWERFUL CLAN. WE ARE CLANLESS...
WE WON'T BE IF YOU JUST TOLD ME MY FATHER'S CLAN NAME.
NOT UNTIL YOU FORMALLY CLAIM IT.
YOU KNOW I CAN'T.

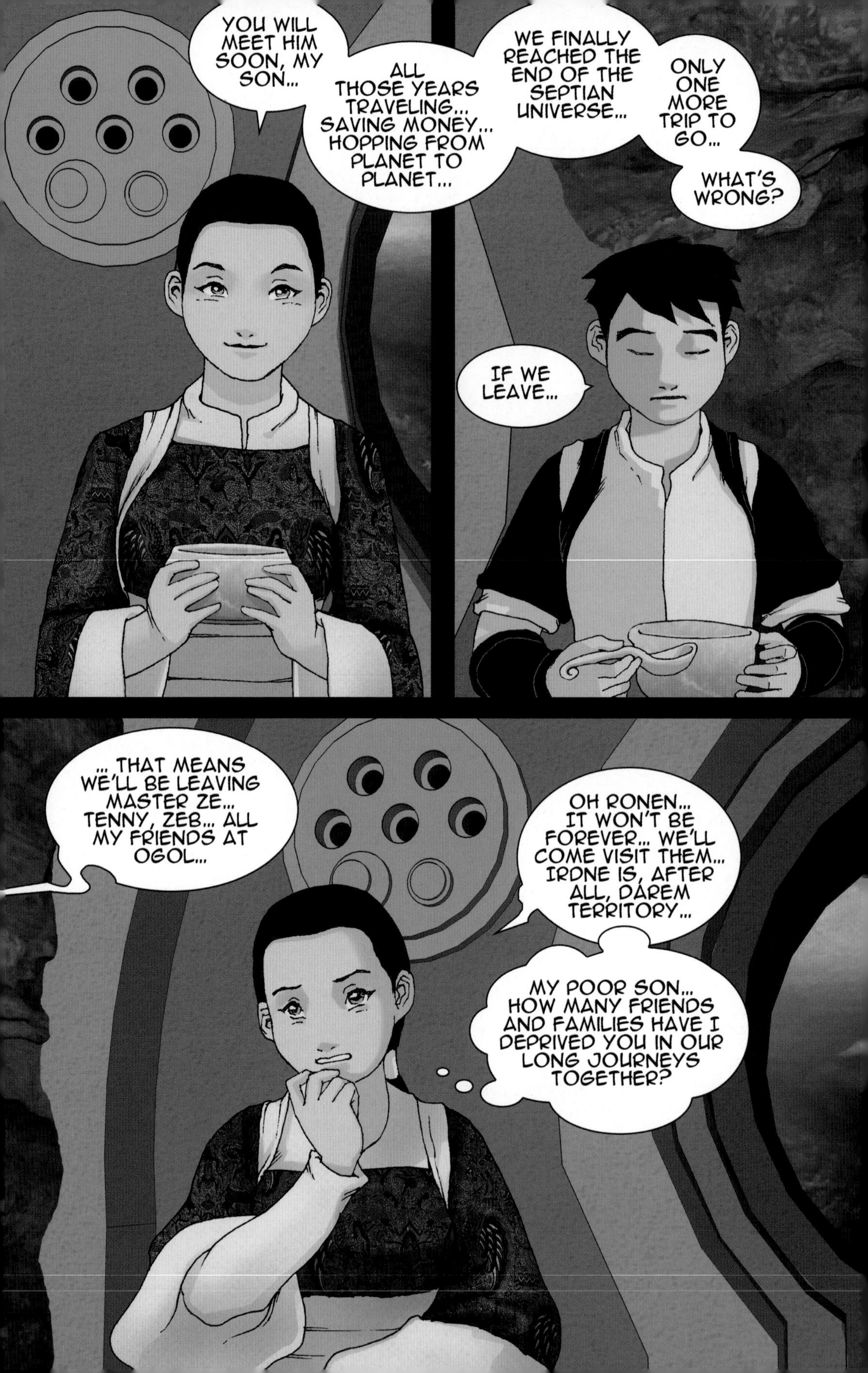
YOU WILL MEET HIM SOON, MY SON...
ALL THOSE YEARS TRAVELING... SAVING MONEY... HOPPING FROM PLANET TO PLANET...
WE FINALLY REACHED THE END OF THE SEPTIAN UNIVERSE...
ONLY ONE MORE TRIP TO GO...
WHAT'S WRONG?
IF WE LEAVE...
... THAT MEANS WE'LL BE LEAVING MASTER ZE... TENNY, ZEB... ALL MY FRIENDS AT OGOL...
OH RONEN... IT WON'T BE FOREVER... WE'LL COME VISIT THEM... IRONE IS, AFTER ALL, DAREM TERRITORY...
MY POOR SON... HOW MANY FRIENDS AND FAMILIES HAVE I DEPRIVED YOU IN OUR LONG JOURNEYS TOGETHER?

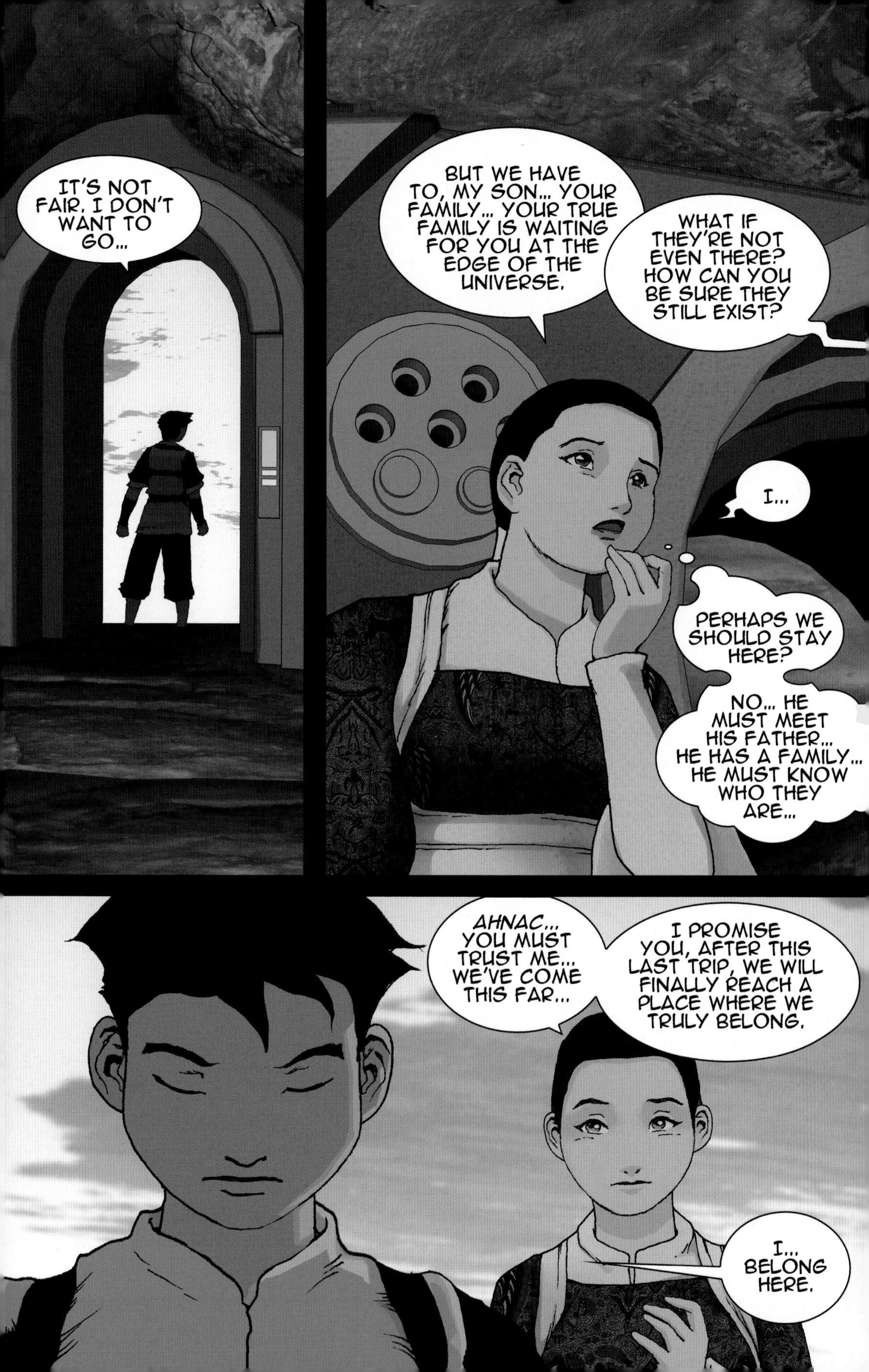
IT'S NOT FAIR. I DON'T WANT TO GO...
BUT WE HAVE TO, MY SON... YOUR FAMILY... YOUR TRUE FAMILY IS WAITING FOR YOU AT THE EDGE OF THE UNIVERSE.
WHAT IF THEY'RE NOT EVEN THERE? HOW CAN YOU BE SURE THEY STILL EXIST?
I...
PERHAPS WE SHOULD STAY HERE?
NO... HE MUST MEET HIS FATHER... HE HAS A FAMILY... HE MUST KNOW WHO THEY ARE...
AHNAC... YOU MUST TRUST ME... WE'VE COME THIS FAR...
I PROMISE YOU, AFTER THIS LAST TRIP, WE WILL FINALLY REACH A PLACE WHERE WE TRULY BELONG.
I... BELONG HERE.

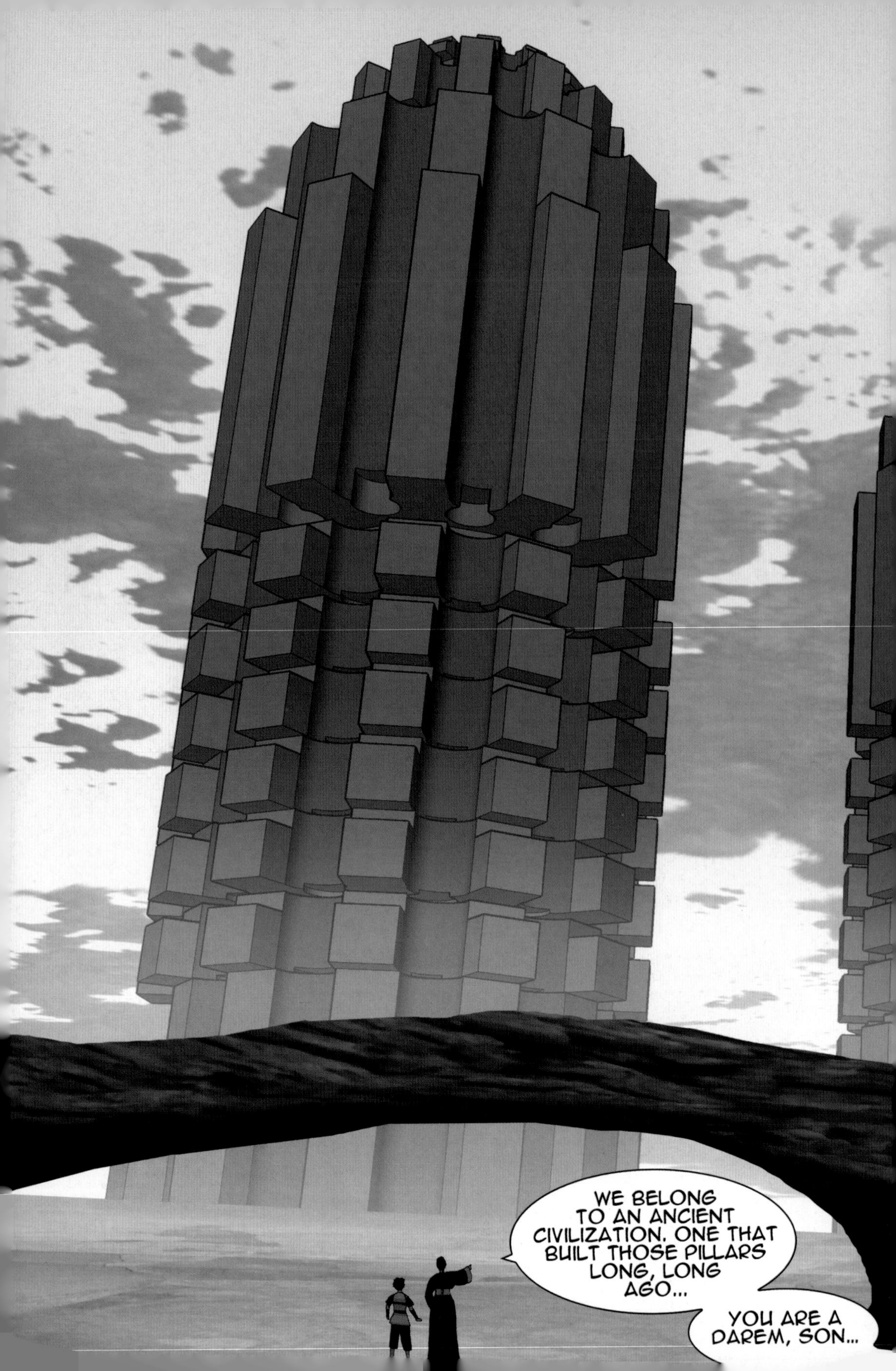
WE BELONG TO AN ANCIENT CIVILIZATION. ONE THAT BUILT THOSE PILLARS LONG, LONG AGO...
YOU ARE A DAREM, SON...

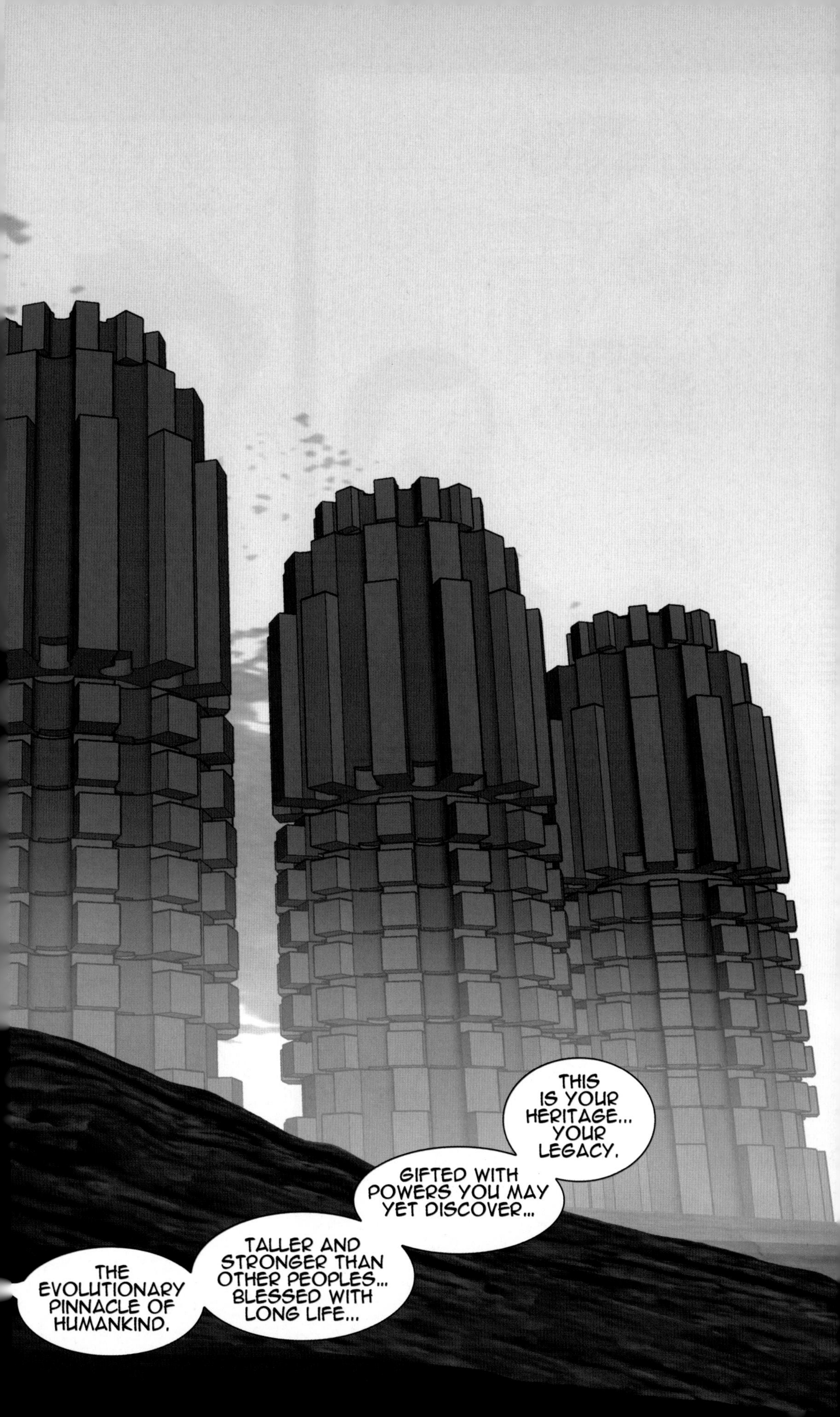
THE EVOLUTIONARY PINNACLE OF HUMANKIND.
TALLER AND STRONGER THAN OTHER PEOPLES... BLESSED WITH LONG LIFE...
GIFTED WITH POWERS YOU MAY YET DISCOVER...
THIS IS YOUR HERITAGE... YOUR LEGACY.

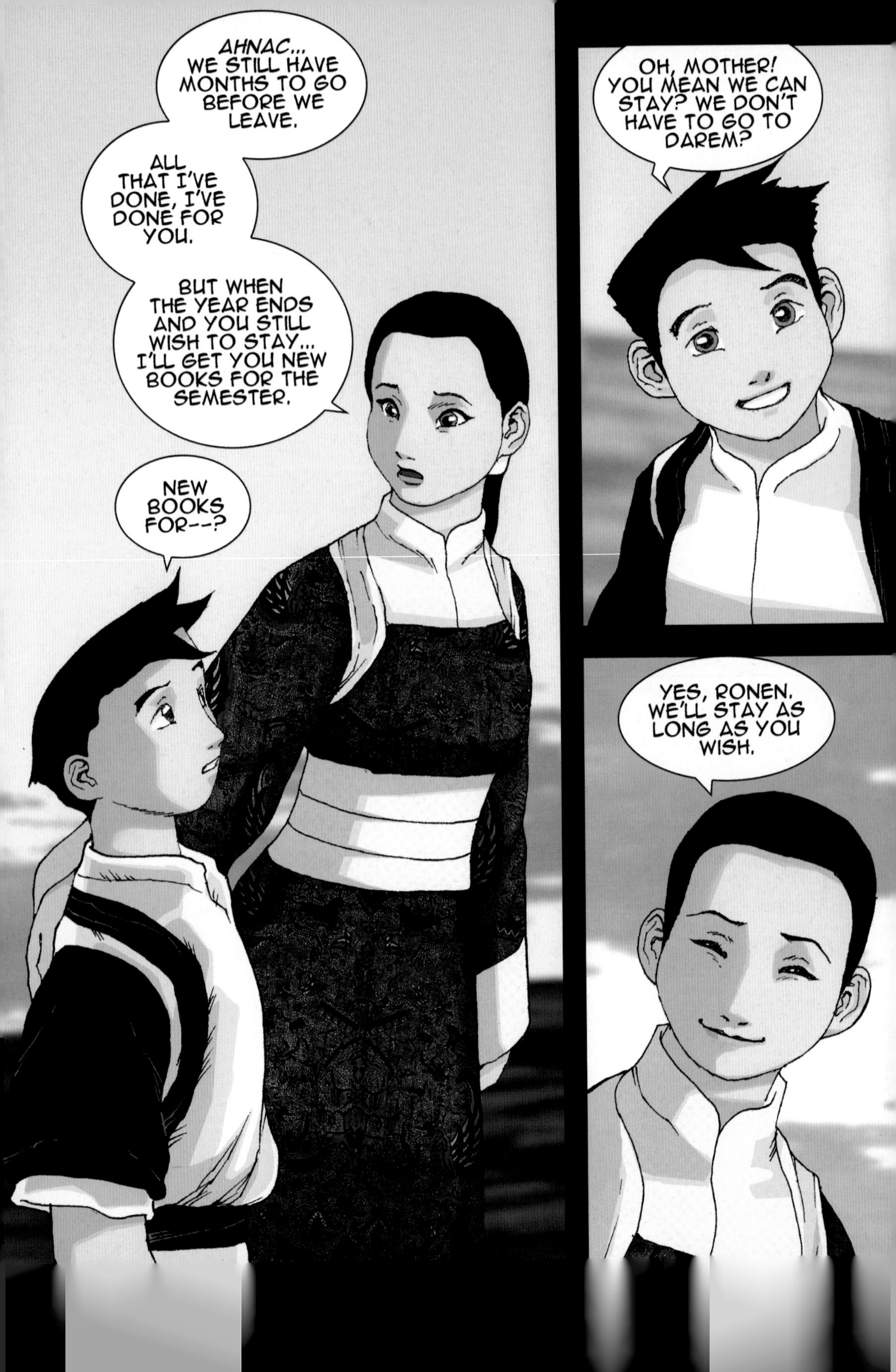
AHNAC... WE STILL HAVE MONTHS TO GO BEFORE WE LEAVE.
ALL THAT I'VE DONE, I'VE DONE FOR YOU.
BUT WHEN THE YEAR ENDS AND YOU STILL WISH TO STAY... I'LL GET YOU NEW BOOKS FOR THE SEMESTER.
NEW BOOKS FOR--?
OH, MOTHER! YOU MEAN WE CAN STAY? WE DON'T HAVE TO GO TO DAREM?
YES, RONEN. WE'LL STAY AS LONG AS YOU WISH.

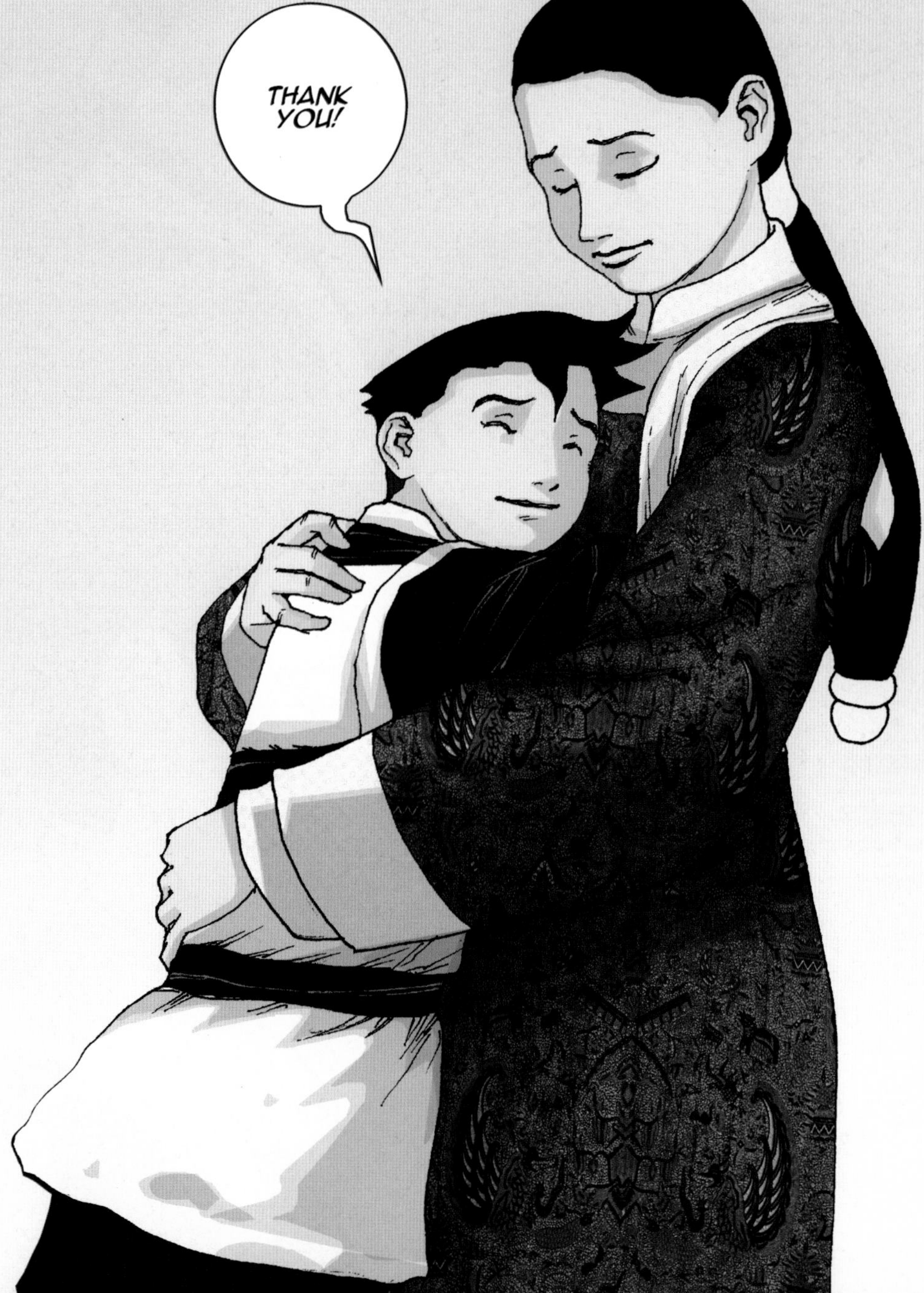
THANK YOU!

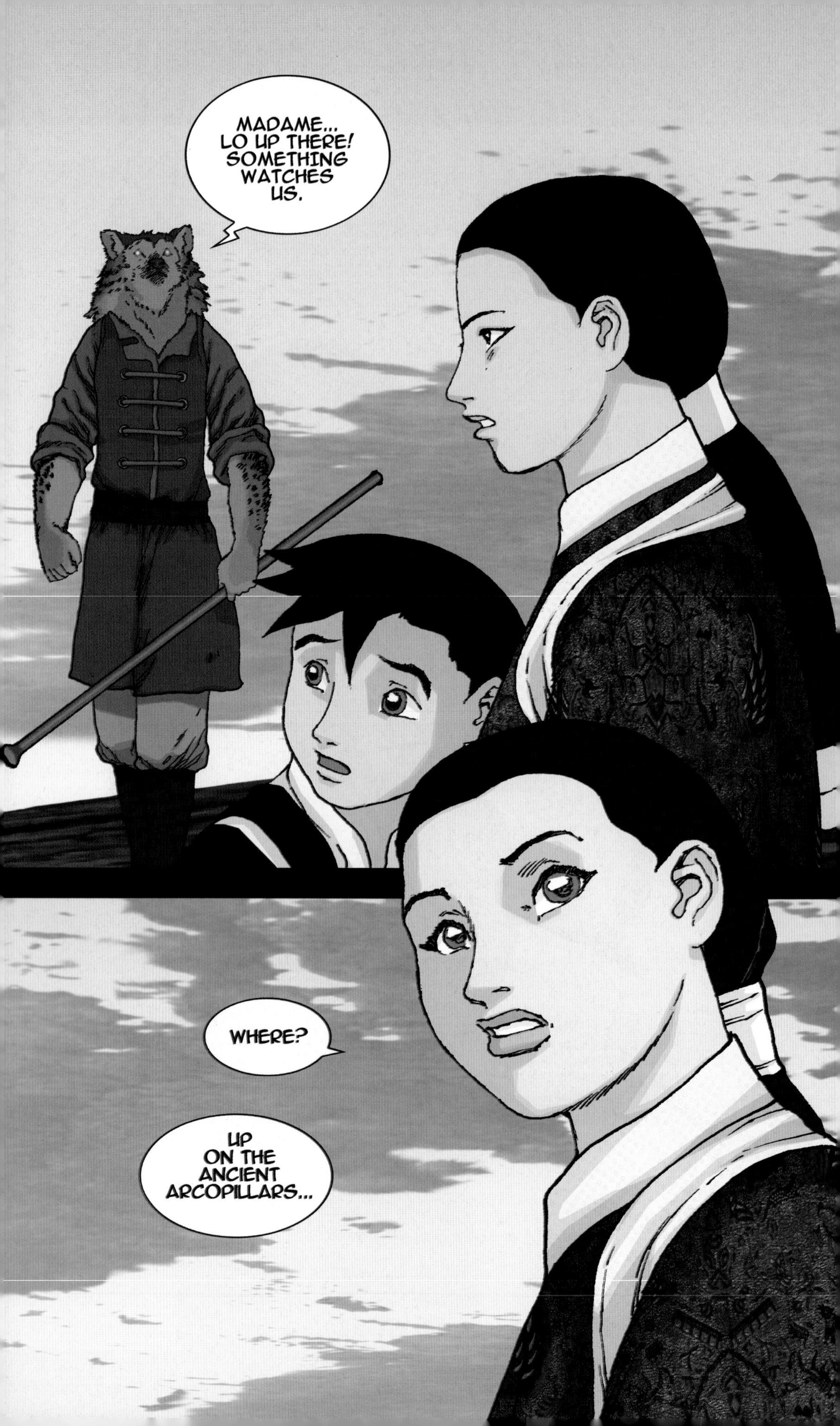
MADAME... LO UP THERE! SOMETHING WATCHES US.
WHERE?
UP ON THE ANCIENT ARCOPILLARS...

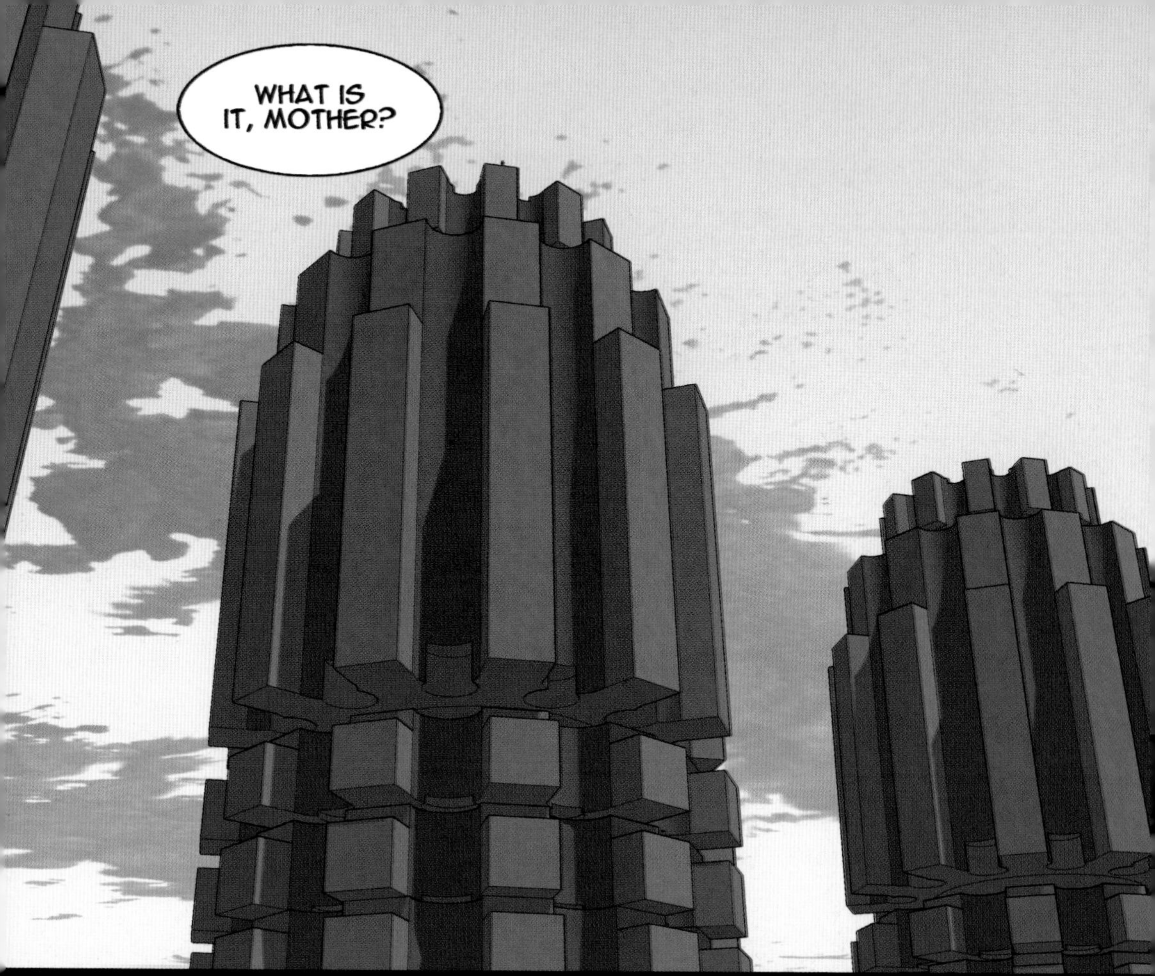
WHAT IS
IT, MOTHER?

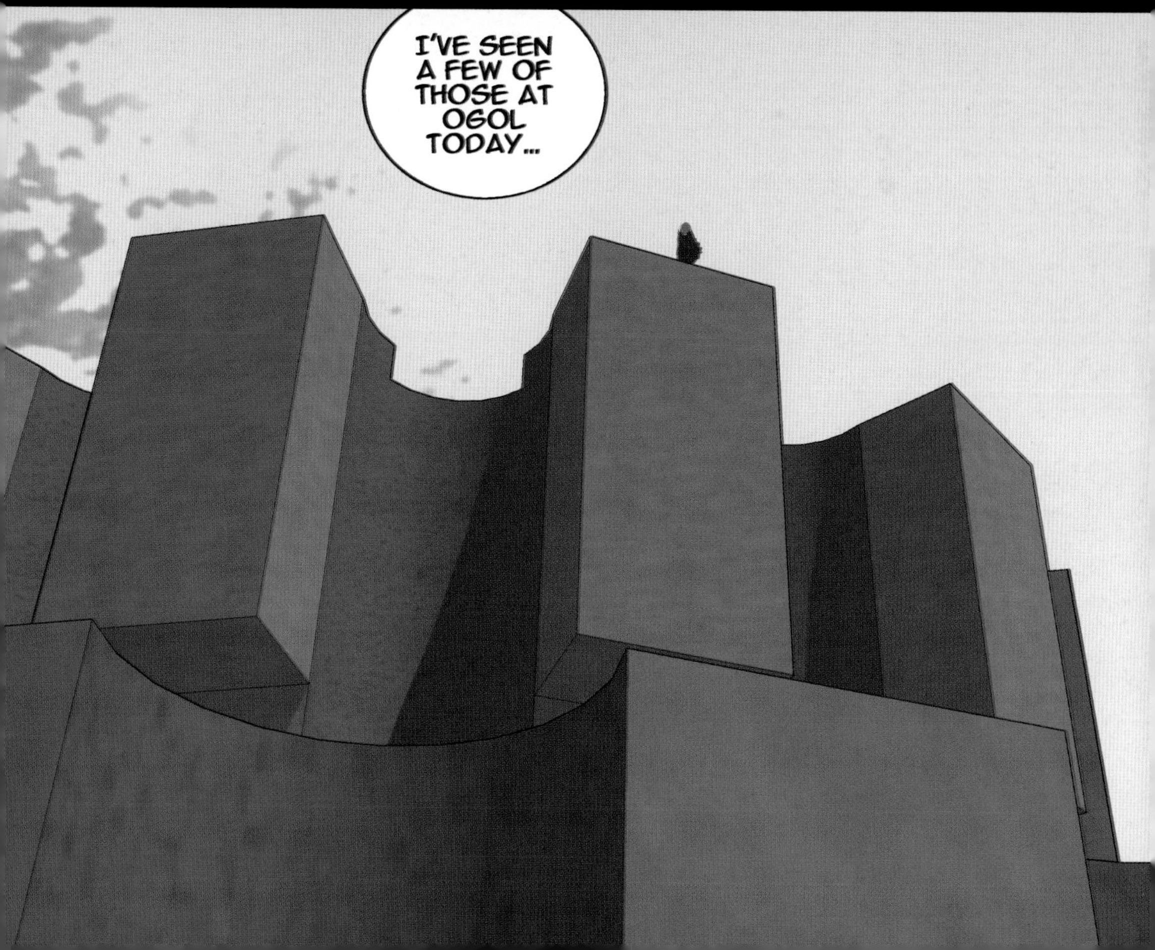
I'VE SEEN
A FEW OF
THOSE AT
OGOL
TODAY...

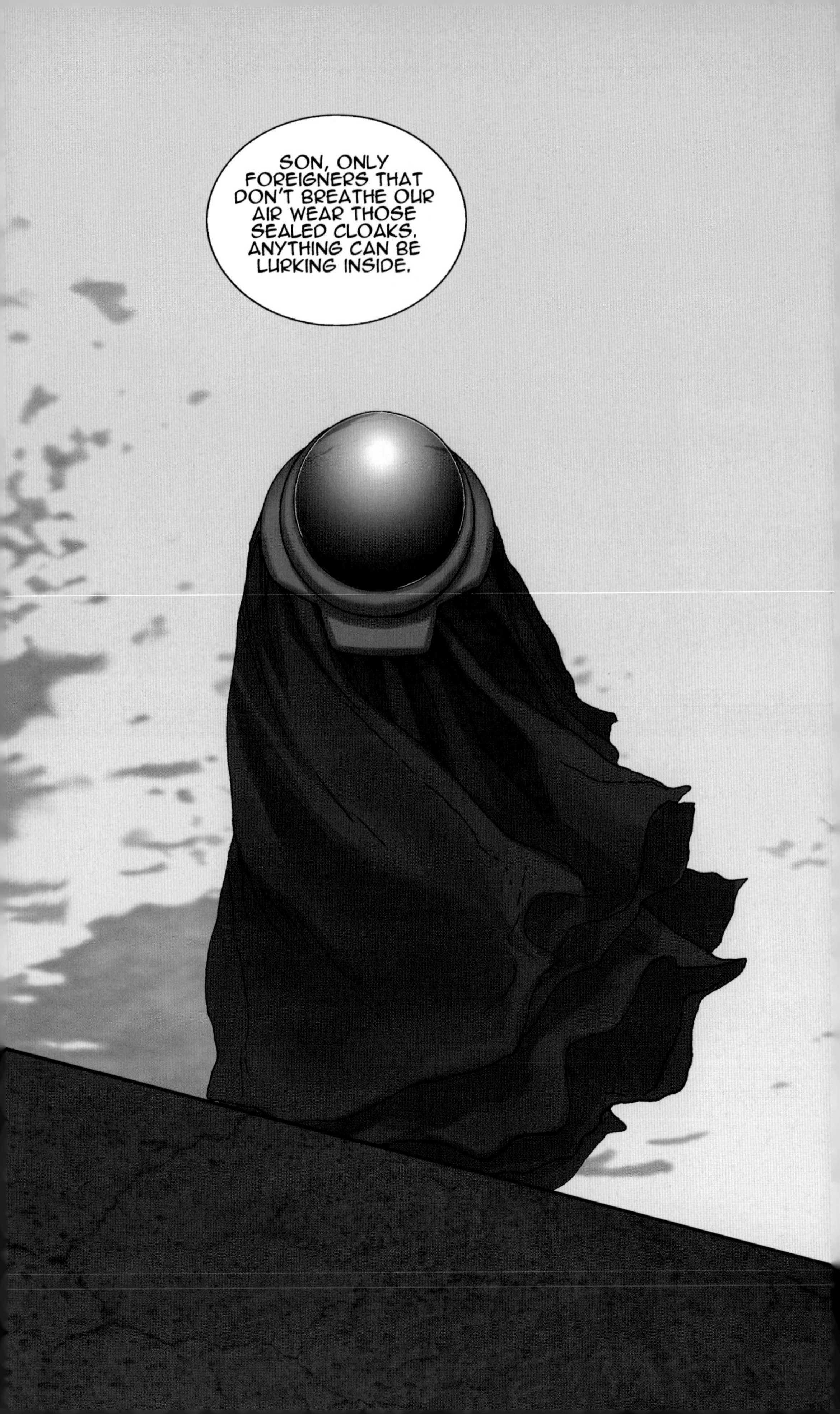
SON, ONLY FOREIGNERS THAT DON'T BREATHE OUR AIR WEAR THOSE SEALED CLOAKS. ANYTHING CAN BE LURKING INSIDE.

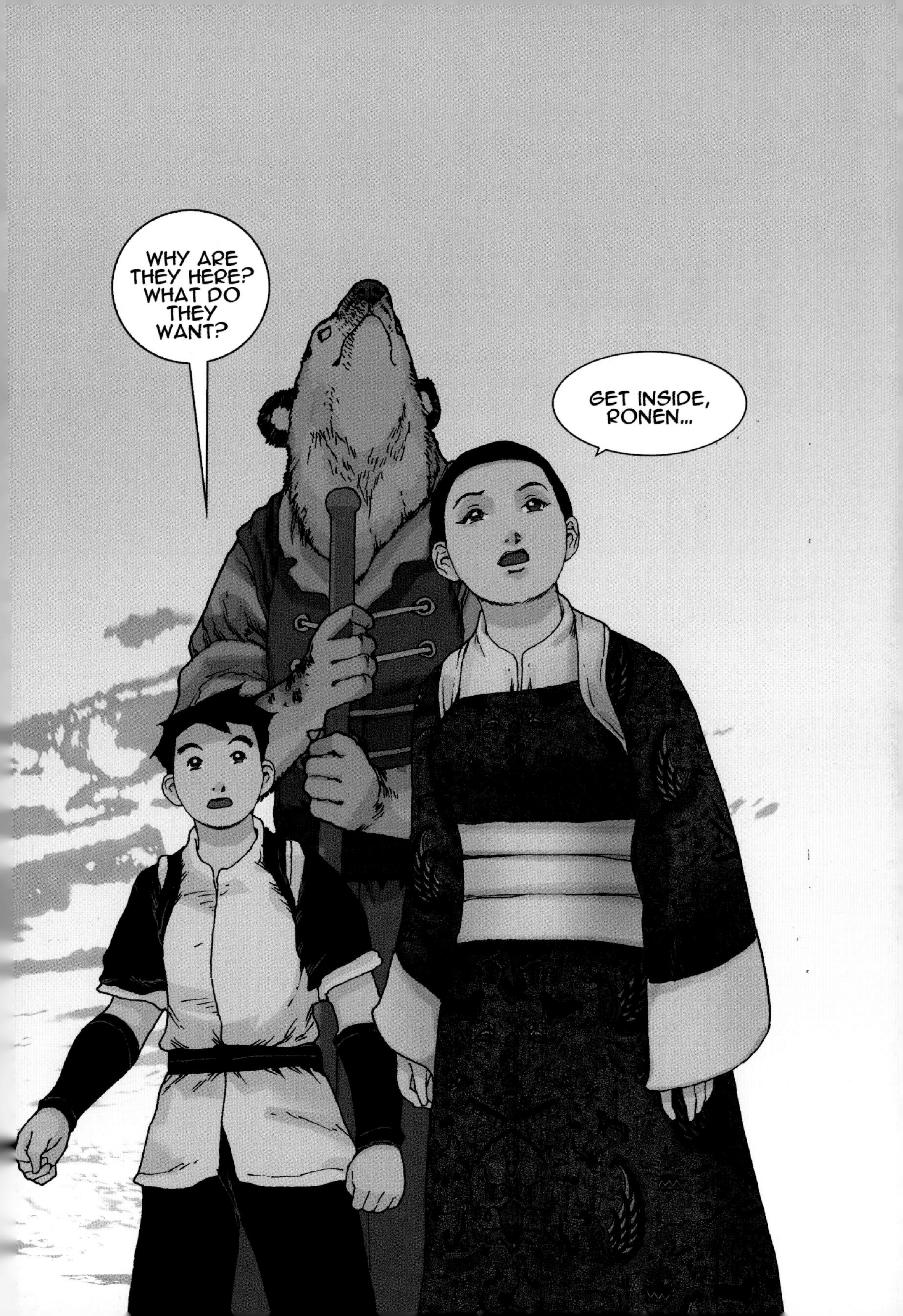
WHY ARE THEY HERE? WHAT DO THEY WANT?
GET INSIDE, RONEN...

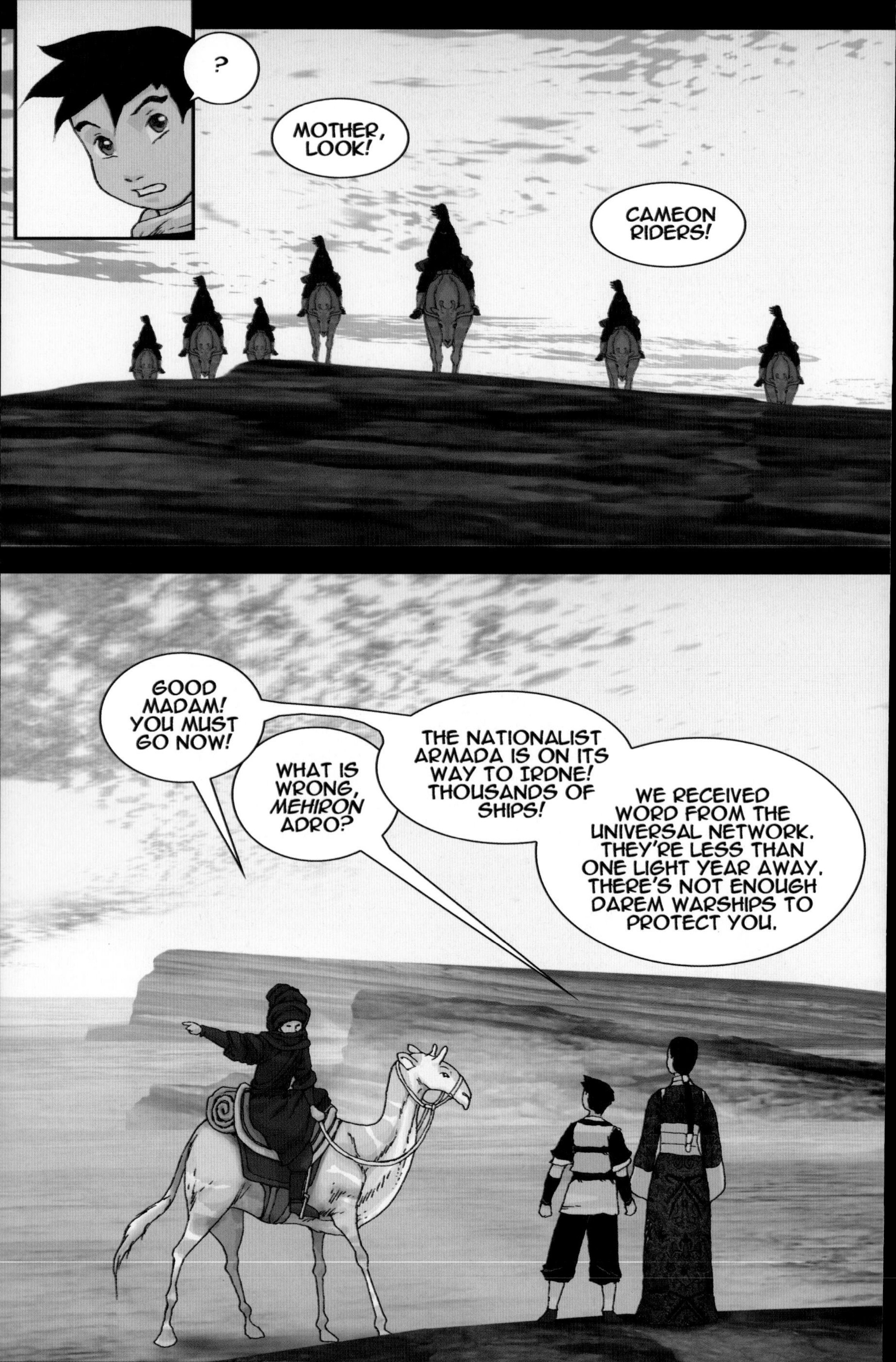
?
MOTHER, LOOK!
CAMEON RIDERS!
GOOD MADAM! YOU MUST GO NOW!
WHAT IS WRONG, MEHIRON ADRO?
THE NATIONALIST ARMADA IS ON ITS WAY TO IRDNE! THOUSANDS OF SHIPS!
WE RECEIVED WORD FROM THE UNIVERSAL NETWORK. THEY'RE LESS THAN ONE LIGHT YEAR AWAY. THERE'S NOT ENOUGH DAREM WARSHIPS TO PROTECT YOU.

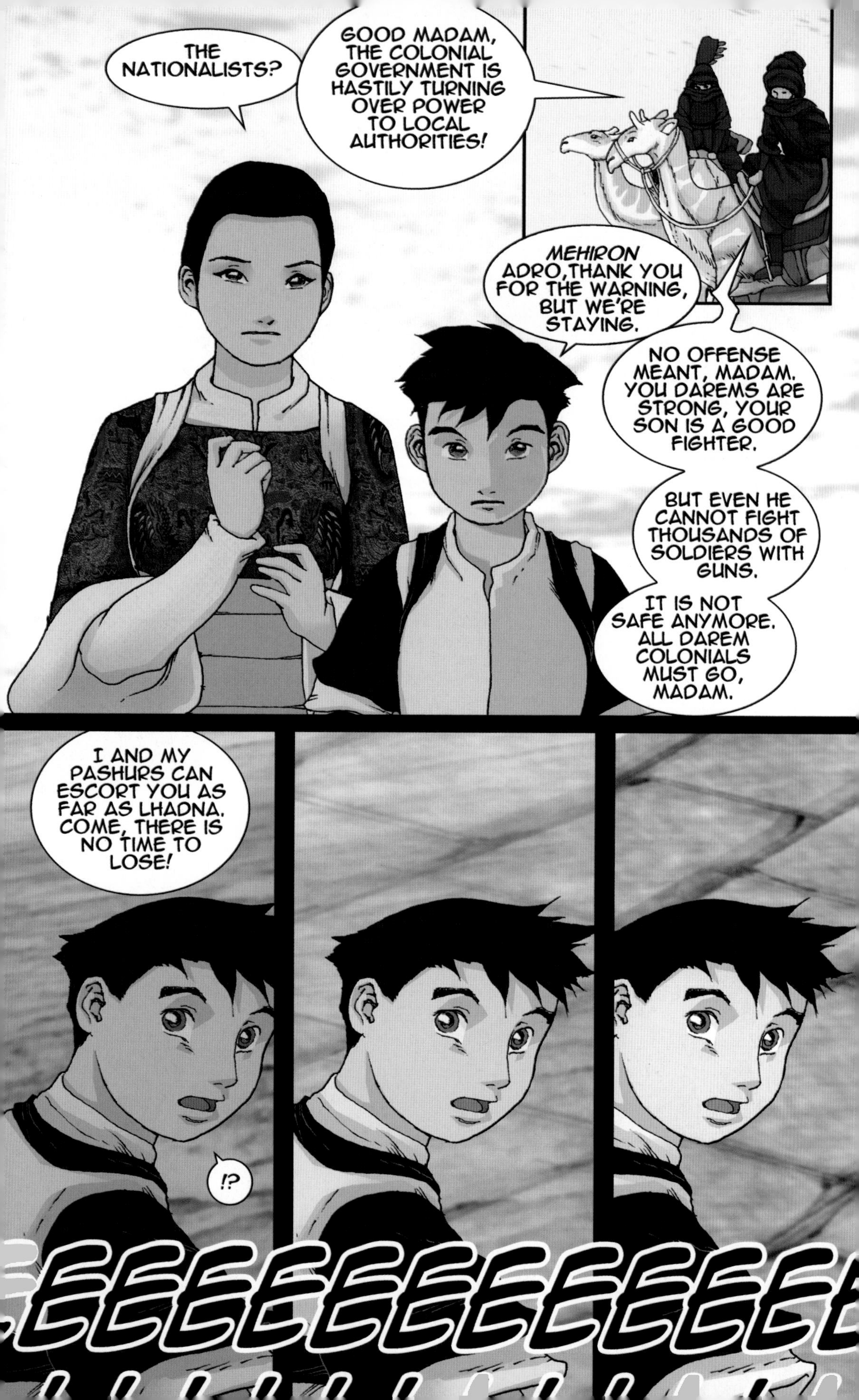

THE NATIONALISTS?
GOOD MADAM, THE COLONIAL GOVERNMENT IS HASTILY TURNING OVER POWER TO LOCAL AUTHORITIES!
MEHIRON ADRO,THANK YOU FOR THE WARNING, BUT WE'RE STAYING.
NO OFFENSE MEANT, MADAM. YOU DAREMS ARE STRONG, YOUR SON IS A GOOD FIGHTER.
BUT EVEN HE CANNOT FIGHT THOUSANDS OF SOLDIERS WITH GUNS.
IT IS NOT SAFE ANYMORE. ALL DAREM COLONIALS MUST GO, MADAM.
I AND MY PASHURS CAN ESCORT YOU AS FAR AS LHADNA. COME, THERE IS NO TIME TO LOSE!
!?
EEEEEEEEEEEEEE

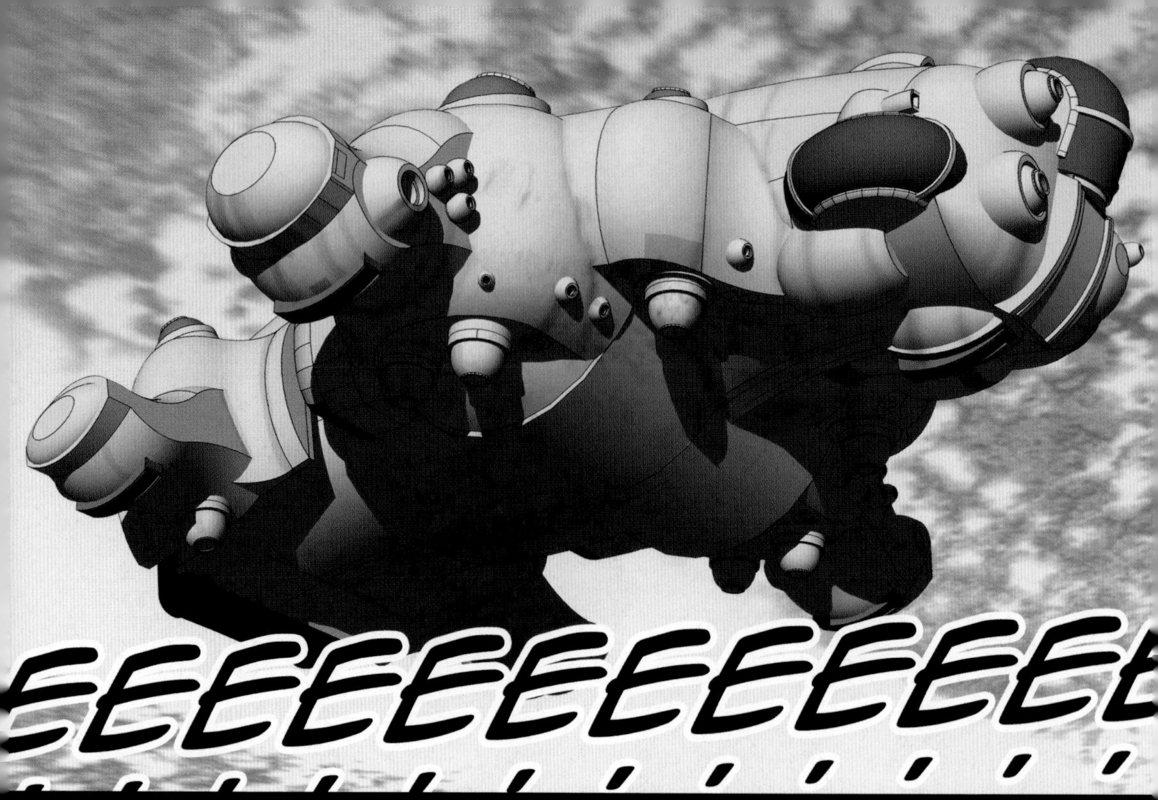
EEEEEEEEEEEEEE

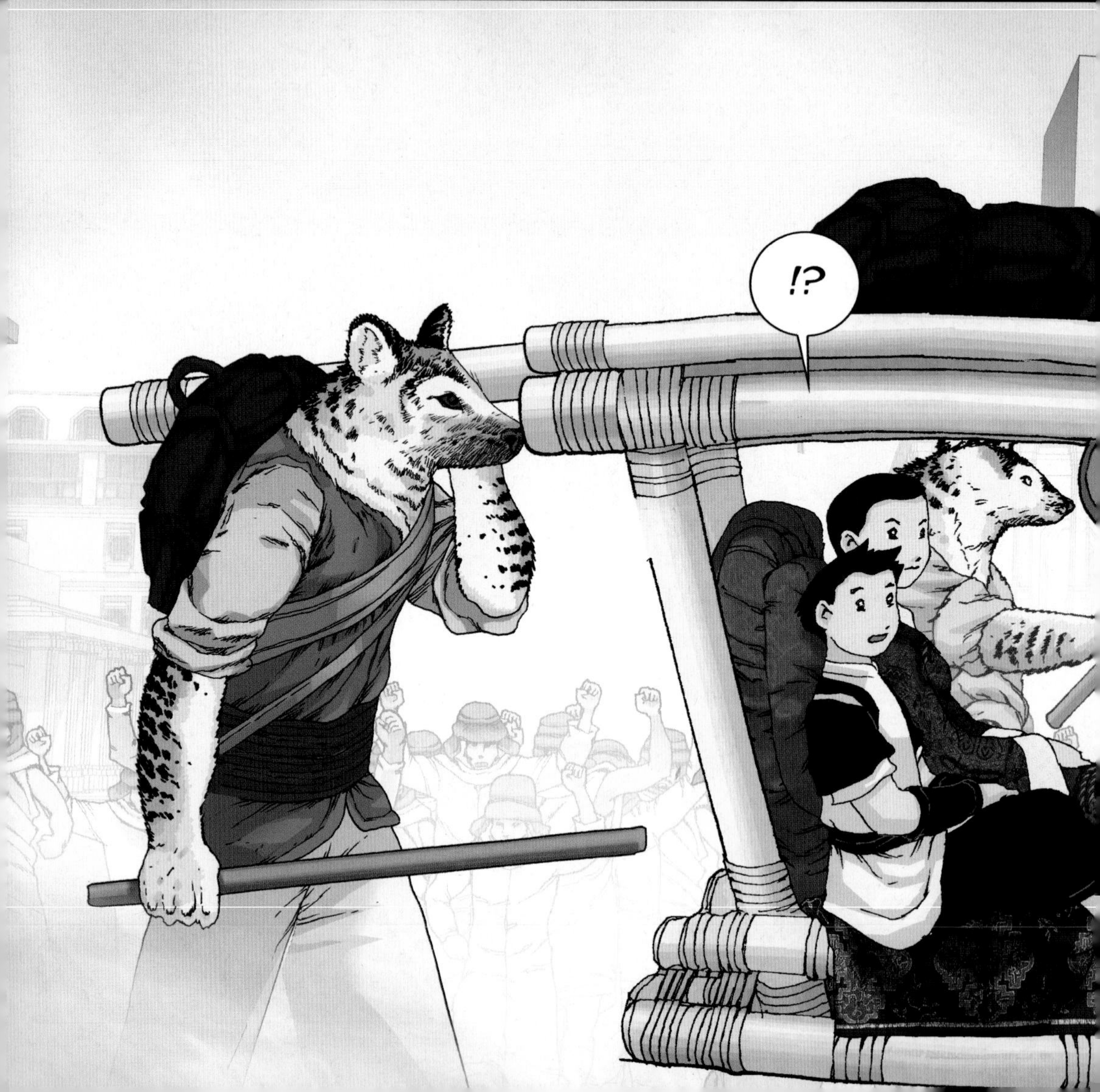
!?

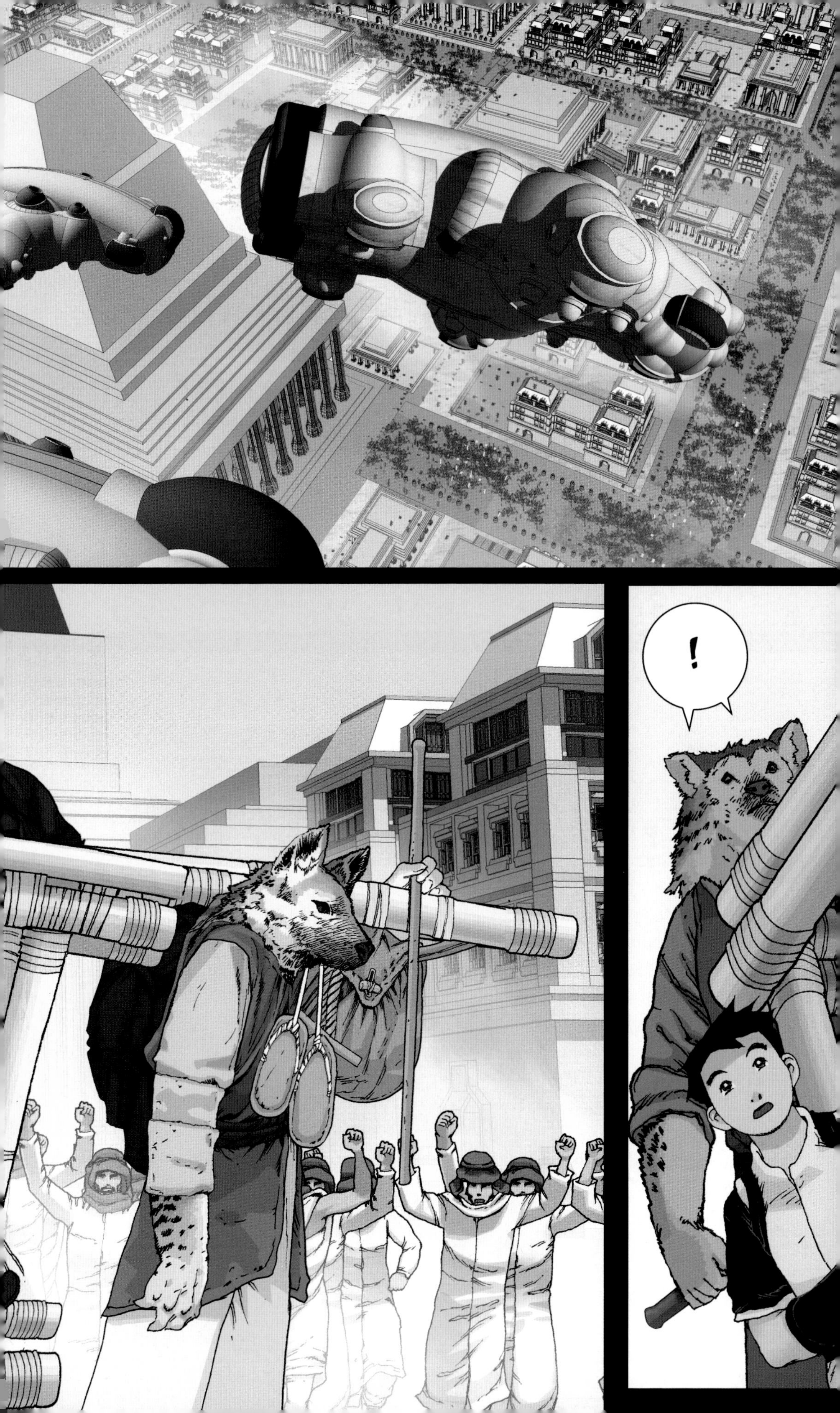
!

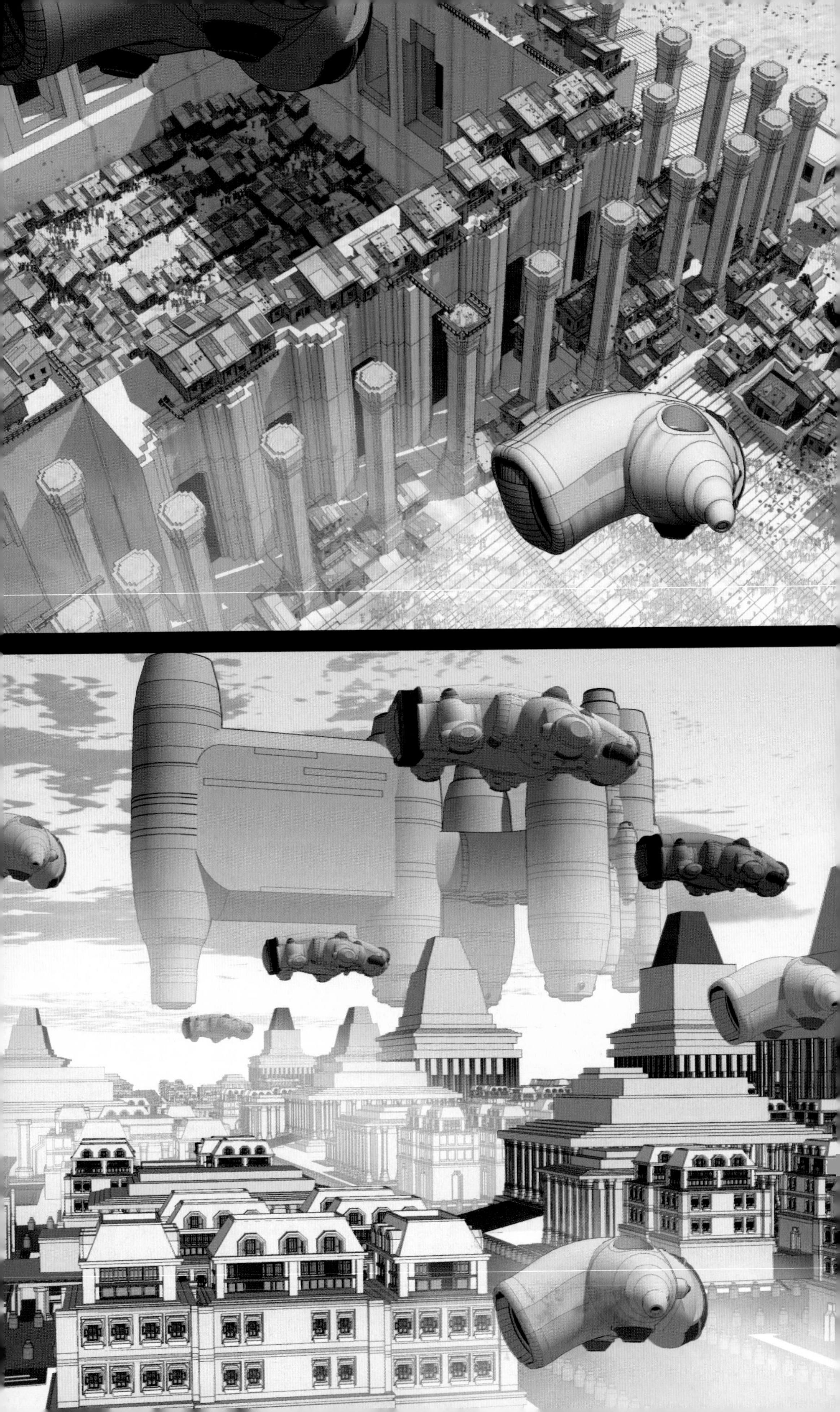

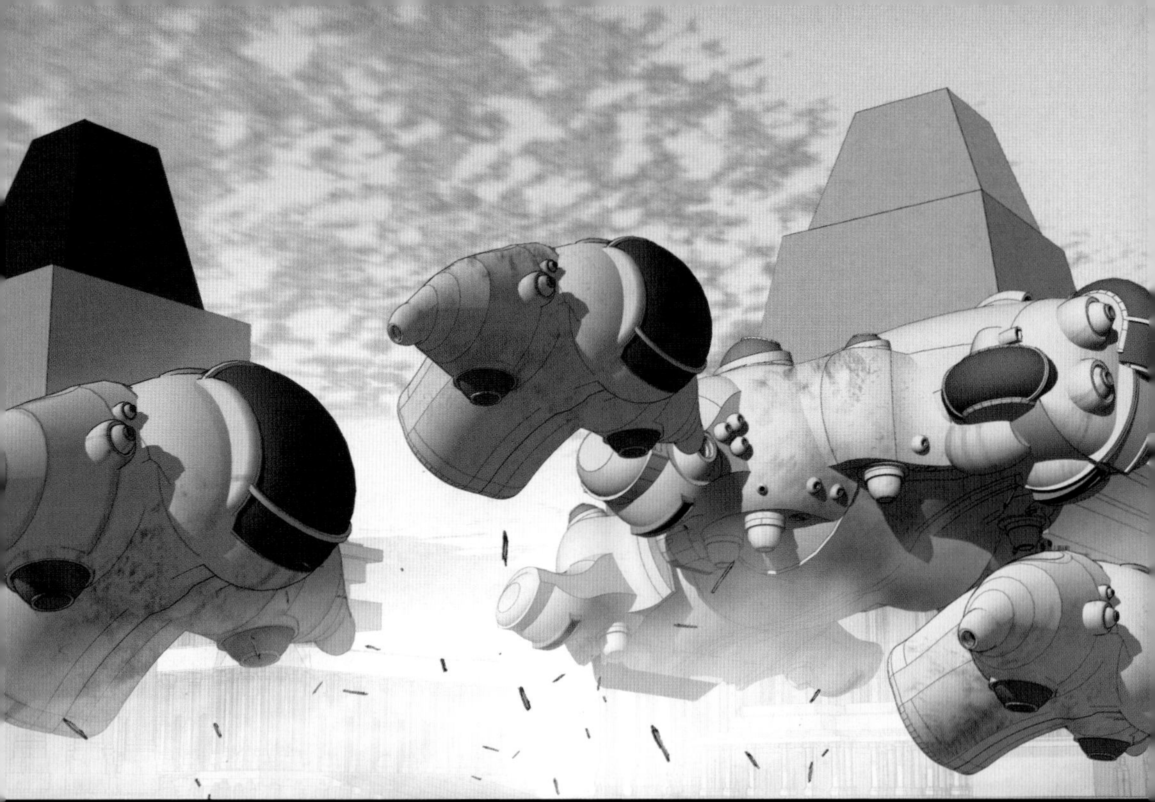

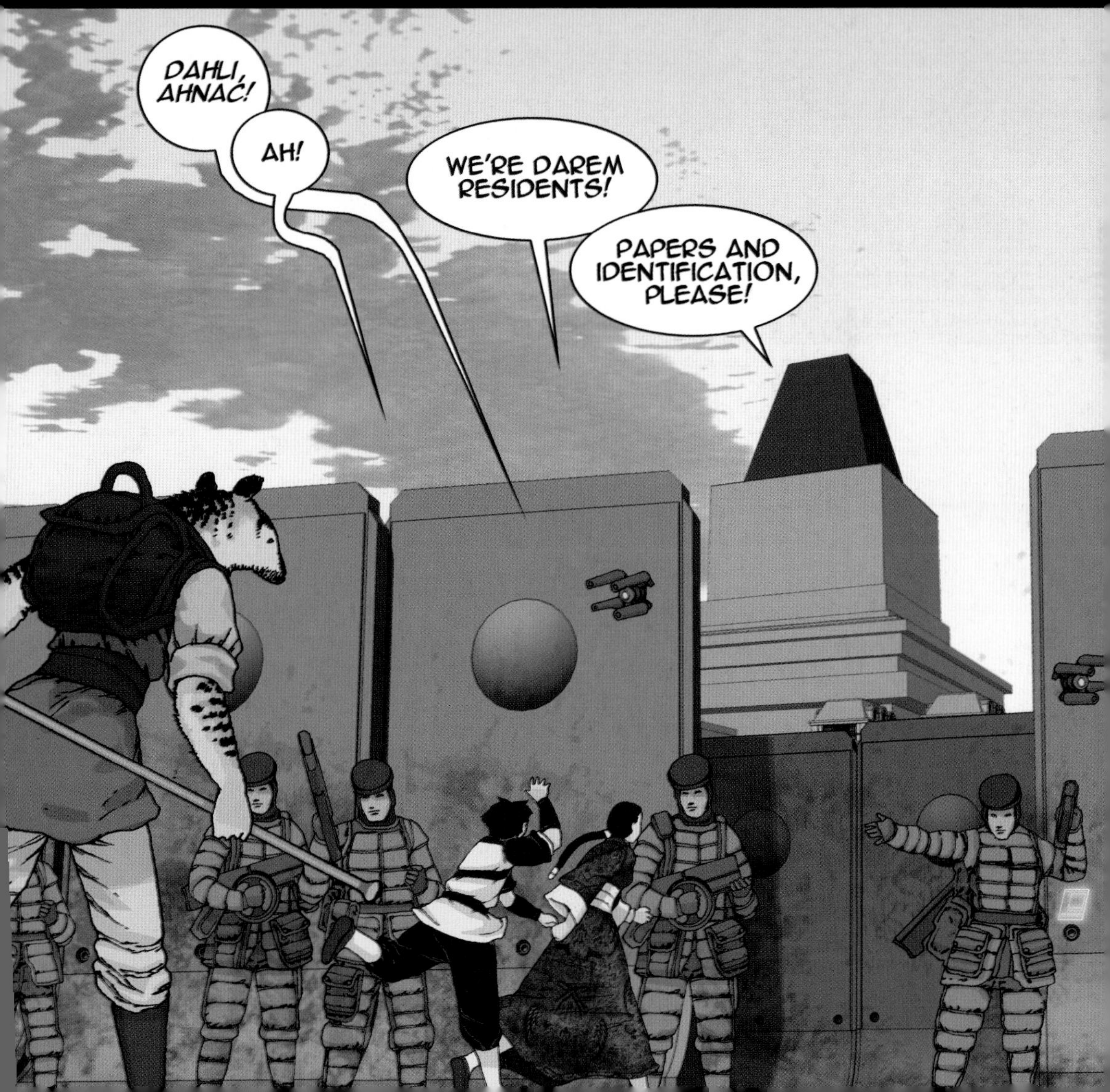
DAHLI, AHNAĆ!
AH!
WE'RE DAREM RESIDENTS!
PAPERS AND IDENTIFICATION, PLEASE!

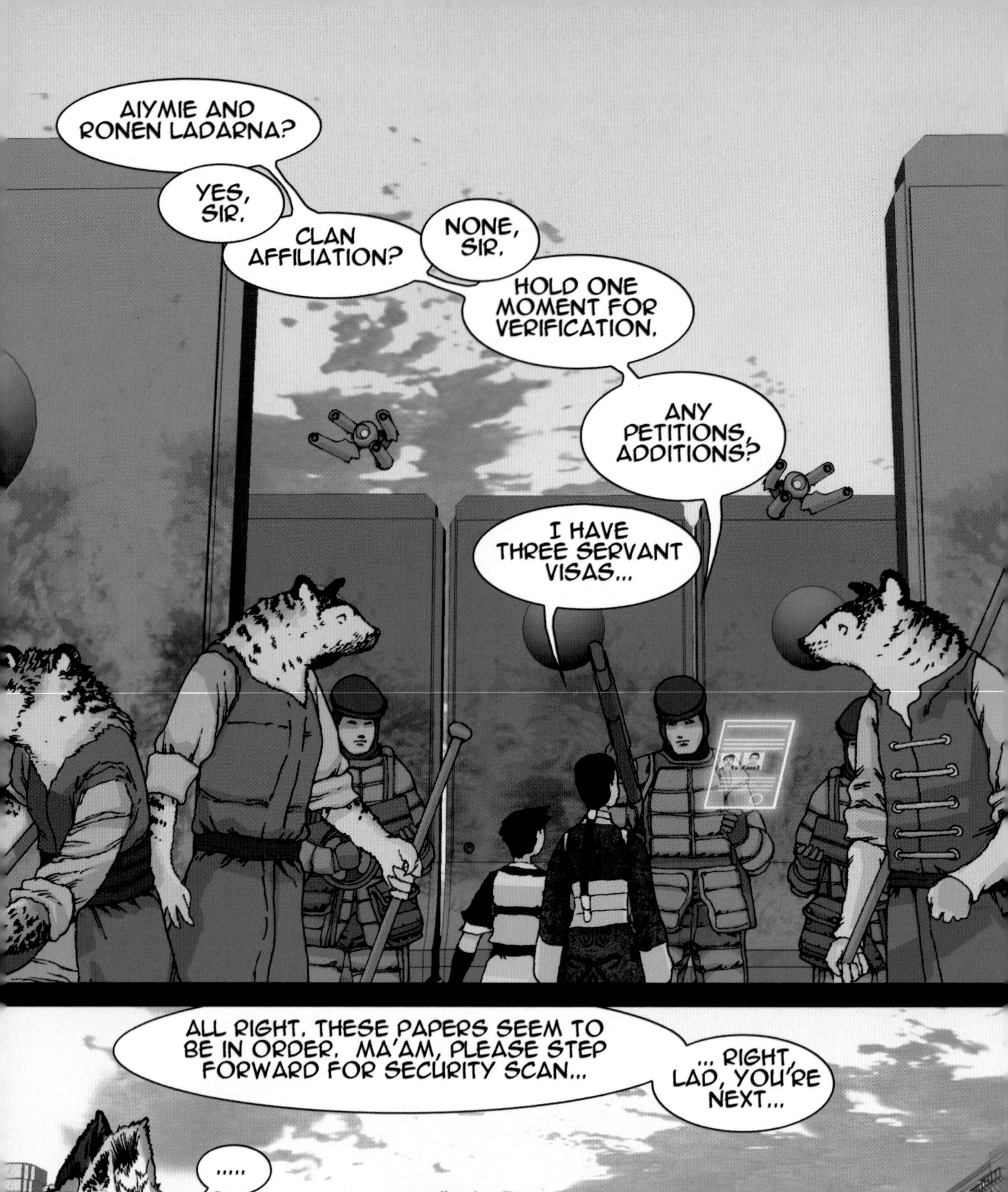
AIYMIE AND RONEN LADARNA?
YES, SIR.
CLAN AFFILIATION?
NONE, SIR.
HOLD ONE MOMENT FOR VERIFICATION.
ANY PETITIONS, ADDITIONS?
I HAVE THREE SERVANT VISAS...

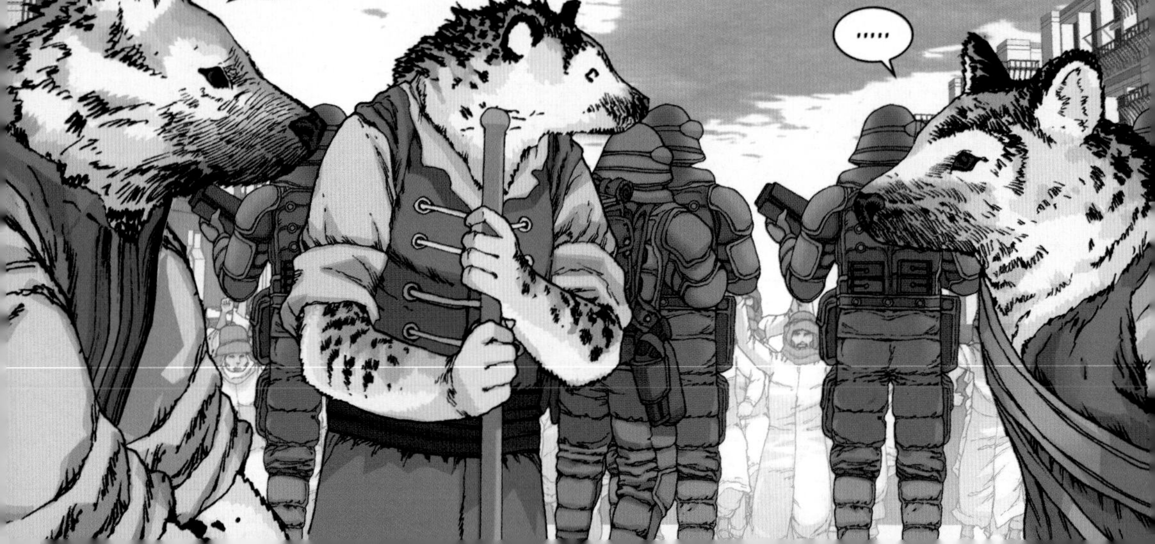
ALL RIGHT. THESE PAPERS SEEM TO BE IN ORDER. MA'AM, PLEASE STEP FORWARD FOR SECURITY SCAN...
... RIGHT, LAD, YOU'RE NEXT...
.....
.....

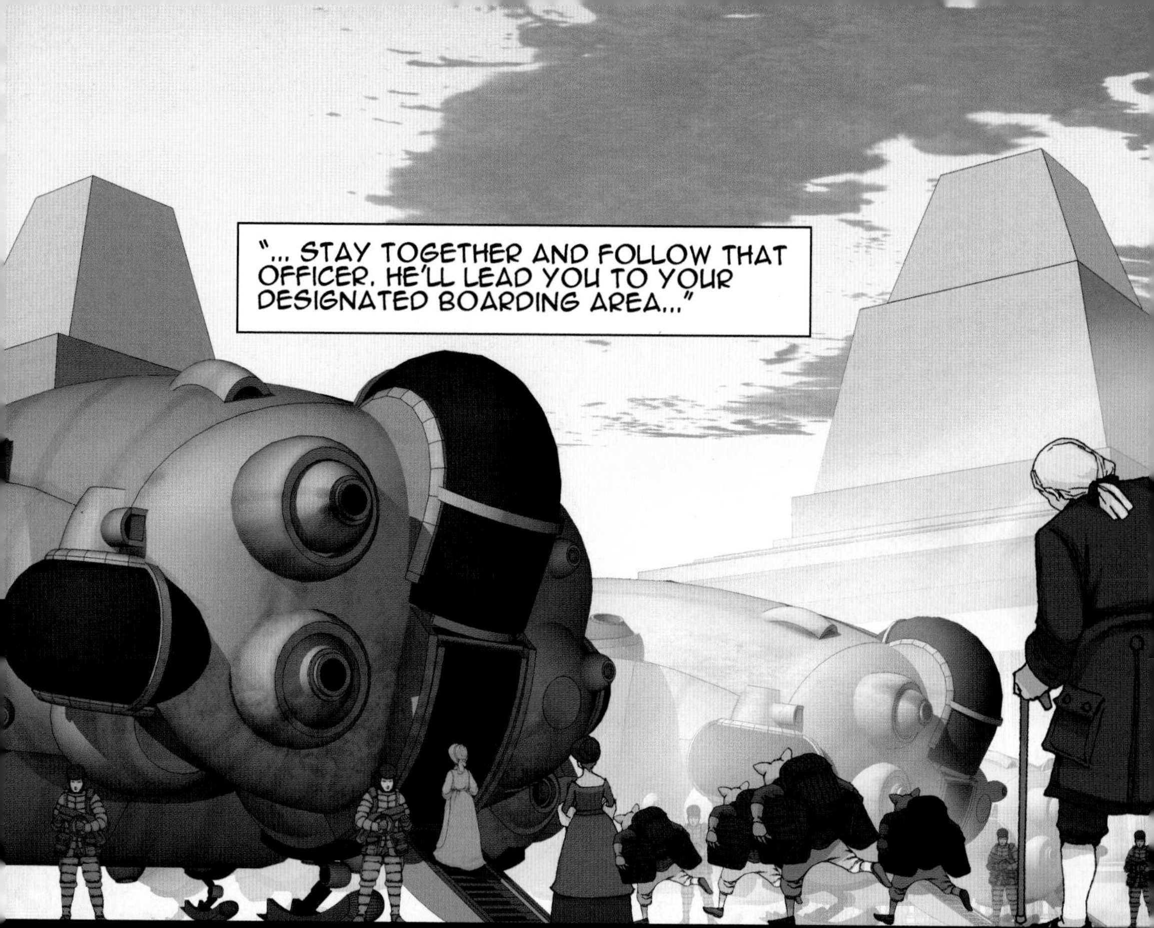
"... STAY TOGETHER AND FOLLOW THAT OFFICER. HE'LL LEAD YOU TO YOUR DESIGNATED BOARDING AREA..."

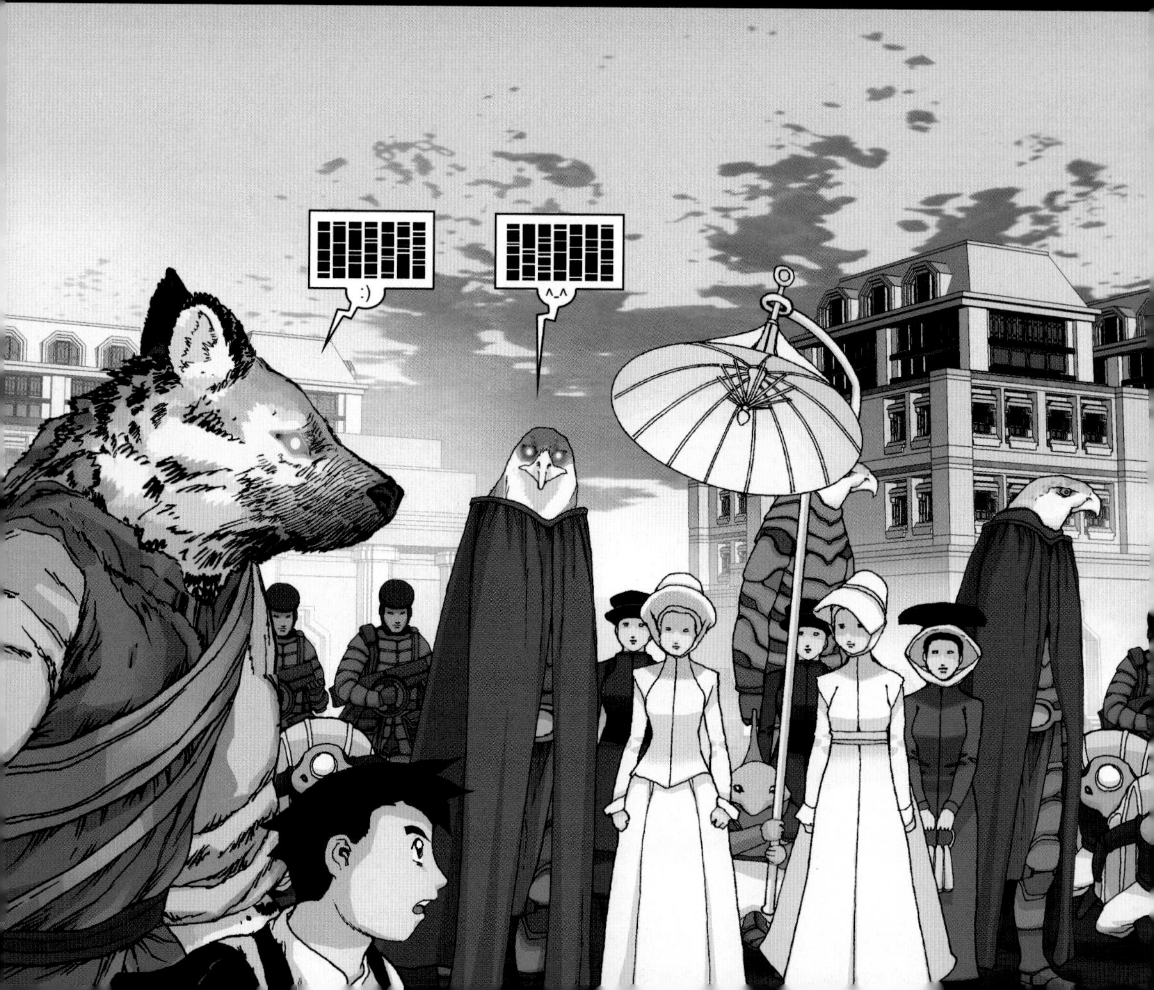
:)
^_^

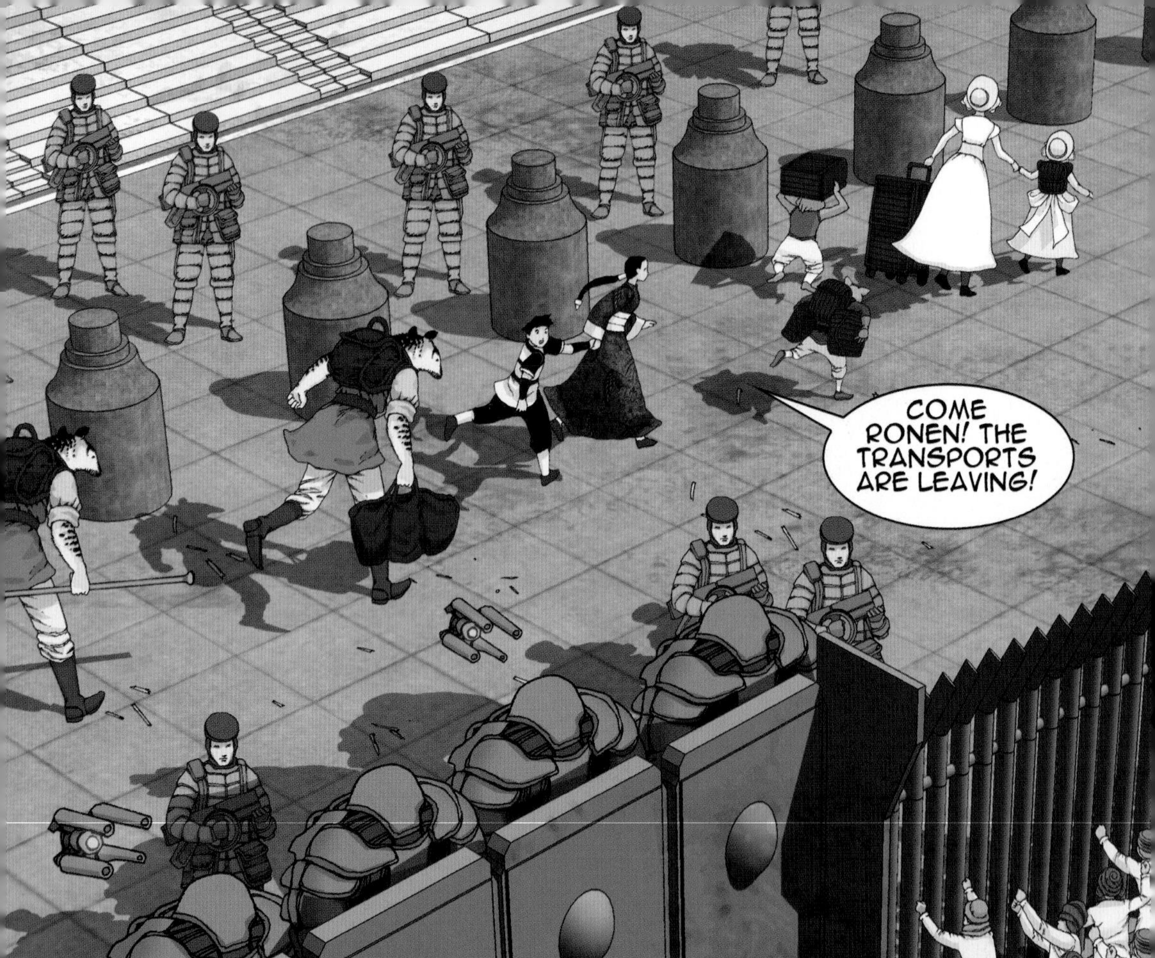
COME RONEN! THE TRANSPORTS ARE LEAVING!

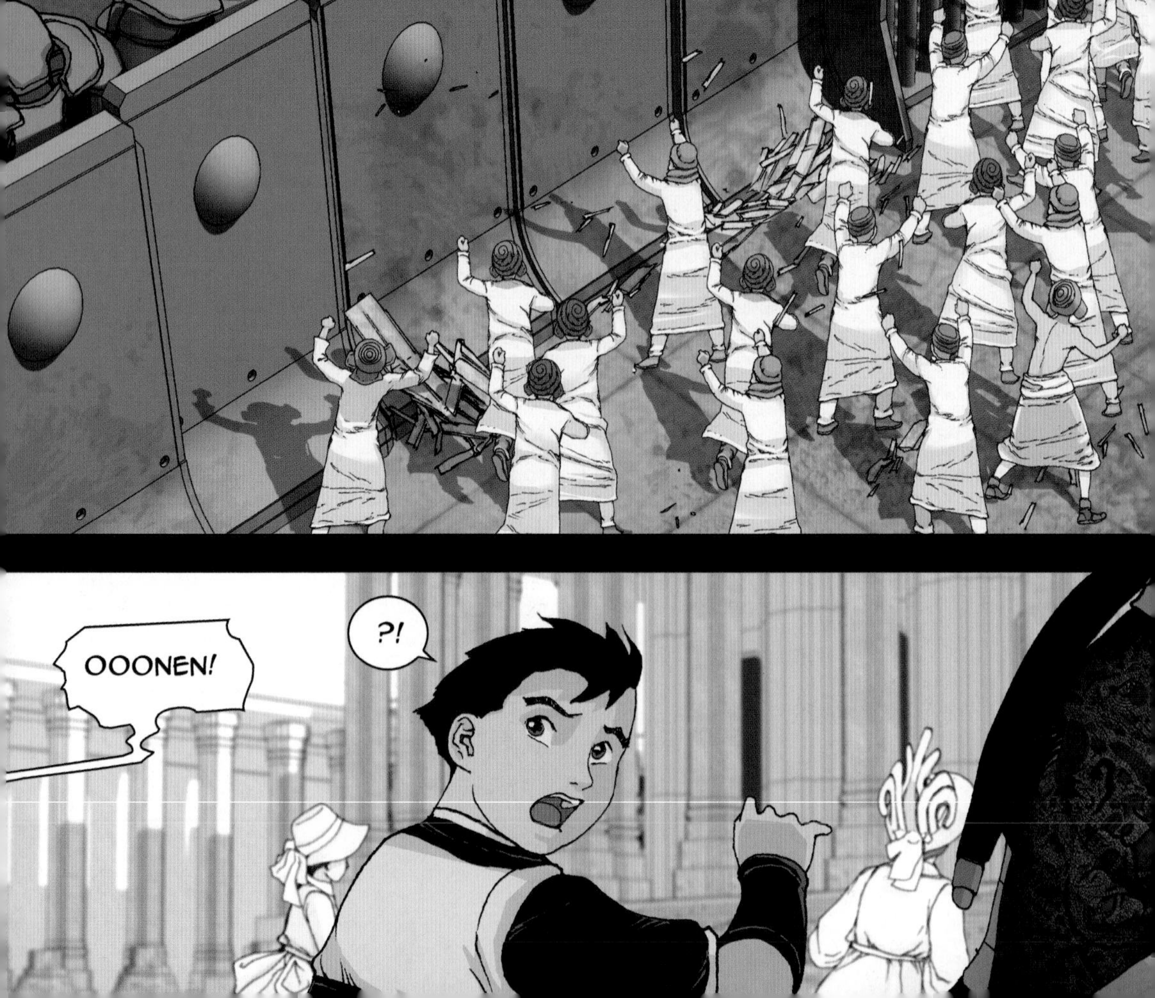
OOONEN!
?!

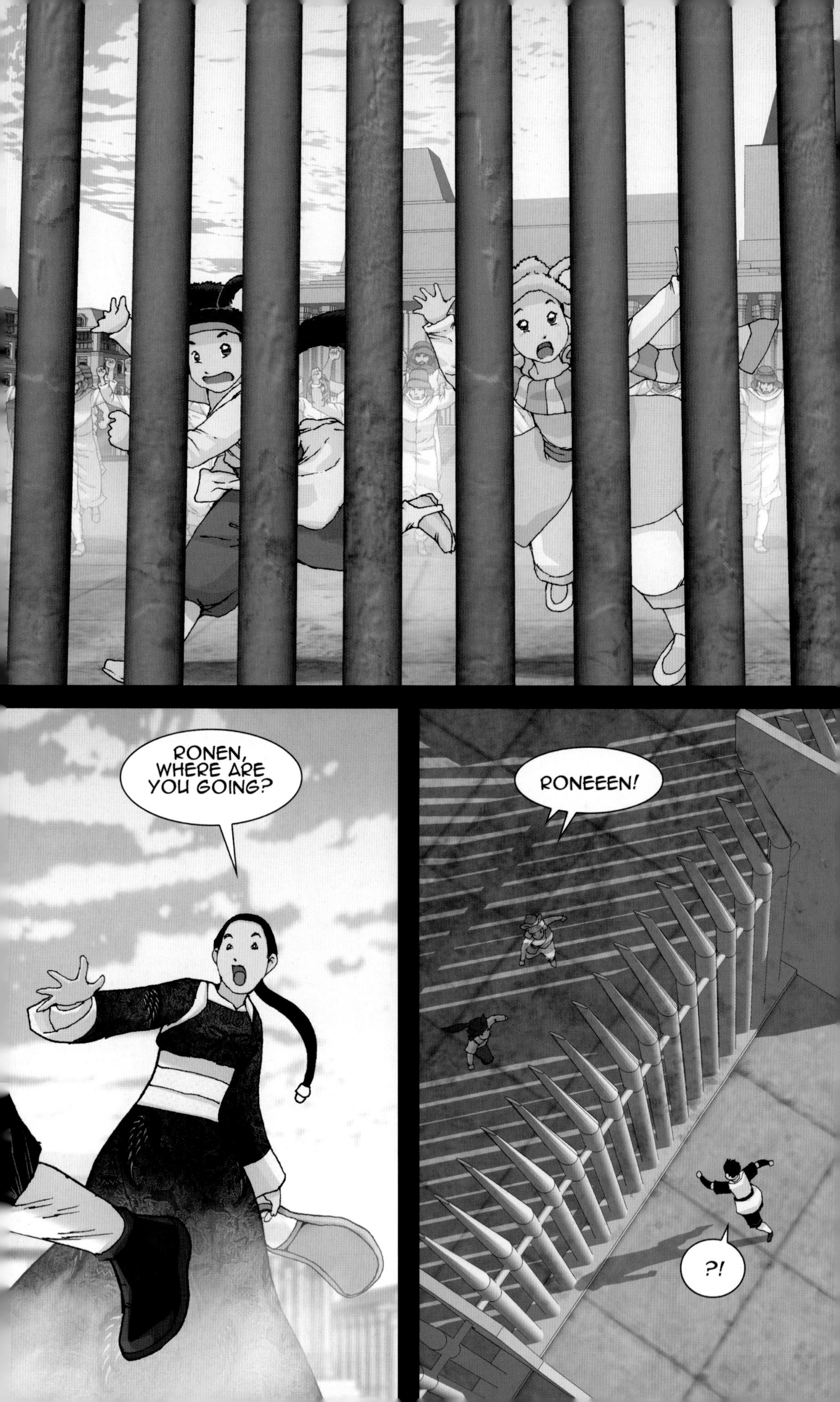
RONEN, WHERE ARE YOU GOING?
RONEEEN!
?!

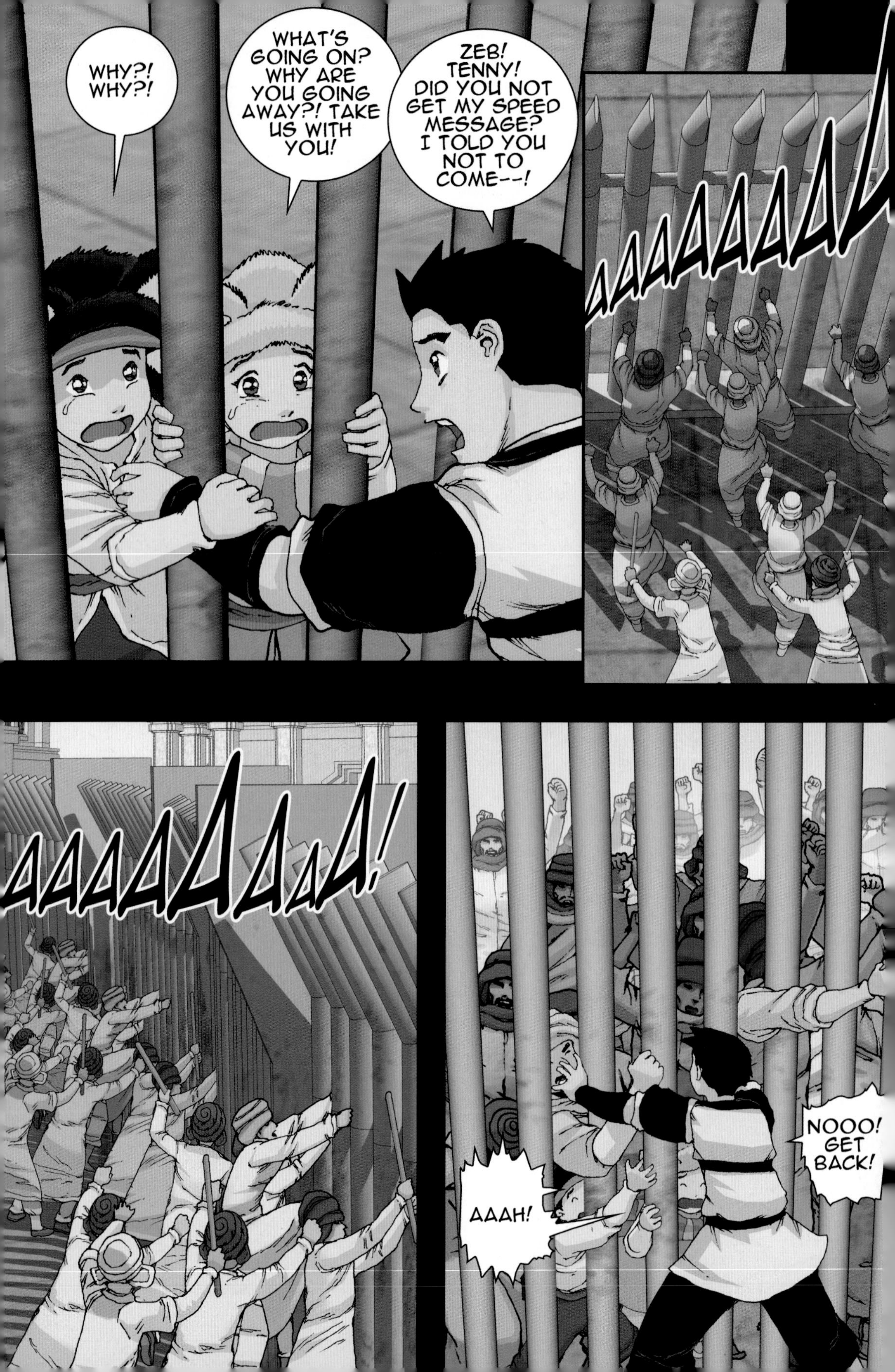
WHY?! WHY?!
WHAT'S GOING ON? WHY ARE YOU GOING AWAY?! TAKE US WITH YOU!
ZEB! TENNY! DID YOU NOT GET MY SPEED MESSAGE? I TOLD YOU NOT TO COME--!
AAAAAAAA
AAAAAAAAA!
NOOO! GET BACK!
AAAH!

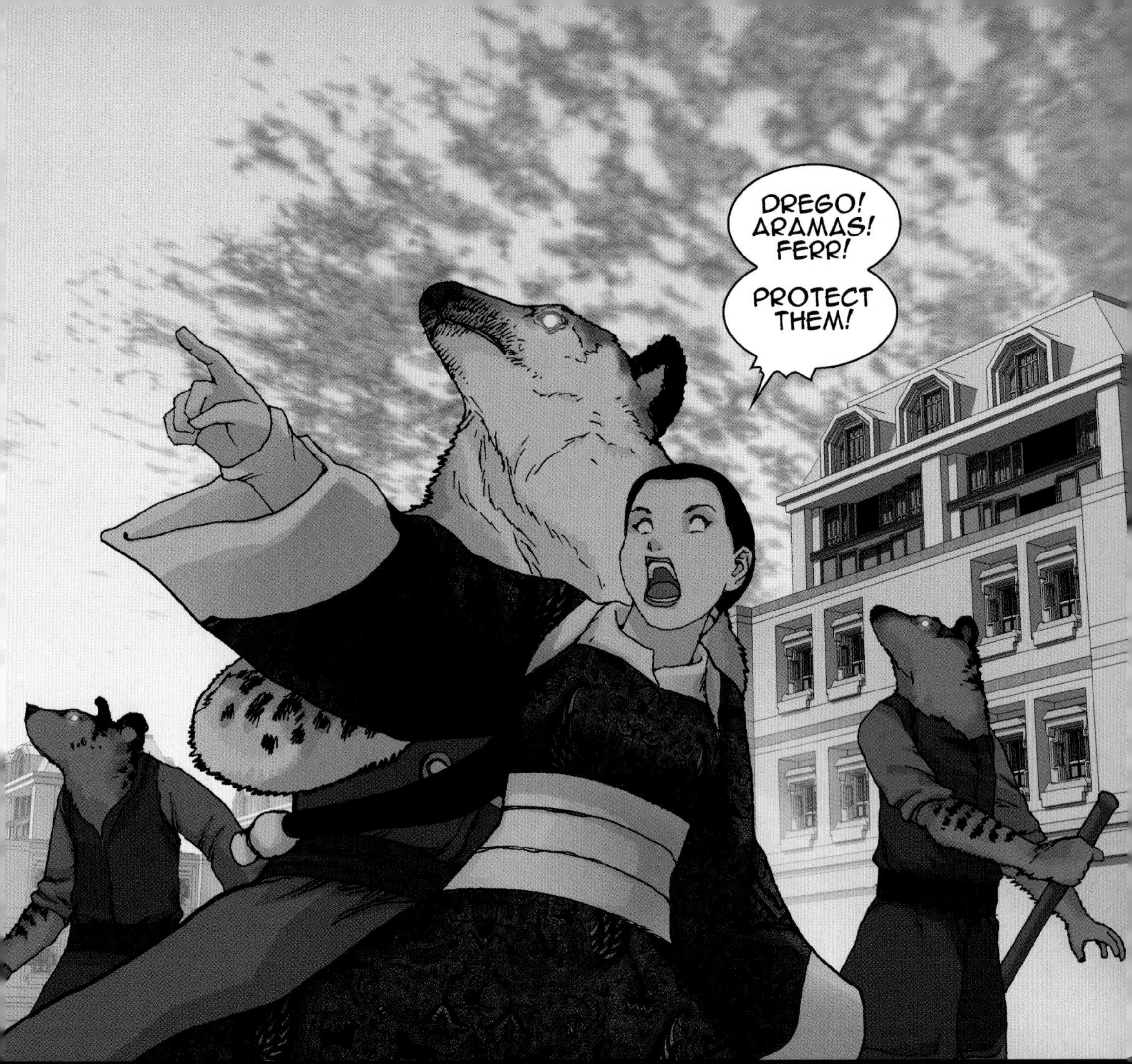
DREGO! ARAMAS! FERR!
PROTECT THEM!

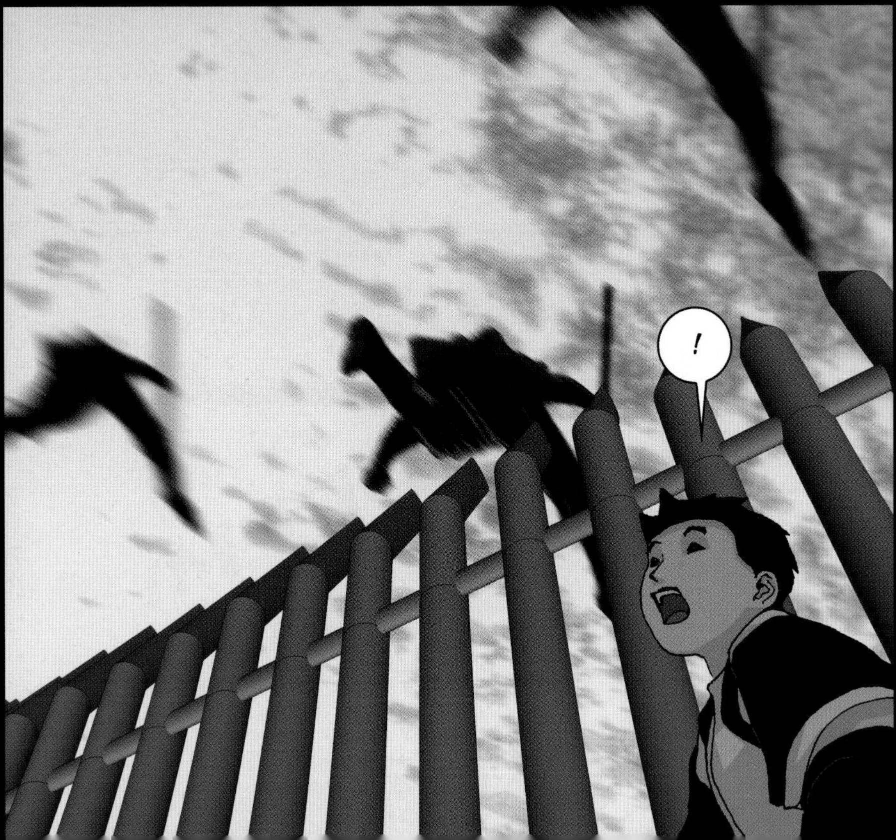
!

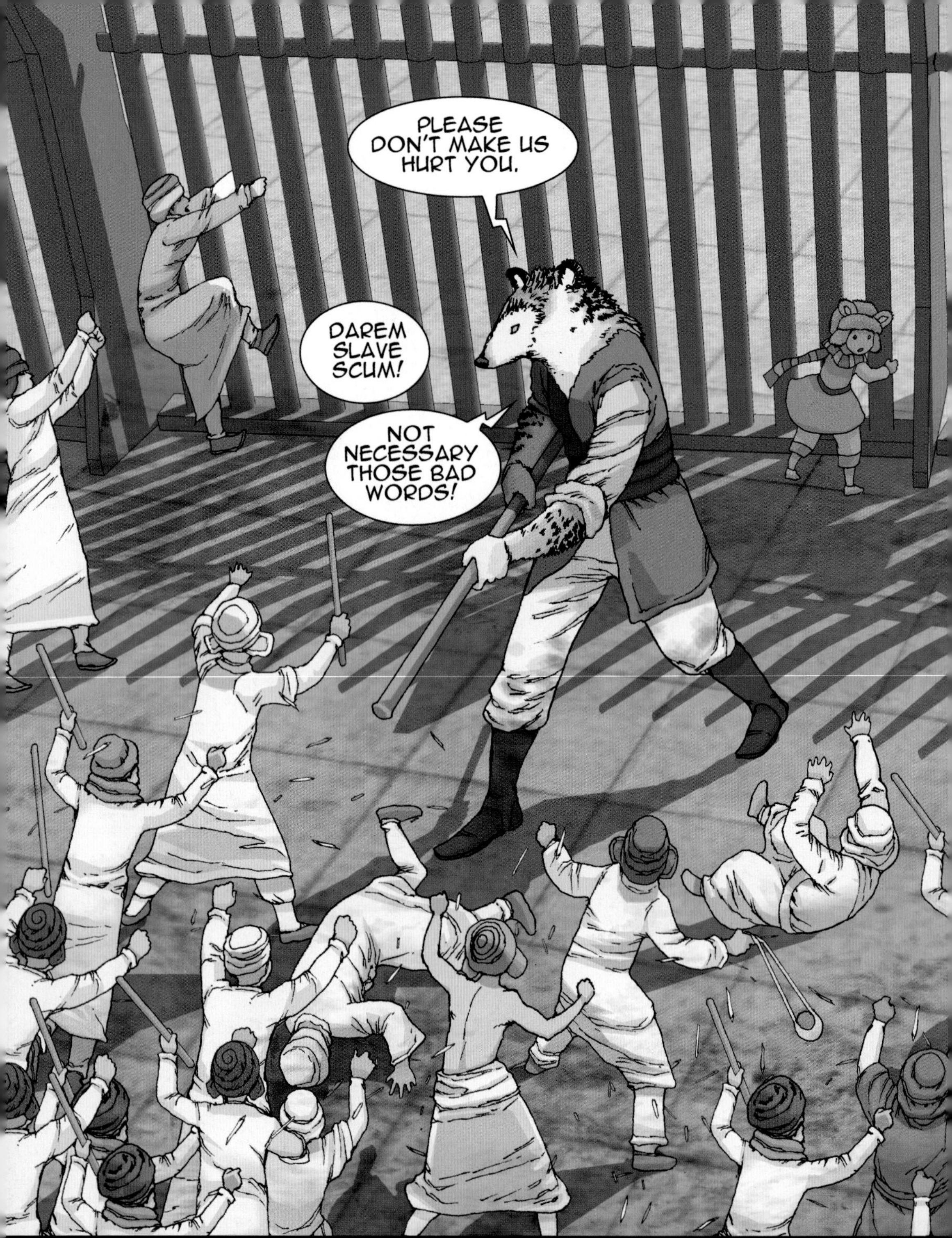
PLEASE DON'T MAKE US HURT YOU.
DAREM SLAVE SCUM!
NOT NECESSARY THOSE BAD WORDS!

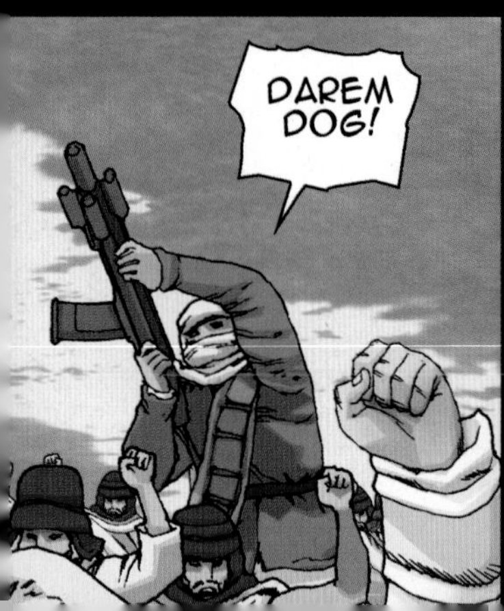
DAREM DOG!

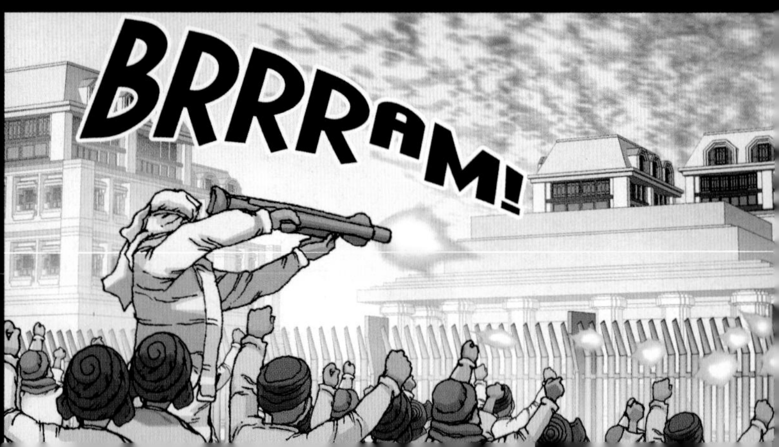
BRRRRAM!

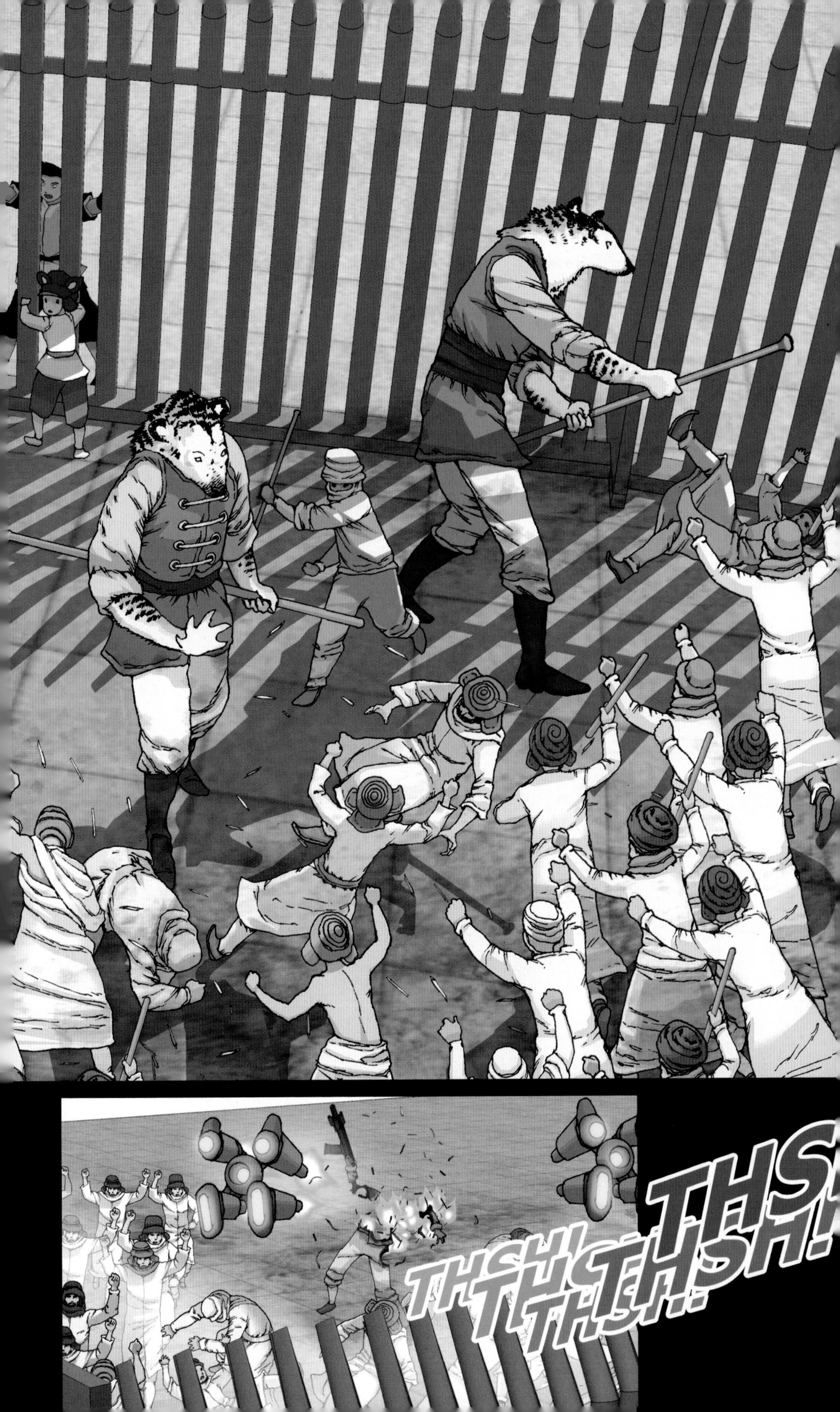
THSH!
THSH!
THSH...

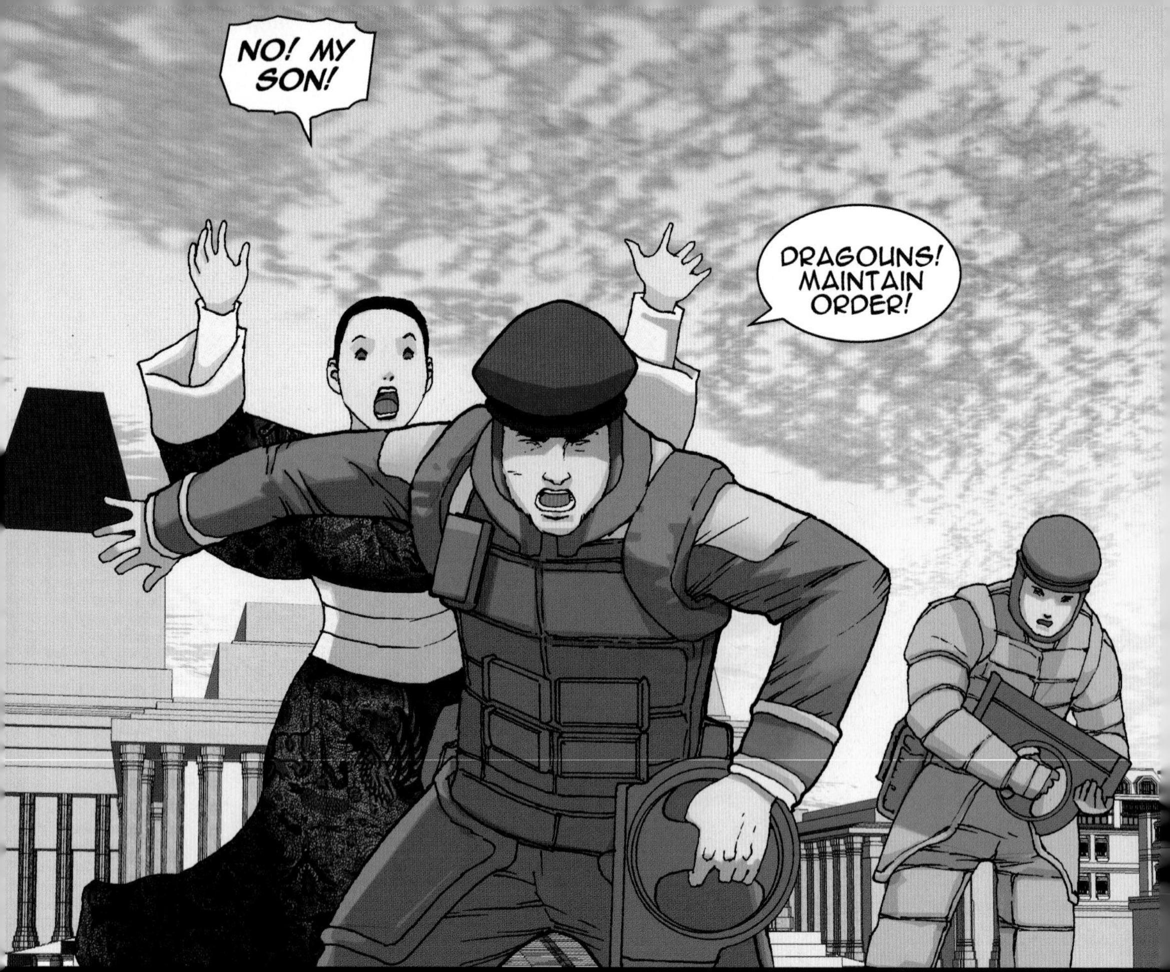
NO! MY SON!
DRAGOUNS! MAINTAIN ORDER!

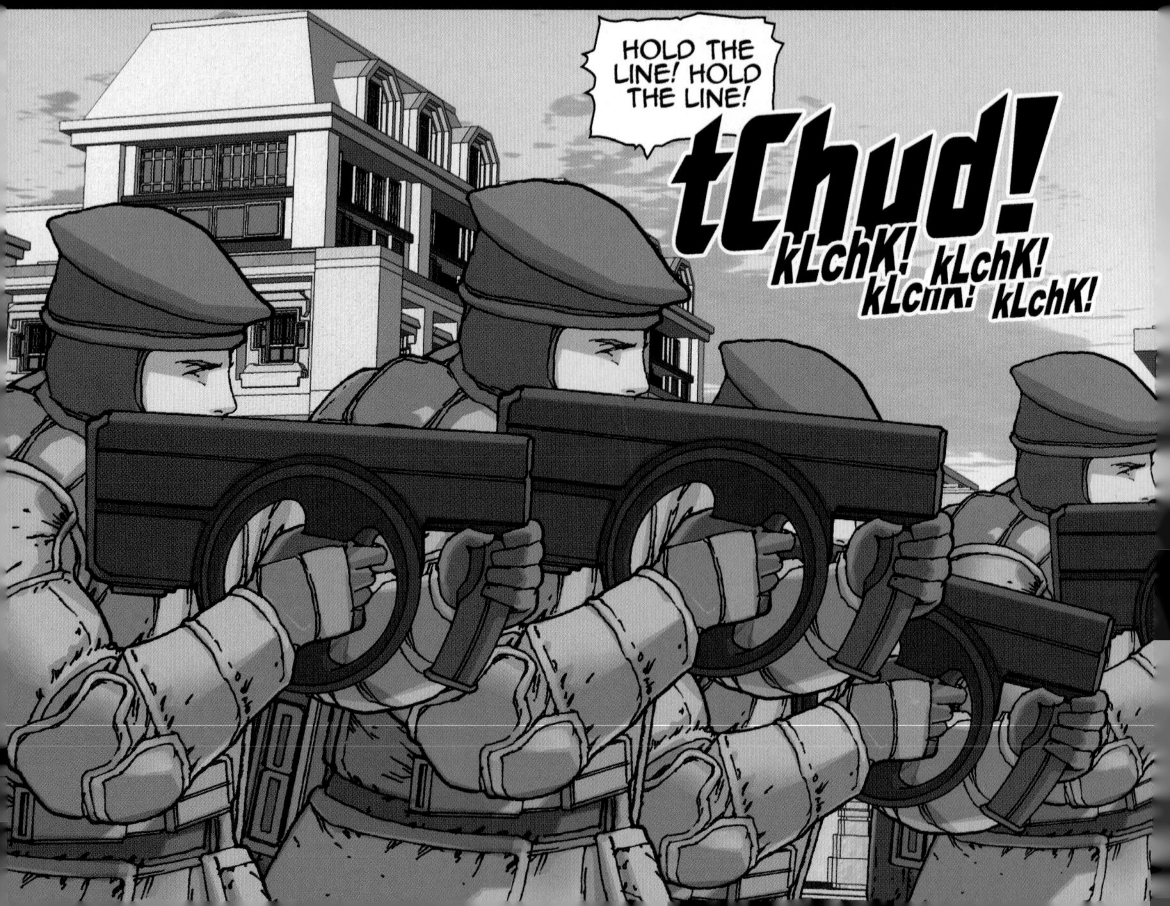
HOLD THE LINE! HOLD THE LINE!
tChud!
kLchK! kLchK!
kLchK!

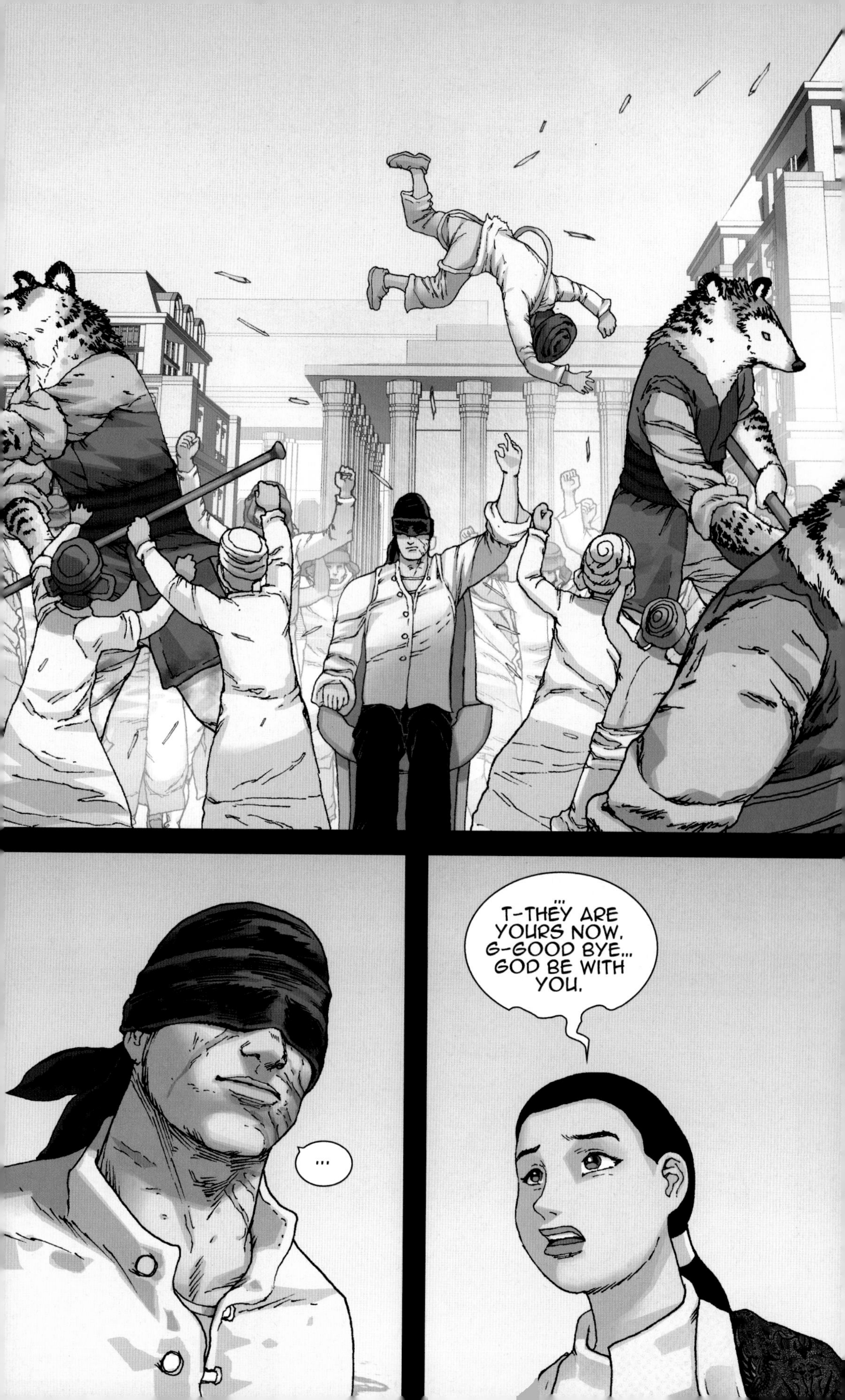
...
...
T-THEY ARE YOURS NOW. G-GOOD BYE... GOD BE WITH YOU.

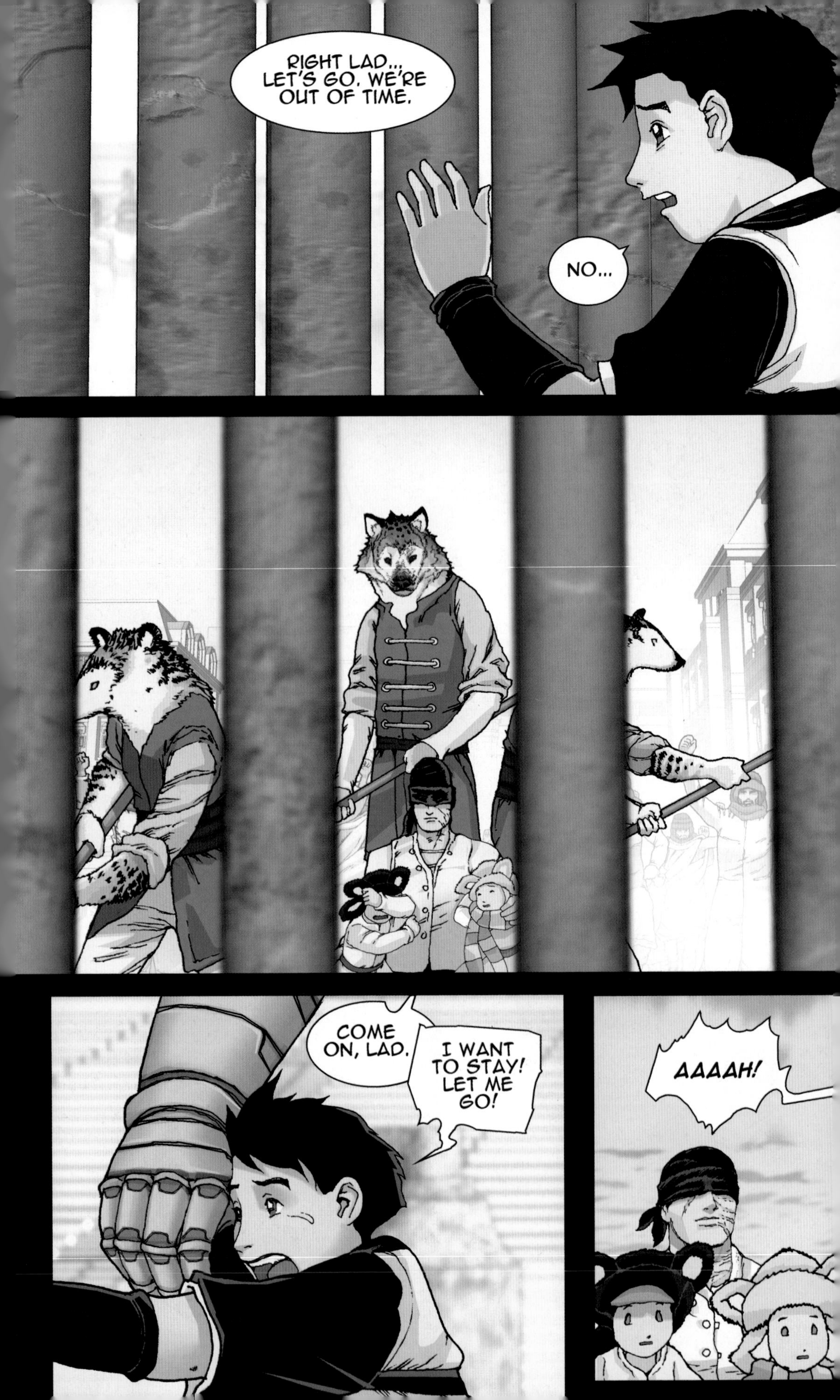
RIGHT LAD... LET'S GO. WE'RE OUT OF TIME.
NO...
COME ON, LAD.
I WANT TO STAY! LET ME GO!
AAAAH!

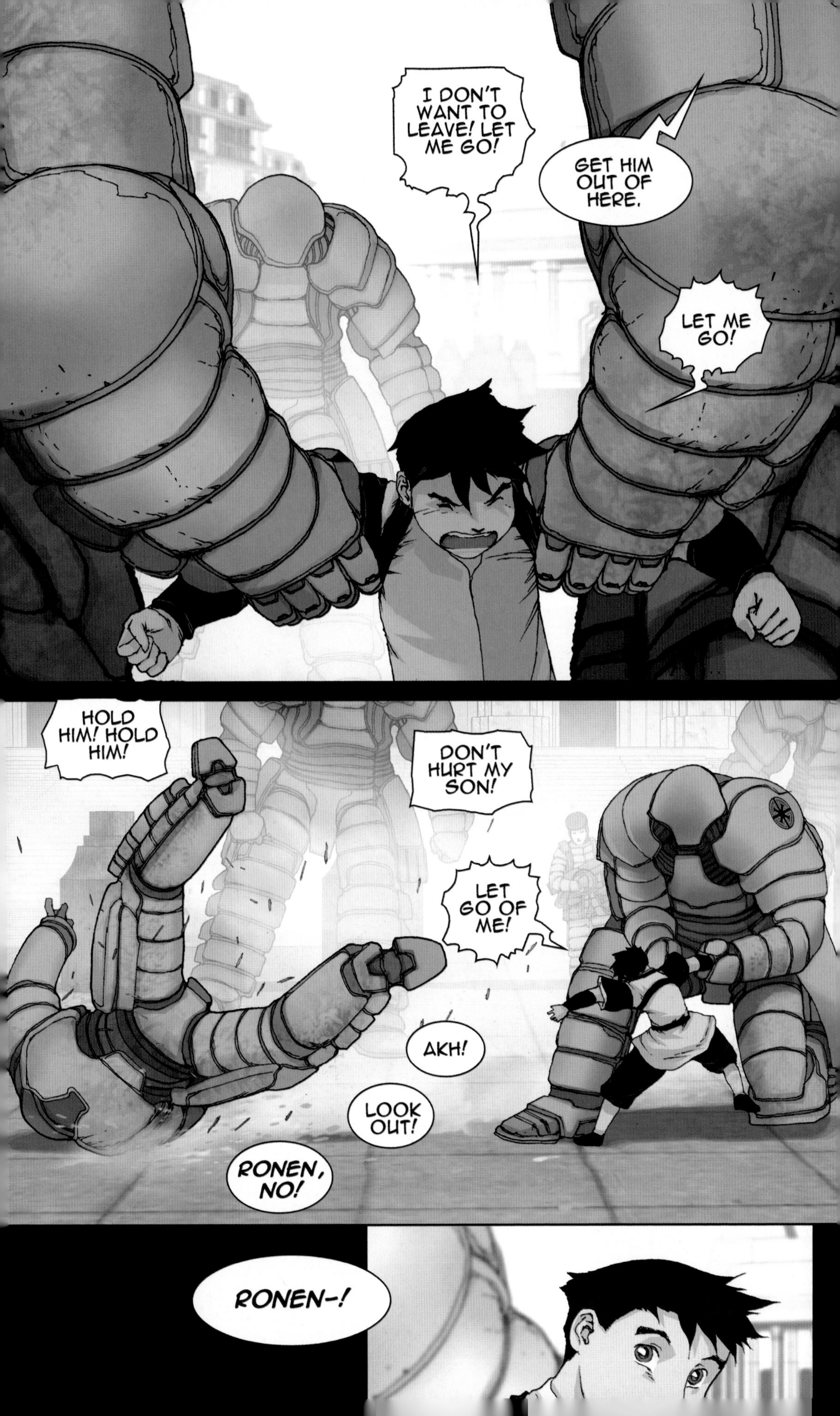
I DON'T WANT TO LEAVE! LET ME GO!
GET HIM OUT OF HERE.
LET ME GO!
HOLD HIM! HOLD HIM!
DON'T HURT MY SON!
LET GO OF ME!
AKH!
LOOK OUT!
RONEN, NO!
RONEN-!

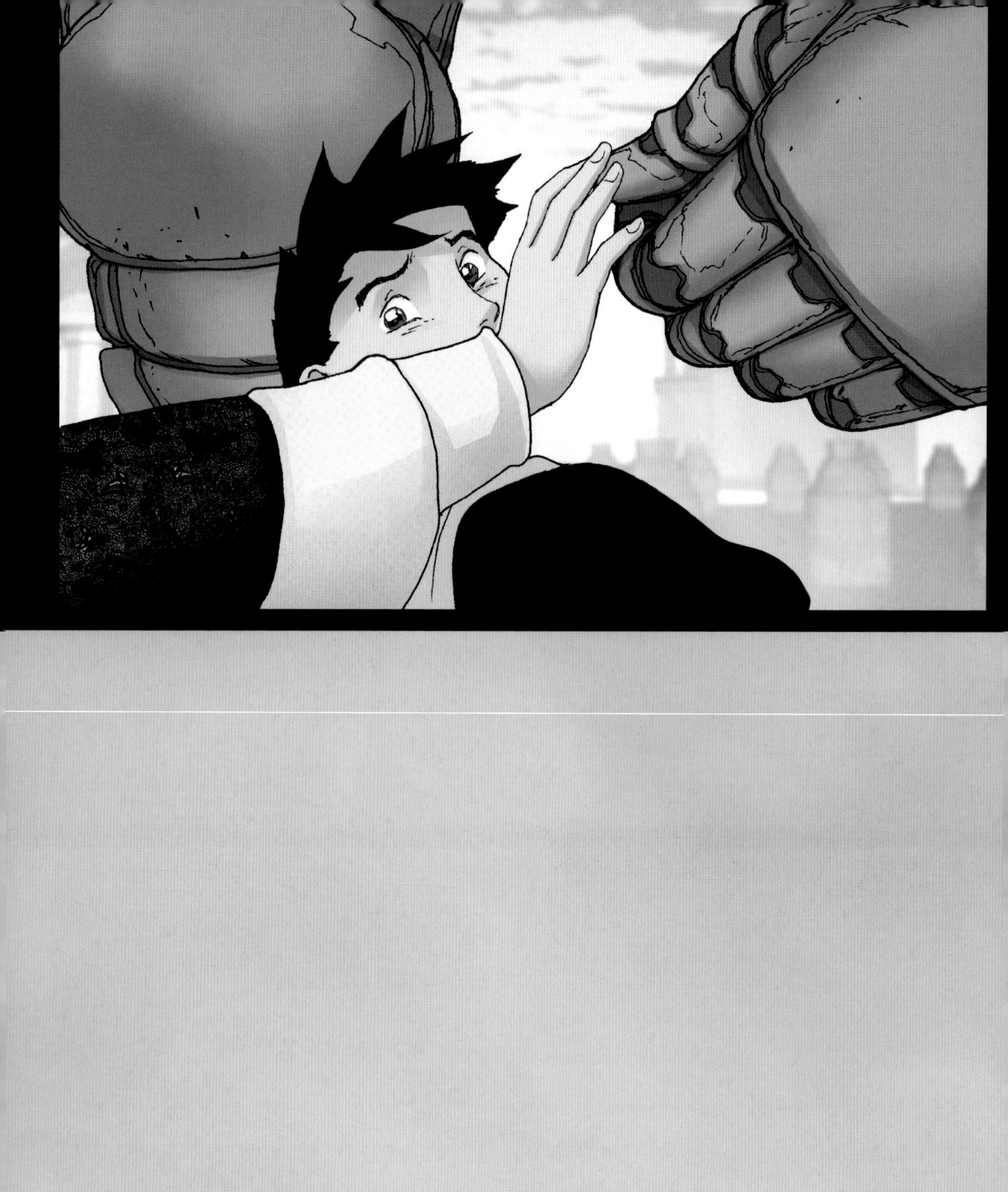

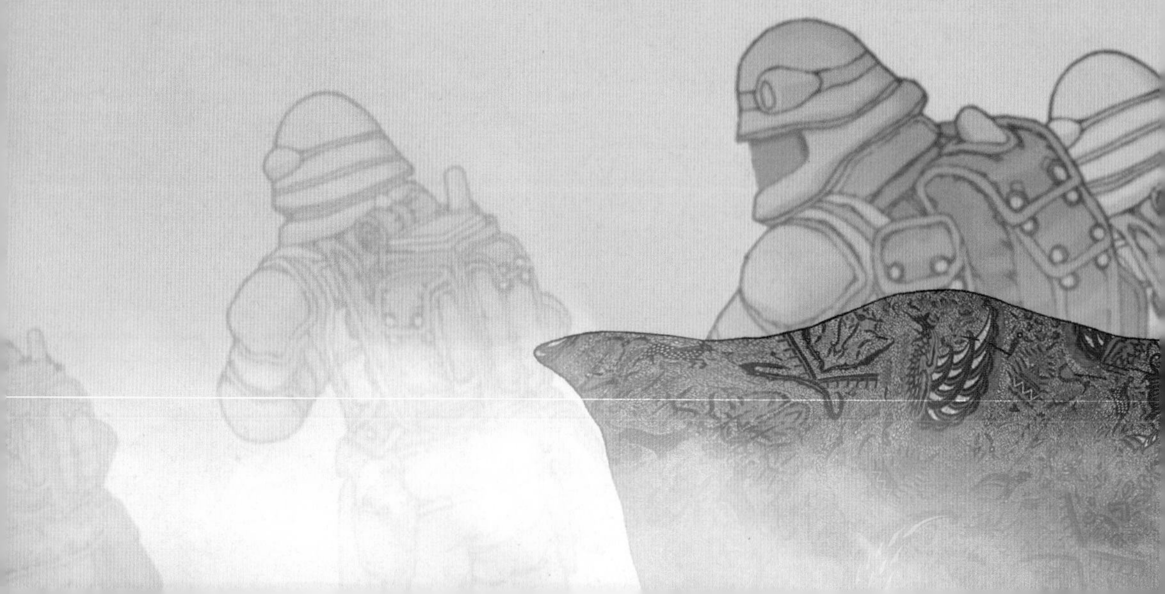

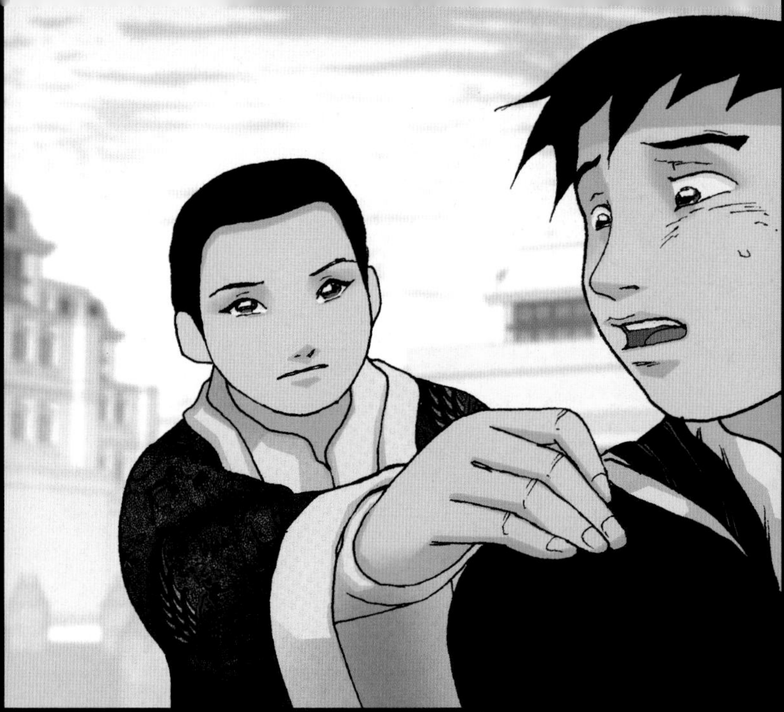
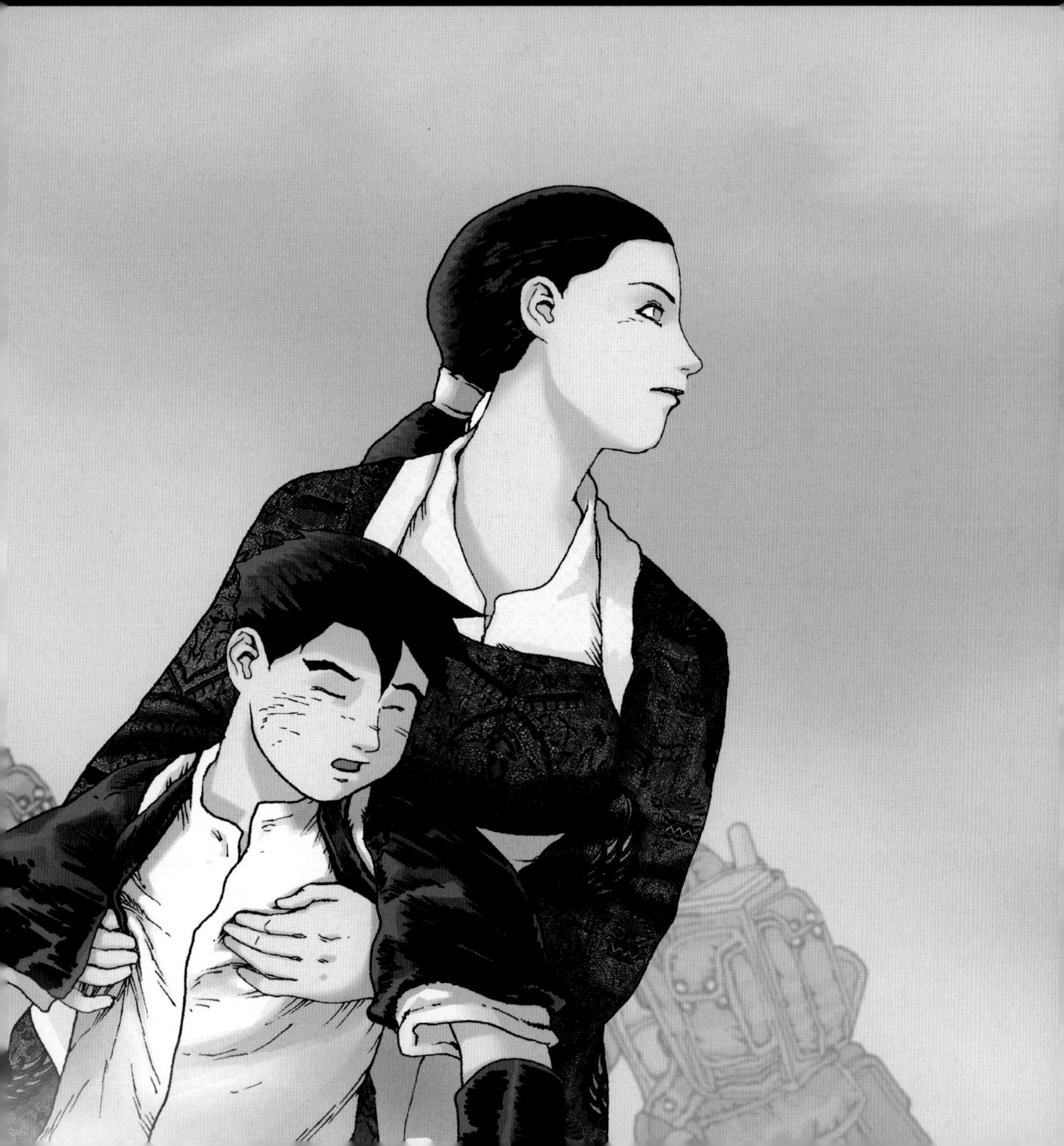

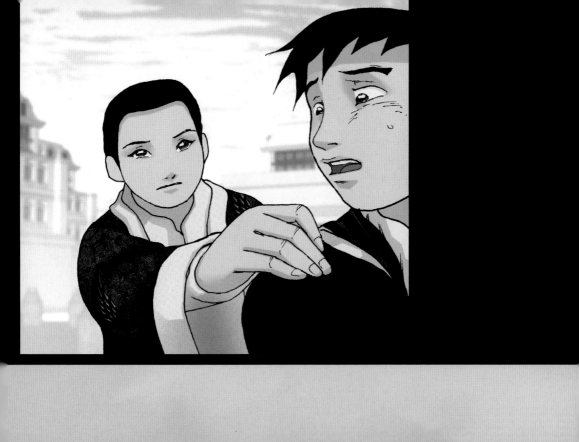

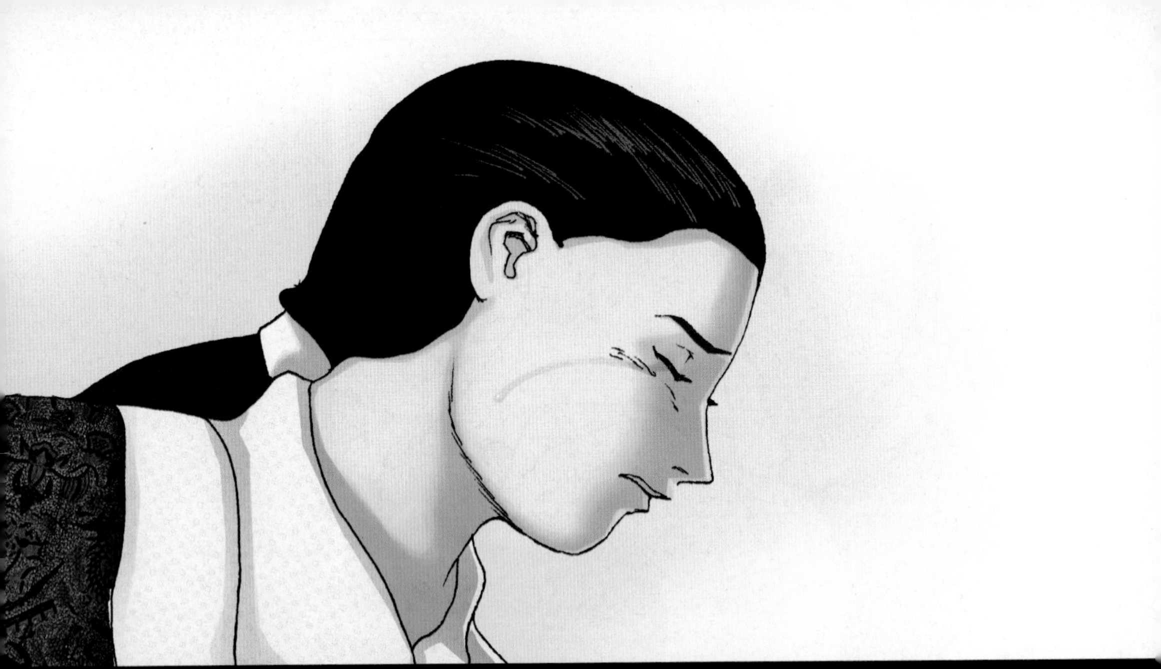
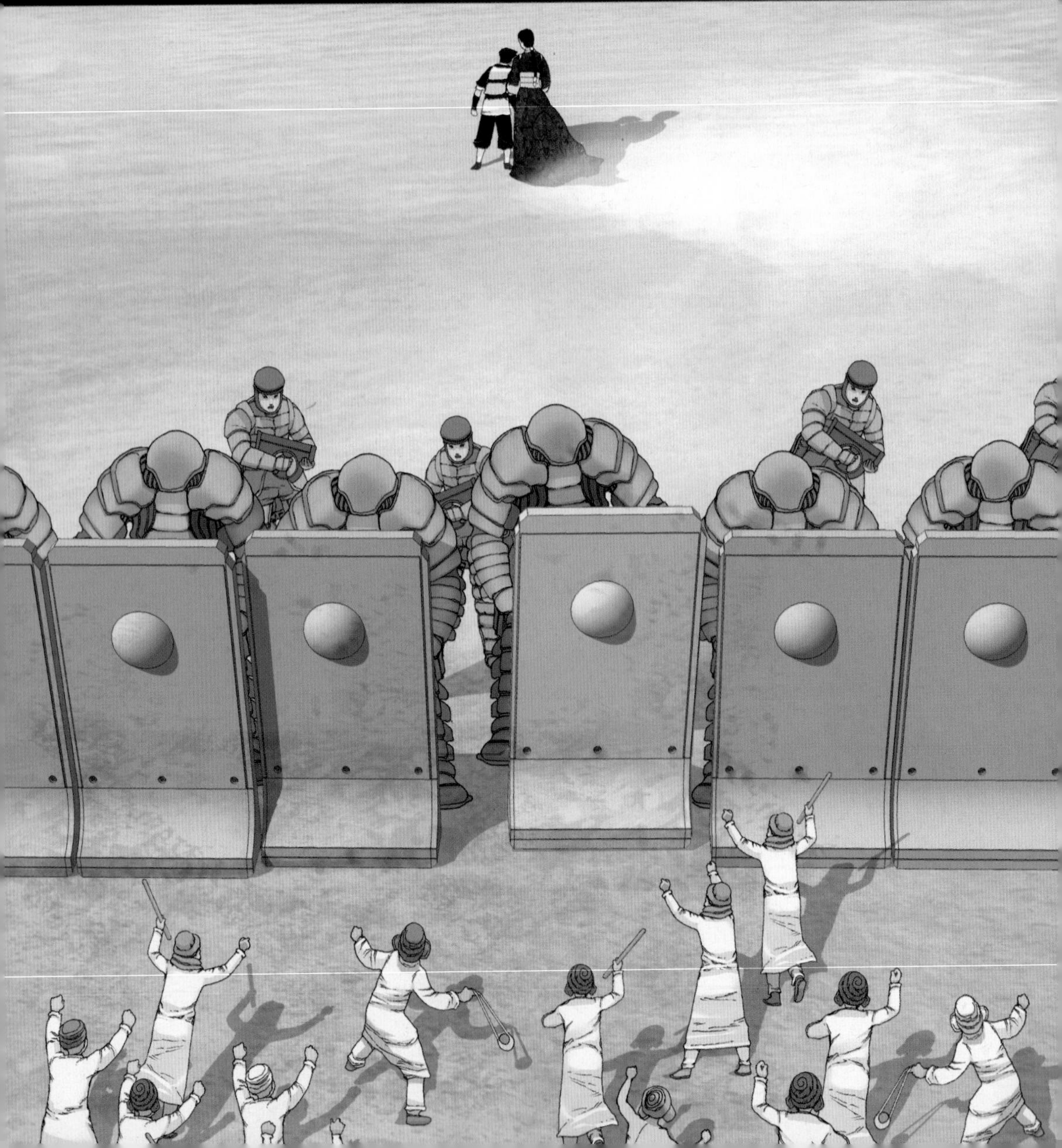

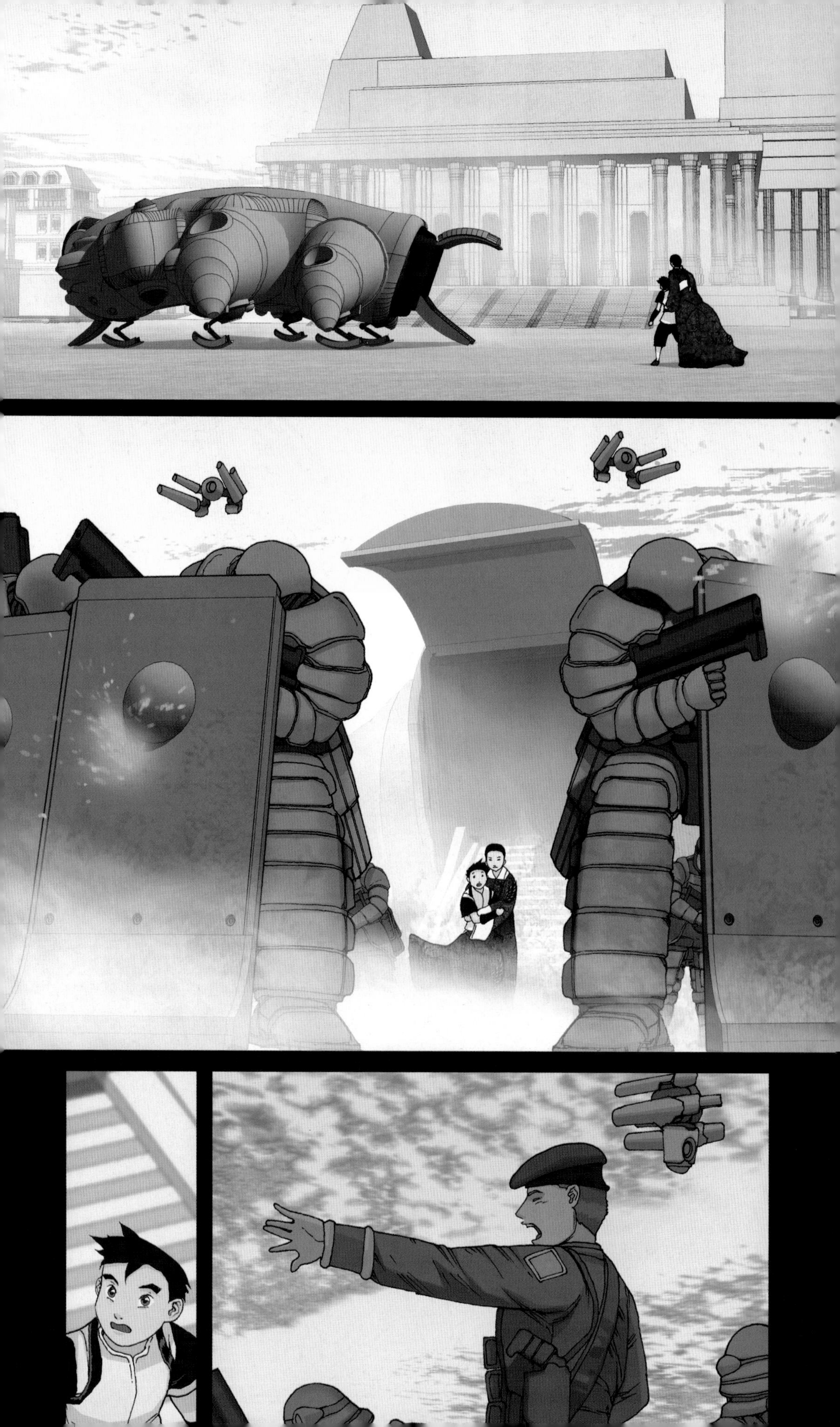

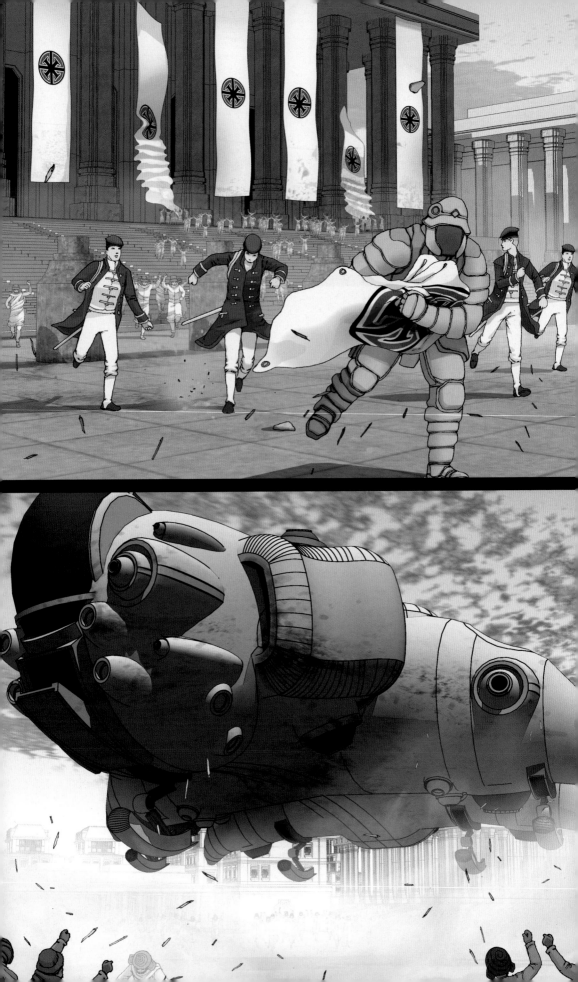

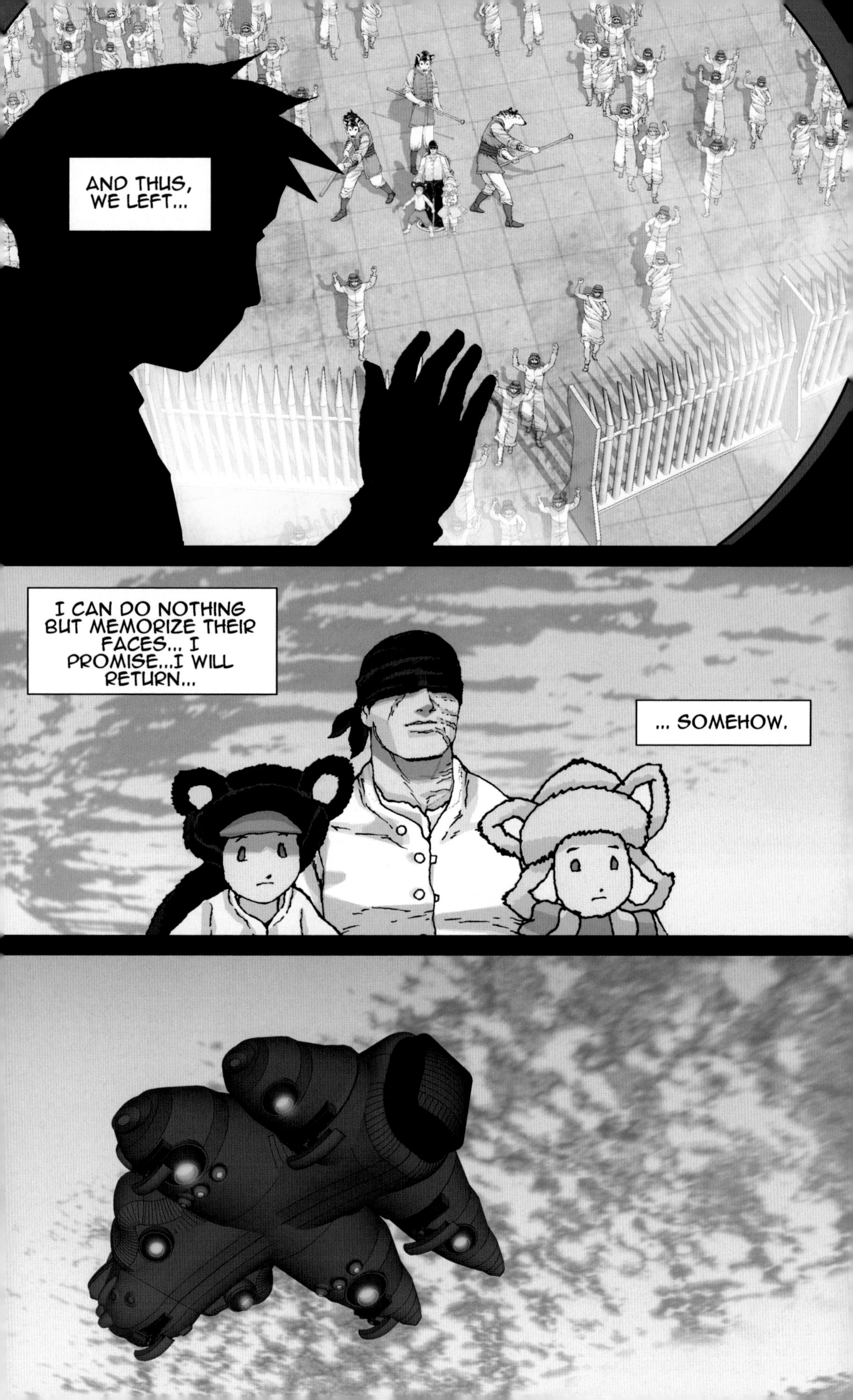
AND THUS, WE LEFT...
I CAN DO NOTHING BUT MEMORIZE THEIR FACES... I PROMISE...I WILL RETURN...
... SOMEHOW.

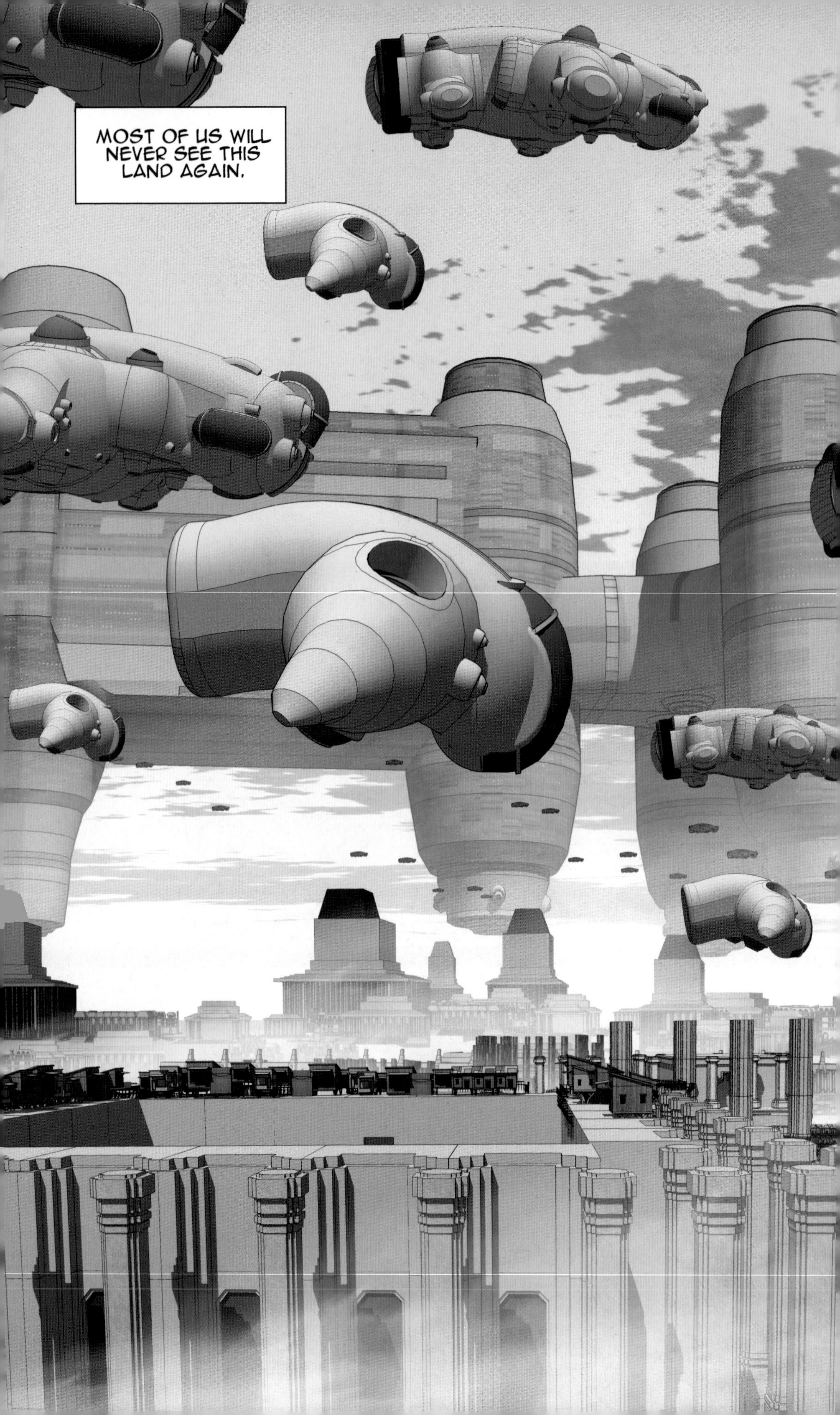
MOST OF US WILL NEVER SEE THIS LAND AGAIN.

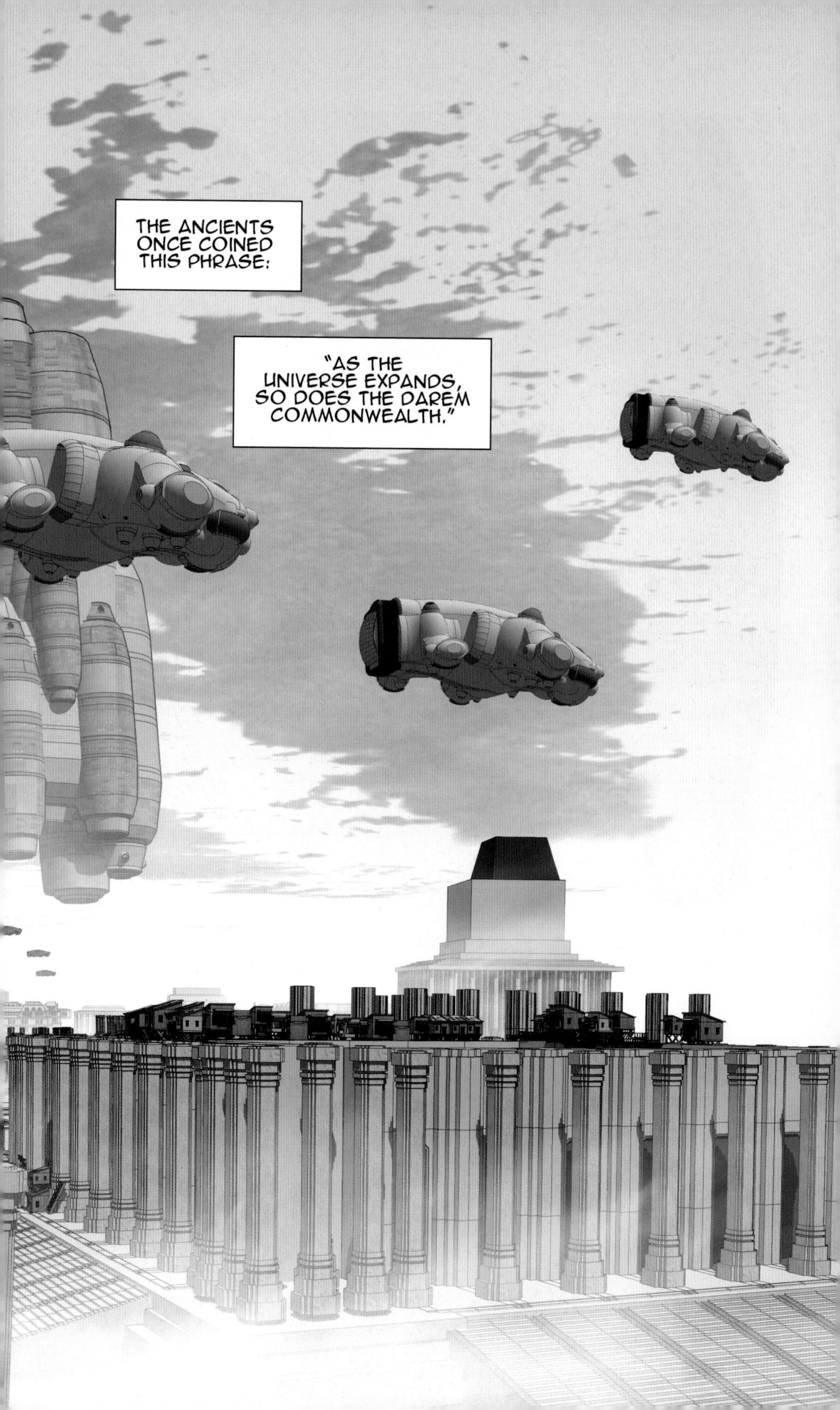
THE ANCIENTS ONCE COINED THIS PHRASE:
"AS THE UNIVERSE EXPANDS, SO DOES THE DAREM COMMONWEALTH."

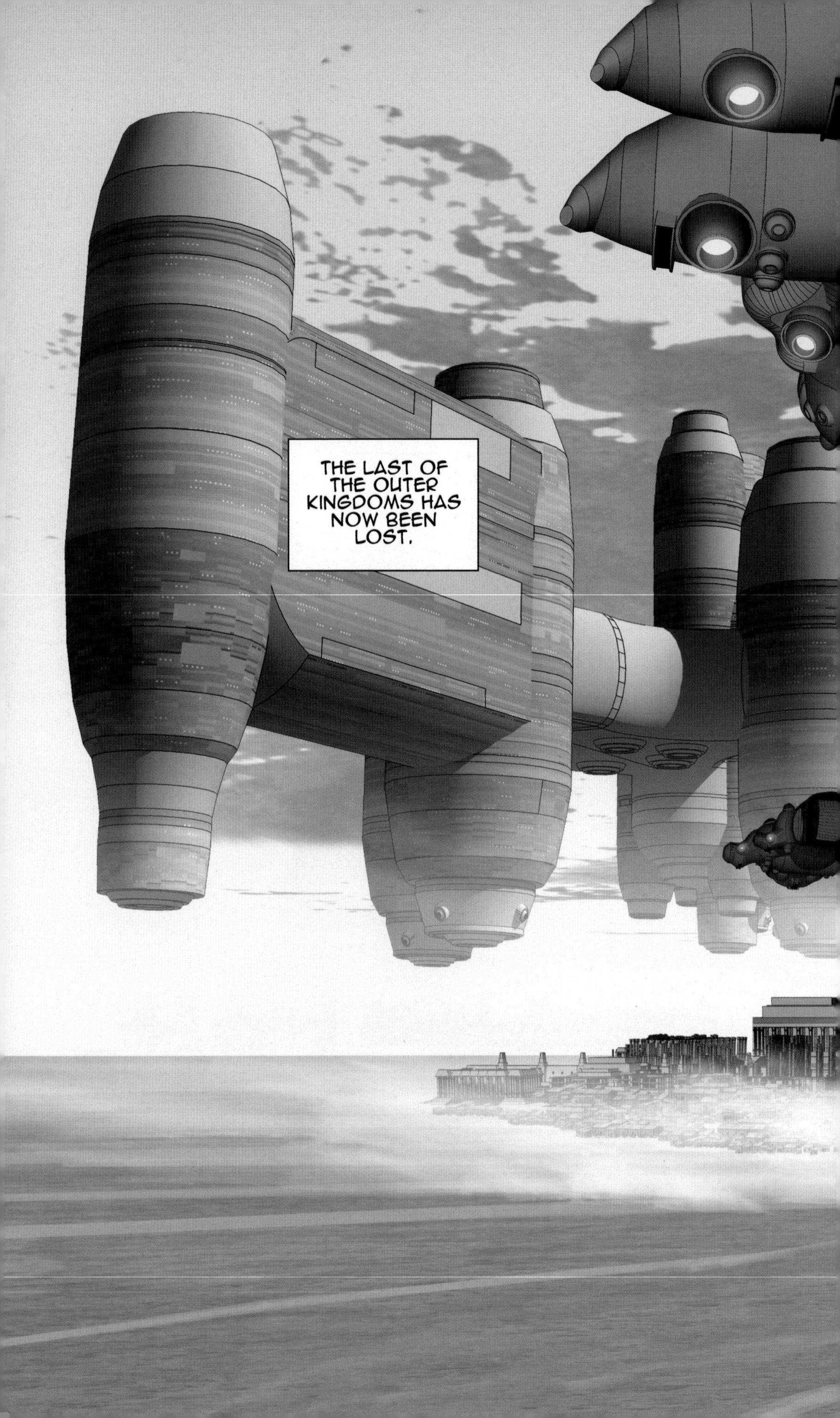
THE LAST OF THE OUTER KINGDOMS HAS NOW BEEN LOST.

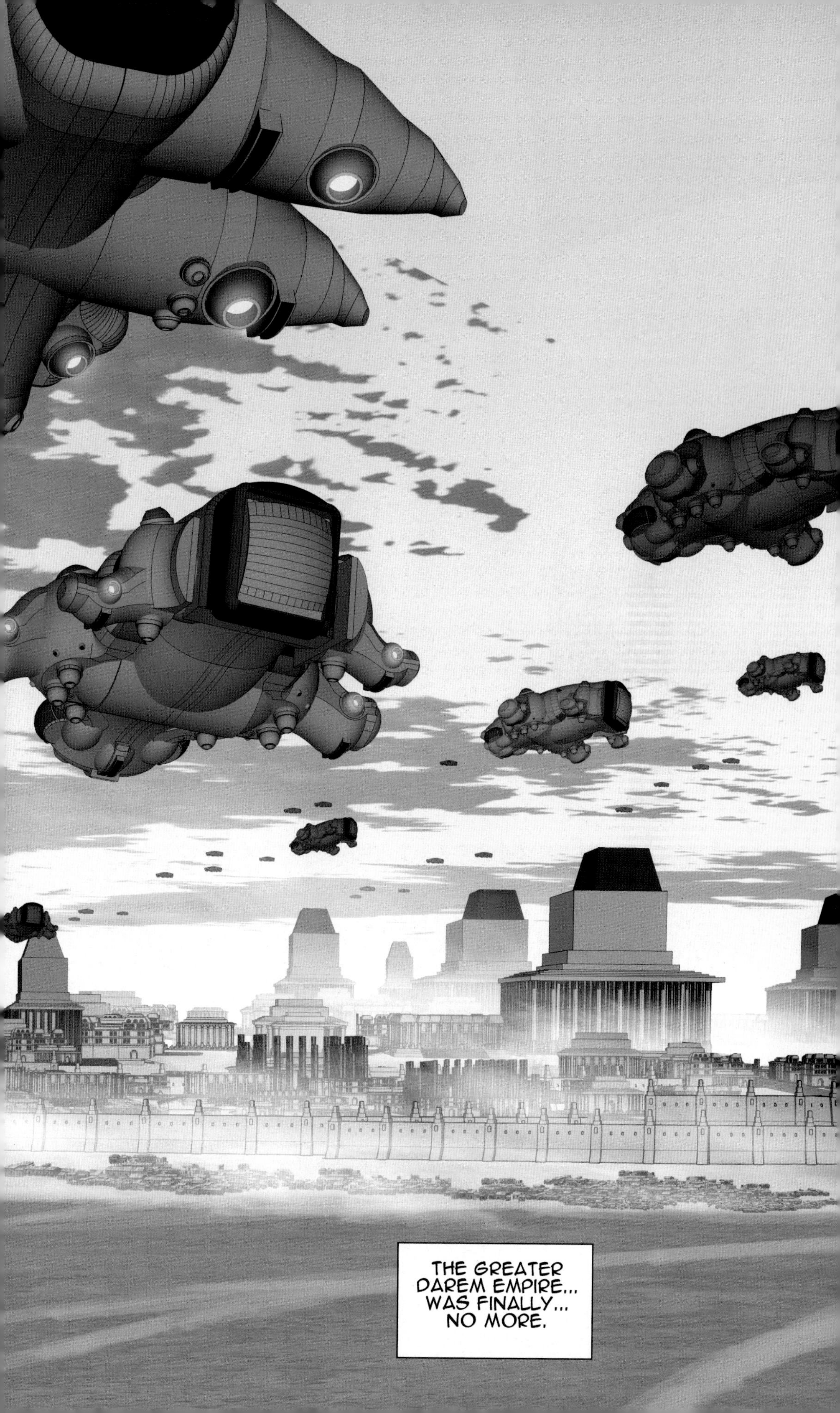
THE GREATER DAREM EMPIRE... WAS FINALLY... NO MORE.

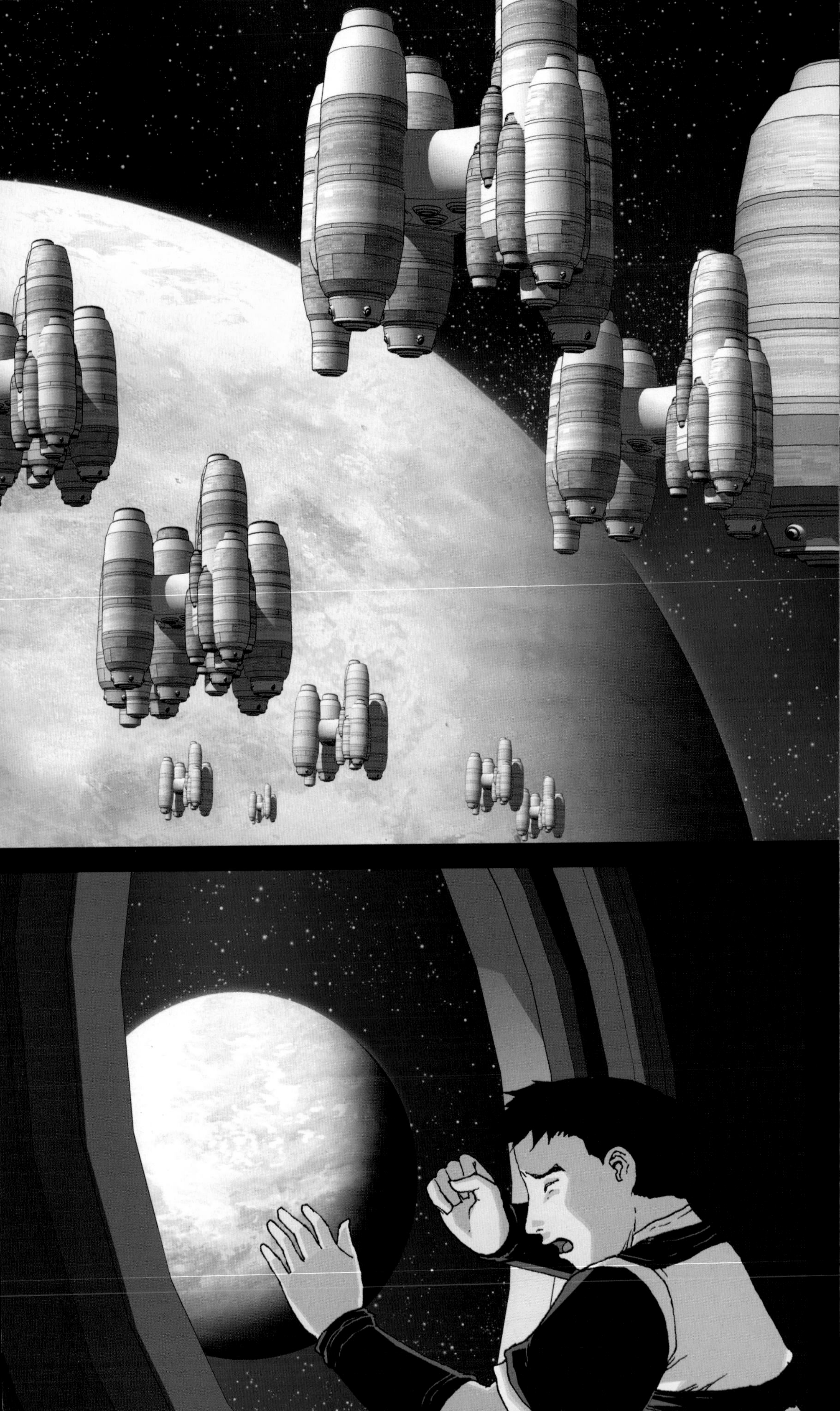

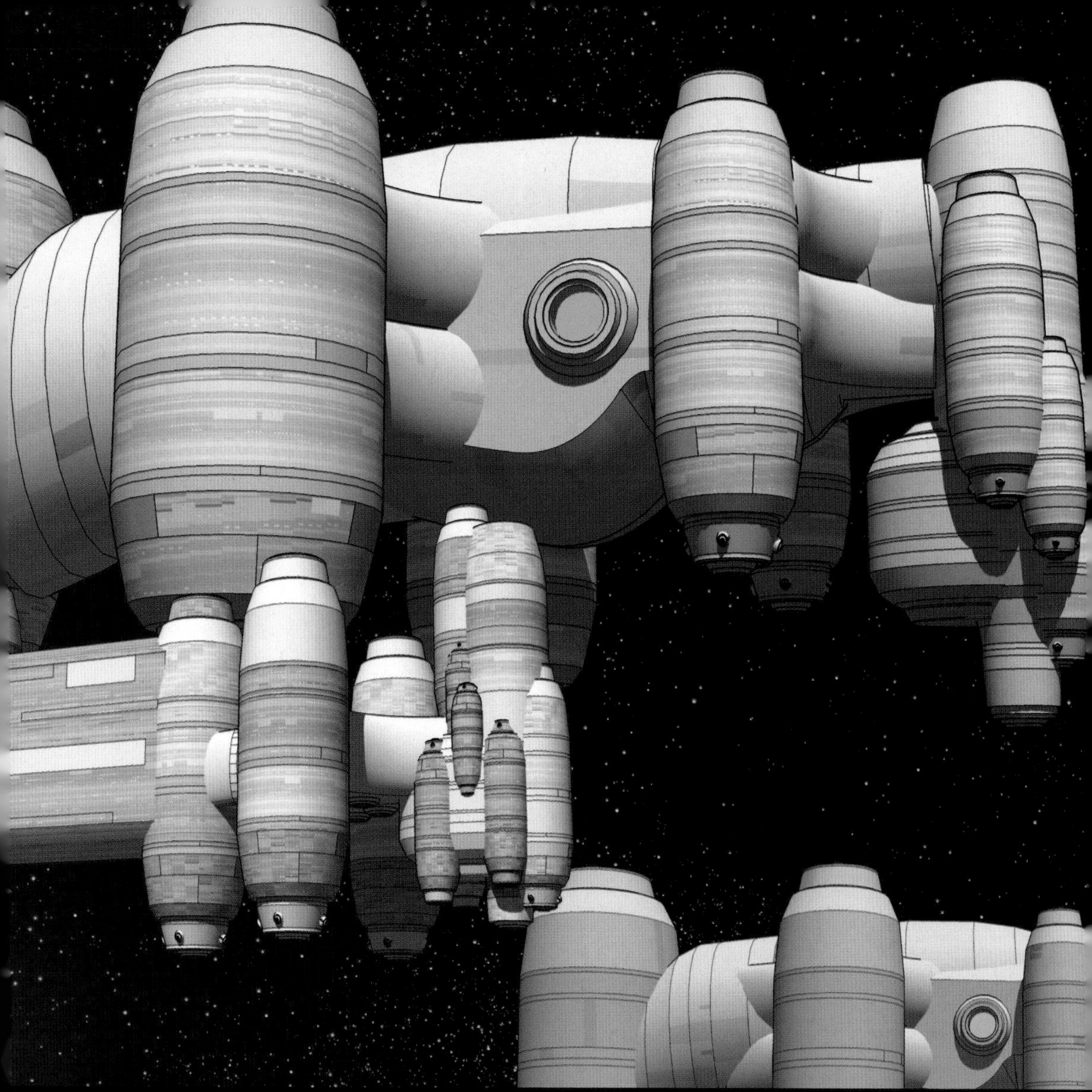

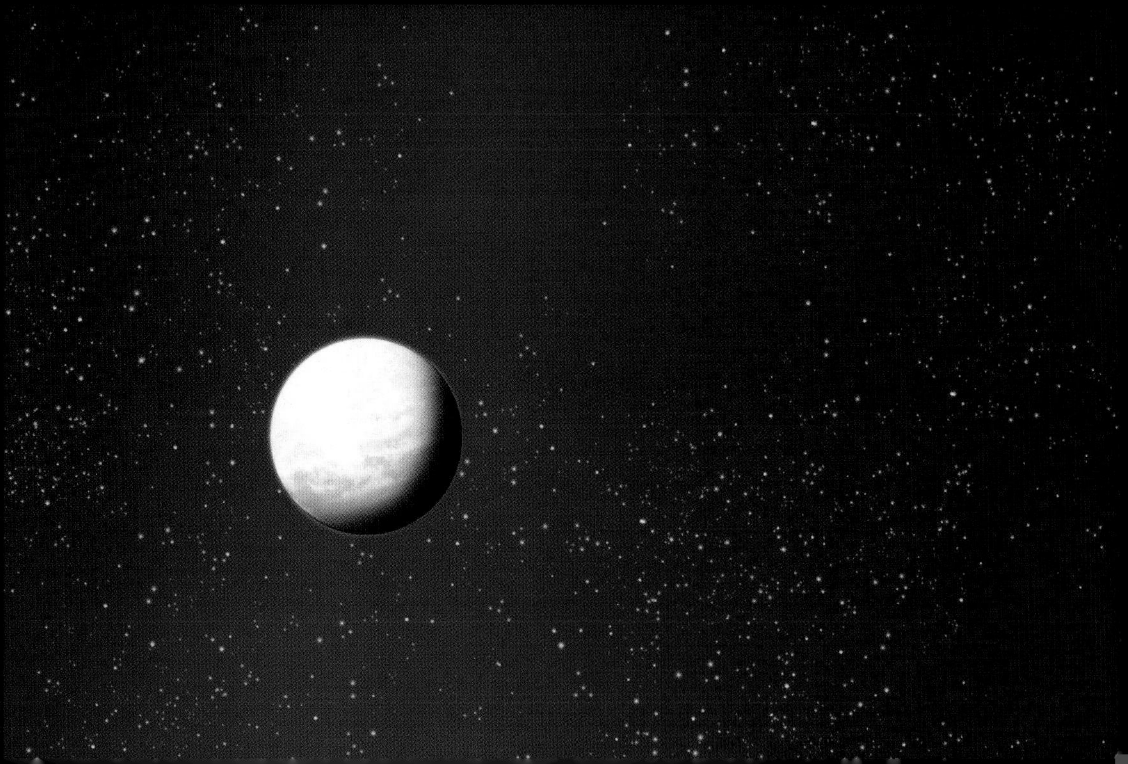

The
Prince of Heroes

Next:

Ronen is on his way to his homeland, but he is unable to let go of Irdne. Traveling in deep space aboard the Nebulous Mirage, *he is accosted by his fellow refugees—among them, even more Mesozorans! Ronen fights for his life as he tries to save a crew member from a terrible fate. The dangers don't end there, as he is kidnapped by a powerful entity even as a mysterious goddess intevenes in an effort to save him! To make matters worse, their ship is about to be intercepted in mid-warp by hostile enemies. Prepare to repel boarders!*

Written and Drawn by Rod Espinosa
Prince of Heroes and all related characters are ™ and ©2008 Rod Espinosa.
Text and Illustrations copyright ©2008 Rod Espinosa. *Prince of Heroes* is published
by Antarctic Press 7272 Wurzbach Suite #204, San Antonio Texas 78240 USA

Publisher / Joe Dunn
Senior Editor / Jochen Weltjens
Sales and Marketing / Lee Duhig

Printed in China by Regent Publishing Services Limited.
ISBN: 978-0-9801255-0-4
www.princeofheroes.com